The Second
Complete Home Decorating Catalogue

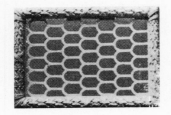

BY JOSÉ WILSON *and* ARTHUR LEAMAN

Decorating American Style

Decorating with Confidence

Color in Decoration

Decorating Defined

Decoration USA

The First Complete Home Decorating Catalogue

The Dollar-saving Decorating Book

The Complete Food Catalogue

The Collector's Catalogue

BY JOSÉ WILSON

American Cooking: The Eastern Heartland

Good Earth & Country Cooking (with Betty Groff)

EDITOR:

House & Garden's New Cook Book

House & Garden's Party Menu Cook Book

JOSÉ WILSON AND
ARTHUR LEAMAN, ASID

The Second Complete Home Decorating Catalogue

HOLT, RINEHART AND WINSTON   NEW YORK

Copyright © 1981 by José Wilson and Arthur Leaman
All rights reserved, including the right to reproduce this book
or portions thereof in any form.
Published by Holt, Rinehart and Winston,
383 Madison Avenue, New York, New York 10017.
Published simultaneously in Canada
by Holt, Rinehart and Winston of Canada, Limited.

LIBRARY OF CONGRESS CATALOGING IN PUBLICATION DATA

Wilson, José.
The second complete home decorating catalogue.

Published in 1976 under title:
The first complete home decorating catalogue.
Includes index.
1. Interior decoration—Catalogs. I. Leaman,
Arthur, joint author. II. Title.
NK2115.W815   1981   747'.029'473   80-26201
ISBN Hardbound: 0-03-055941-3
ISBN Paperback: 0-03-055936-7

*The decorations used throughout the book are ornamental plaster
reliefs reproduced from the catalogue of the Decorators Supply
Corporation, IX-14.*

First Edition

Designer: Helen Barrow
Printed in the United States of America
1   2   3   4   5   6   7   8   9   10

CONTENTS

INTRODUCTION

We compiled the first edition of *The Complete Home Decorating Catalogue* in 1976 because we recognized the need for a fingertip resource book that would eliminate much of the wearisome and time-consuming shopping required when decorating or remodeling a home. Previously, while working on a book about do-it-yourself decorating, we had sent for catalogues and booklets and were amazed to discover the vast range of products for the home and the valuable information and guidance they offered. So we decided to put our discoveries into a book that would provide an easy way for the would-be home decorator to shop by mail, develop decorating ideas, plan purchases, and save time and money.

Today, when inflation and the high cost of gas make it even more desirable to buy wisely and economically and cut down on trips to stores and shopping centers, a second edition seems timely and valid. It is no coincidence that mail-order has become the most popular way to buy and a booming business. Recent figures have shown that Americans now purchase eighty-two billion dollars worth of goods and services by mail every year.

The world of mail-order is seemingly limitless. There is almost nothing for a home or garden that can't be bought by mail—even the house itself can be ordered in a prefabricated package. Our catalogue is not just a source for furniture, fabrics, floor and wall coverings, lamps, art, accessories, and all the things that go into furnishing a home, but also contains moldings and paneling, hardware, tiles, and wood flooring required in building and remodeling. We have included booklets and brochures that provide a wealth of inspiration and ideas for your home projects, and, for those who like to save money and enjoy doing part of the work themselves, all kinds of kits for making furniture, clocks, closets, lamps, curtains, and rugs, and for stenciling walls and floors and recaning chairs.

There are many reasons to send for and study catalogues before making a purchase: it is a simple way to comparison shop, to see what is available in the market to consider before buying, and to save much-needed dollars. Buying furniture, for instance, is a major investment, but unless you live in a big city where you have access to department stores and showrooms, the local selections are seldom large or comprehensive enough and are often overpriced in terms of quality and workmanship. If you don't know what is available or even what style of furniture you want, it makes good sense to write for the catalogues of various manufacturers and companies to see if they have the kind of sofa, table, or storage piece you are looking for. Mail order shopping affords you the opportunity to make your decision at leisure, check out the specifications, finishes, choice of fabrics (most companies will send fabric swatches and finish samples on approval) and dimensions, and work out on graph paper whether it will fit into your floor plan. Many catalogues contain graph paper and scaled-down furniture cutouts in standard shapes and sizes so you can plan the furniture arrangement before ordering.

We have added or expanded certain categories to reflect recent changes in American living patterns and life styles. You'll find such ultimate luxuries as hot tubs, spas, saunas, and whirlpool baths and, on the other hand, energy savers like wood-burning stoves, insulating materials, and devices that cut down on fuel costs. There are also many more products needed in the renovation of old houses, including the special hardware, period trim, and lighting fixtures you won't find in your local building center.

Of course, in such a huge and varied market as home furnishings, not everything can be bought by mail, even though you can write for a catalogue. After each listing you'll find a group of letters that indicate how the merchandise is sold—by mail (MO), through a retail source such as a store or dealer (RS), or, in certain cases, through an interior designer (ID). Manufacturers are happy to supply a list of dealers or stores that carry their products. The relatively few occasions when merchandise is only available through an interior designer present no problem; you can place an order through the decorating department of your nearest department store, provided they carry the line, or contact the local chapter of the ASID (American Society of Interior Designers) for the name of professionals in your area. As the designer's fee represents the difference between the price at which he or she buys (wholesale or trade discount) and the retail price you would normally pay, it costs no more than if you had bought the item yourself. Most major furniture manufacturers sell through stores and interior designers, but many companies that specialize in top-quality contemporary or reproduction furniture sell by mail as well as through their own retail showrooms, and most small cabinetmakers and craftsmen sell only by mail. Then there are mail-order businesses that carry the lines of the biggest names in home furnishings and sell their furniture, rugs, lamps, and wallpapers at a discount.

Apart from well-known companies in the home furnishings field whose products are familiar to us, we have no way of judging the merchandise in the catalogues other than by the photographs and descriptions; this book should therefore be regarded as a guide to what is available, not as an endorsement or recommendation. The prices quoted came from recent catalogues, but with inflation these are naturally subject to change, as are the prices of the catalogues themselves, which may be updated seasonally or annually, often with old merchandise dropped and new added. The items selected as worthy of mention are an indication of what the company offers and their typical price range.

&&&&

There are in this edition, as in the previous one, certain unavoidable omissions. Some companies to whom we wrote for a catalogue and up-to-date information never replied, despite follow-up letters. Others had discontinued their catalogues or were in the process of redoing them and had no copy available as we went to press. Then there is always the possibility that before this book reaches the stores a company will move to a new address or go out of business, something over which we have no control.

Now for some pointers on ordering by mail, learned from personal experience, that can save you time, money, and headaches.

If the catalogue costs $1.00 or more, it is safest to send a check rather than coins.

Should you find it more convenient to send coins for a 25-cent or 50-cent brochure, wrap them and tape them to your letter.

After receiving the catalogue, look carefully at the description of whatever you want to order and ask yourself if you need any further information. For instance, if you are going to buy something that must be installed, such as a major appliance, a hot tub or spa, a wood-burning stove or fireplace, find out from your electrician, plumber, carpenter, or mason what you should check regarding such matters as installation, weight, wiring, plumbing connections, and so on, and write requesting complete information before ordering. There is no point in buying something you can't use without going to great expense or tearing your house apart. For your own protection as well as the company's information, always include on an order blank all information required (size, weight, color, material, etc.) and in your payment all shipping charges indicated on the order blank or in the catalogue. While out-of-state sales carry no sales tax, if you live in the state from which the merchandise is ordered you will have to add the tax to the purchase price.

Most mail-order houses have their regular shipping methods, and before ordering, you should find out how the merchandise will be sent—parcel post, United Parcel Service (UPS), or by motor or air freight—and whether shipping charges are included in the price or extra. UPS does not ship collect, so their charges must be prepaid with the order. Some freight companies will ship collect, which makes it advisable to find out ahead of time how and when your order will be dispatched and what the charges will be.

Parcel post has a restriction on the weight and size of packages. Parcels can weigh up to 40 pounds, provided they are not more than 84 inches in length and girth (or circumference). Larger parcels, weighing up to 70 pounds and 100 inches in length and girth, will only be delivered to towns with second-class post offices. The problem with parcel post is that you have no way of knowing how long a parcel will take to reach you, and nowadays speed is not the word, which is the reason more and more companies are using UPS.

UPS and similar delivery companies take parcels of up to 50 pounds, with size stipulation of 108 inches, length and girth combined, and are pretty fast on delivery, sometimes only three days from coast to coast. Because they require a signature, you must be at home to receive the package, otherwise it is returned to the sender. Before that happens, however, if you are not home, they leave a card that tells you when they will be around next. Signing the card gives UPS permission to leave the package at your home or at a friend's house. Parcel post works about the same way—you have to either be home or a card is left telling you that the package can be picked up at the post office. (Only insured packages require a signature.)

Freight lines, which handle heavier packages of 50 to 500 pounds, deliver by truck or air express. Again, you must be home to receive the shipment or let the trucking company know when to deliver or redeliver.

We can't emphasize too strongly how essential it is to keep a record of your order, the name and address of the company, the description and catalogue number of the merchandise, the date ordered, and so on. Make a couple of photostat copies, one for yourself and one in case your original order gets misplaced or you need proof of what you ordered. Include in your records any sales tax and handling and shipping charges sent with your payment and the number of your personal check or money order, which will provide proof of payment. Never send cash through the mail.

Many mail-order companies let you charge merchandise on a credit card such as American Express, MasterCard, or Visa, and have toll-free numbers you can use to do so. Although the buy-now, pay-later routine is simple and seductive, it is our experience that you are smarter paying by check. Once the mail-order house has passed the charge on to the credit-card company, you'll have a devil of a time straightening things out with the computer should you have to return the merchandise or should it arrive damaged or too late. Often there are delays on orders if the company is temporarily out of stock on the item or is handling a lot of business. You aren't going to pay for something you haven't received or have returned, right? Computers don't take this into account. Chances are the credit-card company will not only bill you but will also slap a finance charge onto your next statement if you haven't paid by then. For returned merchandise you must give the credit-card company all the details and proof of return, such as a credit slip from the mail-order company, within the 30-day limit for notice of statement errors before you get a credit. You can usually save yourself this kind of aggravation and time-consuming correspondence and calls if you pay by check.

Some companies have a time limit on returns, ranging from 10 to 30 days; others don't mention this in their literature. Always make a point of checking the company policy on returns, substitutions, and guarantees before ordering, since there is always the possibility that your order will arrive damaged, too late or prove in some way unsatisfactory or not what you ordered. To get a replacement or refund, act quickly. Provided there isn't a no-return policy, as there is on special sale items, you should return it at once, or at least within 10 days of receipt, if possible registered and with return receipt requested. Write a letter (keeping a copy) stating clearly and precisely what was wrong with the order and whether you want a replacement, exchange, or refund. If you don't hear from the company within 30 days after returning the merchandise, write to the customer service department or the president (whose name you can get by calling the company or consulting a business directory in your public library) by registered mail, return receipt requested.

Should the contents of the package arrive damaged or broken, first write to the company explaining the problem and asking what they want you to do with the package. Don't throw away the original packaging, as this is necessary to prove that the damage occurred in transit and not through any fault of yours.

In some cases, you may order something you absolutely must have on or before a certain date, such as Christmas or a birthday. When you send your order, write on the check "This order is canceled if the merchandise cannot be delivered by . . ." and give a date. If your order arrives too late to be of any use, don't open the package. Write on the outside "Refused—return to sender" and send it back. If you open the package, you must pay the return postage, in which case send it registered and request a return receipt as proof of delivery.

In the unlikely event that you don't receive a reply, refund, or replacement after 30 days in answer to your complaint about undelivered, damaged, or returned merchandise, you have various recourses. You can inform your city or state Department of Consumer Affairs or your State Attorney General's office. Or, if your local newspaper or radio or TV station has action reporters who follow up on consumer complaints, you can contact them. Or, here are other consumer agencies to which you can refer complaints:

● Mail Order Action Line of the Direct Mail/Marketing Association, 6 East 43rd Street, New York, NY 10017. This international trade association puts out a free booklet, *Consumer Guidelines to Shopping by Mail,* containing information about ordering and about following up if the order doesn't arrive, is damaged, or otherwise unsatisfactory, and a form for getting your name off or on mailing lists.

● Council of Better Business Bureaus, 1150 17th Street, Washington, DC 20036, the watchdog for illegal or unethical business practices and false or misleading advertising of national retailers and manufacturers.

● U.S. Postal Service's Consumer Affairs Office, Washington, DC 20260.

However, before you make a complaint to a consumer agency, first try to settle the matter with the manufacturer or company. If you don't get an answer from the customer service department, a letter to the president will often bring immediate results. He, after all, has the biggest stake in the reputation of his product and his company.

Happily, the odds for avoiding disappointment over mail order purchases are stacked high in your favor with most outfits and manufacturers guaranteeing—and living up to—efficient, trustworthy service. In fact, wise consumers all across the country have found that mail order is truly today's answer to saving money without sacrificing quality in home decorating.

So if you are among those who have not yet discovered the pleasure, ease, and practicality of this unique kind of shopping, we hope this new edition of our book will introduce you to an exciting, vast source of new products for the home.

JOSÉ WILSON AND ARTHUR LEAMAN, ASID

IDENTIFICATION OF ABBREVIATIONS

MO   mail-order sales
RS   retail stores and dealers
ID   through an interior designer

A careful selection of catalogues from this book can help you create rooms like these. The cheerful garden room/ office has bright yellow painted furniture, green tile floor, and lots of plants. Ethan Allen, I-4.

An elegant period bed/sitting room is furnished with handsome reproductions from Historic Charleston Reproductions, I-47.

A sleek studio apartment, decorated by Michael Sherman, has mirror-framed window wall of vertical blinds from LouverDrape, III-22; two sofas, one a sleeper, from Workbench, I-92; and unpainted chests clad in silver lizard vinyl with chrome nailheads and stainless steel pulls from Furniture-in-the-Raw, I-39.

I

Furniture

I-1
ABACUS PLASTICS
102 West 29th Street
New York, NY 10001

Abacus Plastics, $2, updated annually, 20 pages, illustrated, black and white.

A comprehensive line of contemporary Lucite furniture and accessories. Included in the catalogue are cocktail, console, dining, and end tables in a variety of sizes and shapes, the classic curving one-piece molded chair, folding chairs, upholstered armchairs and a rocking chair, serving and bar carts, stools, pedestals, bookshelves, shelving, and picture frames. Prices begin at $1.25 for a 3" x 5" single frame. A set of four folding chairs is $125 and a lighted 5-shelf curio cabinet at $1,235 is the most expensive piece. Packing and trucking charges are extra. MO/RS/ID

I-2
ABITARE
212 East 57th Street
New York, NY 10022

Abitare, $10, published annually, 234 pages in ring binder, illustrated, black and white.

Abitare is Italian for living and the New York store of this name brings together the best and newest designs for the home and office from all parts of the world. While $10 may seem a lot to pay for a catalogue, this one is extremely stylish, beautifully and clearly designed, with photographs of each piece backed by a sketch on graph paper, and the name, designer, description, material, finish, colors, and dimensions, making it worth every penny to anyone interested in modern furnishings of the highest quality. The loose pages are divided into sections on low seating, chairs, tables, storage systems, lighting, and accessories. The accessories are a diverse collection including a portable radio, an umbrella stand, a wastebasket, an Andy Warhol Campbell's soup can stool (labeled in Italian "zuppa di Pomodoro") with lid that doubles as a storage piece, as well as mirrors, bathroom accessories, ashtrays, a folding ashwood clothes stand, and natural or painted large terra-cotta pots with saucers and platforms on wheels. The furniture ranges from the familiar Wassily chair by Marcel Breuer to striking mushroom-like marble coffee tables to good-looking storage systems and pieces. Everything is clean-lined and exceptionally well designed, and while this could hardly be considered inexpensive furniture, it represents value for the money. Price list included. MO / RS

I-3
ADLER BILLIARDS
820 South Hoover Street
Los Angeles, CA 90005

Pool Tables by Adler, brochure, $1 (refundable with purchase), published annually, illustrated, black and white.

All kinds of pool tables, from standard run-of-the-mill models to some that are highly unusual and fanciful, with elaborate bases and amusing names. The Adler Heirloom Series consists of authentic replicas of the Brunswick and English Thurston tables built prior to 1900. There are also some completely restored antique billiard tables. Adler pool tables are individually handcrafted, with a choice of finish, cloth frieze, and pocket treatment, in a wide range of prices. RS/ID

I-4
ETHAN ALLEN, INC.
Ethan Allen Drive
Danbury, CT 06810

The Ethan Allen Treasury of American Traditional Interiors, $7.95, published every two years, 394 pages, illustrated, color.

A lavishly illustrated, comprehensive color catalogue of Ethan Allen's enormous range of coordinated home furnishings, including furniture as well as unique and beautiful decorative accessories from around the world, in brass, ceramic, and Murano glass. The furniture adaptations in the major collections (Georgian Court, Royal Charter, Classic Manor, and Heirloom) cover various traditional styles such as Early American, Tudor, William and Mary, 18th Century, and Federal. The Antiqued Pine Collection ranges from adaptations of Colonial designs with single-paneled doors, apothecary drawers, and porcelain knobs to later designs with plinth bases, multi-paneled doors, and bonnet tops, and the Hand Decorated Collection consists of a variety of painted and stenciled pieces, including rockers and chairs, tables, and bookcases. The collections can be bought in retail stores and the more than 300 Ethan Allen Home Galleries throughout the country and in Canada that offer a complete range of home furnishings—furniture, floor coverings, wall coverings, lamps, draperies, bedspreads, pillows, and accessories. The catalogue is packed with decorating ideas, room settings, consumer information on furniture finishes, what to look for when shopping for furniture, a guide to upholstered furniture, the care of furniture, rugs and metals, a vocabulary of traditional furniture terms, floor-plan graph paper and cut-out templates for planning rooms. A detailed pictorial index helps to identify the furniture pieces with specifications and page numbers. RS

I-5
AMCO CORPORATION
901 North Kilpatrick Avenue
Chicago, IL 60651

Amco Wire-Works, *free color brochure.*

With the advent of the high-tech school of decorating Amco's good-looking and functional chromate-wire, free-standing shelving emerged from the commercial kitchen and is now being widely sold in retail stores for display anywhere in the home. The shelving, some of which is shown in the brochure, can be used in almost unlimited ways, and the wide range of sizes allows a custom fit to the available space. The shelving snaps together, can be assembled in minutes with only a hammer, and is strong enough to support up to 1,000 pounds per shelf. Shelves come in 12", 18" and 24" widths, 36", 48" and 60" lengths, and standard height of 75½". There are also wall shelf units and hooks to attach to shelves. Write for the name of your nearest retail source. RS

Dark traditional woods and contemporary white upholstery and background create a warm setting for relaxation and entertainment. Photograph: Ernest Silva. Ethan Allen, I-4.

I-6
AMERICAN DREW
P.O. Box 489
North Wilkesboro, NC 28659

The Catalog Catalog, *10 cents, published annually, 10 loose pages in folder, illustrated, color.*

Each page in the folder shows a piece of furniture from one of American Drew's collections in a room setting, with a listing on the reverse side of the different pieces in the collection. Heirloom is a selection of eighteenth-century style adaptations of special pieces such as a silver chest, curio console, semainier chest, lady's writing desk, and Chippendale mirror. Tanglewood, Surrey County, Millers Creek, New Kinsmen, Domicile, Wilshire Place, Lenox Court, Cherry Grove, and Chaumont consist of bedroom and dining furniture with some auxiliary pieces, in traditional and country styles. Domicile is contemporary but rustic. All American Drew furniture is crafted entirely of solid hardwoods and selected veneers, sanded, waxed, and polished by hand. No prices are given, but an order form in the folder offers a complete color catalogue of any one of the collections for $2. RS/ID

I-7
ATELIER INTERNATIONAL LTD.
595 Madison Avenue
New York, NY 10022

AI Cassette, *$2, published annually, 90 pages, illustrated, black and white.*

Atelier International has a neat new way to show their furnishings on illustrated cards packaged in a clear plastic cassette-size box. The collection includes contemporary furniture, lighting, art, and accessories produced from original designs created by an international group of architects, artists, and designers, many of whom have received awards from museums, professional societies, and institutions. Among the pieces shown are Le Corbusier's classic chaise lounge, sling chair, lounge chair, sofa, and table (these are in the permanent design collection of the Museum of Modern Art); a highly flexible seating system designed by Mario Bellini, consisting of ten units that can be arranged as armchairs, sofas, and a zigzag seating piece; an upholstered canvas sling and folding chair by Giovanni Offredi that converts from a dining chair to a lounge and has a handle for carrying or hanging up; and high and low circular glass-topped ta-

Delicately carved frames teamed with cane or upholstery in dining or occasional chairs from Tomlinson, I-81.

Dramatic rattan chairs designed by Hall Bradley for Brown Jordan, I-19.

bles with a unique weblike chrome steel base. No prices are given. ID

I-8
ROBERT BARROW
412 Thames Street
Bristol, RI 02809

Robert Barrow, Furnituremaker, brochure, $1 (refundable with purchase), illustrated, black and white with color swatches.

Robert Barrow's specialty is the handcrafted continuous arm Windsor chair, a style originally developed in the United States toward the end of the eighteenth century. Each chair is a faithful reproduction of a Rhode Island Windsor, circa 1780, with its own number and Mr. Barrow's signature stamped on the bottom. He uses native woods such as pine, maple, oak, and ash, and his tools, with few exceptions, are those that a Windsor-chair maker of the period would have used. Various styles are available: continuous arm, continuous arm and brace back, bow back, bow back with brace, in a stained and varnished finish or, for traditionalists, milk-paint finishes in barn red, mustard, green, blue, or black. Mr. Barrow also makes a continuous arm child's chair, a youth chair with foot rest, and a settee. Prices range from around $200 for the child's chair to around $600 for the settee, amazingly reasonable for such fine workmanship. MO

I-9
BEDLAM BRASS BEDS
19-21 Fair Lawn Avenue
Fair Lawn, NJ 07410

Color catalogue, $3; *black and white parts catalogue,* $1 (either refundable with purchase).

This company produces many styles of brass beds, which are illustrated in the color catalogue. The design ornaments are reproductions of antique parts and an infinite number of variations can be obtained by simply interchanging tubing diameters. The beds are available in single, double, queen, and king sizes and range in price from around $260 to $1640. There is an additional charge for a lacquered finish. For restoring antique brass beds, the company has a parts catalogue which includes solid brass tubing with bends, brass caps, ornaments, balls and fittings, threaded fasteners, round-head machine screws, and threaded rods. They also have round, square, and spiral brass tubing and will custom-bend scrolls to your specification. MO

I-10
BEDS 'N THINGS BY R.V. COLE, LTD.
16 East 30th Street
New York, NY 10016

OJ Systems/Beds 'N Things, free brochures, published annually, 12 pages, illustrated, color, with additional black-and-white leaflets.

The OJ System, shown in settings in the color brochure, consists of all kinds of modular units; base and wall cabinets, shelves, record-storage compartments, drop-leaf desks, tables, and bar shelves that can be mixed and matched in all kinds of ways to suit your needs. The company even provides a diagram on which you can place the modular cutouts to arrange your own system. The stackable modules come in 24" and 48" widths and a choice of teak, natural oak, rosewood, and white, with some available in decorator lacquers. White units have chrome hardware, the wood units have matching wood hardware. Prices are reasonable, from around $60 to $299 for a hi-fi buffet with inlaid teak veneers, 71" long x 29" high x 18" deep. The black-and-white leaflets show a wide range of platform beds, daybeds, bunk beds and trundle beds combined with headboard and under-bed storage, bedroom cabinets and dressers in laminated plastic, and a couple of teak desks with file drawers, again all reasonably priced. MO

I-11
BENICIA FOUNDRY & IRON WORKS
675 East H Street
Benicia, CA 94510

Iron Beds from Benicia, $2 (refundable with purchase), published semi-annually, 3 illustrated sheets, price list and background information.

The Benicia Foundry and Iron Works has an interesting history. It is on the site of the first foundry built in Benicia in 1853 for the Pacific Mail Steamship Company, which later became Baker and Hamilton's Benicia Agricultural Works, producing farm equipment and tools for the local ranches and farms. Now the foundry produces iron beds and accessories, each cut by hand and with each connecting joint formed by hand pouring molten metal into a mold.

Benicia has embraced modern technology as an improvement over earlier iron-bed production in one way; the coating is a baked-on epoxy which has greater durability and scratch and

Platform bed with bookcase headboard, prefinished and ready to assemble. Sugar Hill, I-76.

Whimsical high-back brass bed called "Kansas," a turn-of-the-century adaptation from Isabel, I-52.

chip resistance than enamel. The iron beds also come with a totally modern bed frame designed to take a box spring and mattress; they are otherwise traditional in appearance. The styles shown are The Classic, The Legacy, The Crown and Victorian II, which come in twin, double, queen and king sizes and are sold with headboard only, headboard with frame, and complete (headboard, footboard and frame), with canopy for twin and double sizes ($50 extra). The first three models have curving headboards. Victorian II is a straight-lined bed topped with brass ball finials and a horizontal brass bar (all styles of beds are also available with pure brass ball finials for $10 per post). Prices range from under $100 for a twin-size headboard for Victorian II to $400 for a complete king-size bed in the Legacy design. There's also a very attractive daybed frame that takes a twin mattress and boxspring for $250 and a charming Victorian-style crib for $325. MO

I-12
BEREA COLLEGE STUDENT INDUSTRIES
CPO 2347
Berea, KY 40404

Early American & Colonial Handcrafted Reproductions, $1, published annually, 20 pages, illustrated, black and white.

Simple, beautiful Colonial handcrafted furniture made by master craftsmen and the student apprentices of Berea College is shown in this cata-

Outdoor or indoor dining group combines tubular aluminum frames with baked polyester enamel finish and vinyl straps. Thinline, I-79.

logue. The reproductions include a Governor Winthrop secretary, with or without top; corner cupboards; Welsh dresser; an Early American buffet and dry sink; tables and chairs in various styles; rockers, chests, beds and mirrors. All pieces are handcrafted in either walnut, cherry or mahogany and because the work is done by hand they can be made to the customer's specifications, even if changes in design or selection of woods are desired. Prices range from $160 for an Empire mirror to around $5,600 for a Colonial corner cupboard with pediment in mahogany or walnut. MO

I-13
THE BERKLINE CORPORATION
Box 100
Morristown, TN 37814

Don't Just Recline . . . Berkline, free brochure, illustrated, color.

Not only are the familiar Berkline reclining chairs, updated with new lines, new fabrics and vinyls, and the rocking-chair recliners shown here, but also included are contemporary Berkline casual furniture groups for dens and family rooms with coordinated sofas, sofa beds, lounge and reclining chairs, tables, ottomans and more. No prices are given. RS

I-14
THE BIGGS COMPANY
Mail Order Department
Attn. Mrs. Frances W. Street
105 East Grace Street
Richmond, VA 23219

Biggs Reproduction Furniture, $5 (refundable with purchase), published annually, 90 pages, illustrated, black and white.

Since the company was founded in 1890, Biggs has specialized in reproductions and adaptations of fine American traditional furniture selected from museum and private collections, which are shown in their mail-order catalogue. (Their showrooms also have contemporary furniture and a wide range of fabrics and decorative accessories.) The catalogue illustrates a wide variety of eighteenth-century chairs, tables, sofas and loveseats, footstools, lowboys, highboys and chests, cabinets, breakfronts, sideboards, cupboards, desks, beds, and occasional pieces and includes reproductions from Old Sturbridge Village and Thomas Jefferson's Monticello. Prices of the furniture vary according to the wood finishes (standard, premium and custom) which are shown in color on an accompanying sheet. Wood samples are available on request.

Prices range from just over $100 to around $2,500 for the Hull sideboard, and all relevant information about ordering is on the back of the price sheet. Among their other services, Biggs will refinish or reupholster any of their reproductions at certain times of the year. MO / RS

I-15
BLACKWELDER FURNITURE COMPANY
Highway 21 North
Statesville, NC 28634

Blackwelder's Fine Home Furnishings, $3, published annually, 108 pages, illustrated, color.

This company is not a producer of furniture but carries lines of some of the most reputable American manufacturers of furniture, lamps, mirrors, accent pieces and accessories, which it sells at prices below those in retail stores. No prices are included in the catalogue. You select the piece or pieces you are interested in; for price and availability information write, call (a regular and a toll-free number are given), or use the price quote and/or purchase request form, giving the manufacturer's name, series or group name, series and item number, color or finish, and cover or fabric number listed in the catalogue. As they have such a large inventory, it is often possible to locate a piece from a discontinued series or a hard-to-get item. The list of manufacturers whose products they carry is huge, and includes such well-known names as Thomasville, Kittinger, Knob Creek, Koch & Lowy, Sarreid, Stiffel, Thonet, Woodard, Brown Jordan, Directional, Salterini, Thayer Coggin, and Tropitone. A recent edition of the catalogue, which changes yearly, had beautiful reproductions by Baker, American Colonial furniture by Pennsylvania House, groups by Drexel, Heritage, Henredon, American of Martinsville; many contemporary lines, including Milo Baughman's designs for Thayer Coggin; sectional groups; indoor/outdoor furniture; children's furniture; reclining chairs; brass beds; chinoiserie cabinets; desks, wall units and bookcases; glass-and-metal accent tables by LaBarge; and pianos and organs by Kimball. MO

Butler's tray cocktail table with yewood veneer from Hekman, I-44.

Solid maple butcher block table and beechwood folding chairs with slatted seats from Conran's, I-26.

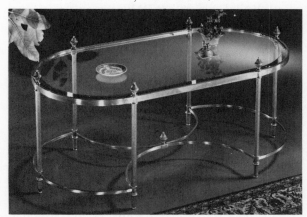

Brass Directoire-style cocktail table with beveled glass top from LaBarge, IV-22.

I-16
THE BOMBAY COMPANY
P.O. Box 53323
920 Valmont Street
New Orleans, LA 70153

The Bombay Company Catalogue, $2,
published annually, 40 pages, illustrated,
color.

A superbly illustrated and interestingly written catalogue from a company that specializes in English antique reproductions, many with a colonial heritage. The settings and background copy, inspired by the far-flung outposts of the British Empire, alone would make this catalogue worth sending for, but an even greater enticement is the astonishingly low price of the furniture, from just over $20 to under $200, including shipping and handling charges anywhere in the U.S. According to The Bombay Company, this is possible because they eliminate import costs and duties on raw materials. Everything is made where the woods are grown—the great mahogany jungles of the Orient and the tropics, and the teak, rosewood, and ramin forests of Brazil, India and Malaysia. By using these abundant hardwoods and local manufacturing companies and craftsmen, they can afford to sell furniture at prices you are unlikely to see elsewhere. The leather, brass, and rosewood campaign chair copied from one used by the commanders of the Khyber Rifles in Pakistan is $119. An English muffin table—a small mahogany accent piece 17" high with an 11½" x 8½" top—is only $19. Most of the furniture consists of small tables, folding tray tables and bar carts, chairs and accent pieces such as a wine-chest end table or a decorated seaman's locker. Every piece is well chosen, classic in design and seems to be inordinately good value. MO / RS

I-17
BON MARCHÉ
55 West 13th Street
New York, NY 10011

Free leaflets.

This New York store specializes in inexpensive, well-designed contemporary furniture, imported and domestic. They have no catalogue but will send on request copies of their newspaper advertisements. Among the offerings shown in the sheaf of ads we received were the ever-popular reproduction of the classic Breuer side and arm chairs, made in Italy of solid beech and natural cane on hand-polished, triple-plate chromium frames; folding chairs with transparent amber plexiglass seats and backs and chrome-steel frames; and high-tech-type vinyl-coated wire drawers that clip together to create stacking units with an étagère to match. Inexpensive track lighting is another of Bon Marché's permanent stock items. MO / RS

I-18
J & D BRAUNER
298 Bowery
New York, NY 10012

J & D Brauner Butcher Block, $1, published
annually, 50 pages, illustrated, two-color.

J & D Brauner introduced butcher-block furniture, which recently has become a fashion unto itself, over twenty years ago and they are still one of the leading manufacturers, with a tremendous selection of designs, sizes, and shapes. They sell butcher-block shelves and brackets, cutting boards, kitchen work tables with stainless steel frames and shelves, professional chopping blocks on legs (with or without knife rack and casters), carts, wall systems, desks, and all kinds of tables, including some with random oak or oak parquet tops. They also offer a very wide range of dining chairs, folding chairs, and stools in different styles and materials, such as Windsor chairs, the Hitchcock side and arm chairs, Colonial ladderback, bentwood side chair, and the classic Italian chrome-tubing chair with cane seat and back. Prices are very reasonable, from $13 for an 18" x 12" cutting board to around $700 for a 48" round parquet table top with two 12" leaves. The catalogue is handsomely designed, printed to show the natural wood tones, and very easy to follow. MO / RS

I-19
BROWN JORDAN
P.O. Box 5688
El Monte, CA 91734

Brown Jordan, $3, published every two
*years, 64 pages, illustrated, color. **Brown***
***Jordan Rattan**, $15, published annually, 27*
brochures and samples in ring binder,
illustrated, black and white.

Brown Jordan makes some of the most elegant leisure furniture and the catalogue shows individually and in settings the various collections of welded tubular and cast aluminum and bronze, which range from sleek, clean-lined contemporary designs to a few romantic and more traditional decorative groups such as French Quarter, Classic, and Calcutta. A back-of-the-book identification section shows every piece with dimensions. A list of representatives and showrooms is also included.

The more expensive rattan catalogue covers a fuller range of furniture—dining groups, game groups, beds, sofas, and seating groups—in styles from modern to Victorian to Chinese Chippendale. This is extremely handsome, well constructed and comfortably cushioned. RS / ID

I-20
BRYAN–ROBESON COMPANY, INC.
4012 Park Road
Charlotte, NC 28209

Quality Furniture . . . Bryan–Robeson, $2, published annually, 52 pages, illustrated, color.

This company offers a wide selection of furniture, mostly traditional in styling, with some contemporary and Oriental pieces included. They have a large assortment of sofas and chairs upholstered in leather or fabric, dining groups, chests, desks, tables, storage pieces, and four-poster or brass beds. The wood furniture comes in a variety of woods and finishes. All chairs are handcrafted. Most fabrics are treated with a protective finish. You may choose from a vast selection of over 900 decorator fabrics (swatches can be requested on the order blank at no extra charge), or you may supply your own. They also have two attractive hand-painted Oriental screens with either four or five panels and four case clocks, one a copy of a 1763 original by Job Brown, a Maryland artisan. Dimensions are given with each piece, as is the weight, so you can estimate the freight charges in various zones across the country. An up-to-date price list is included with each catalogue. Prices are moderate to fairly high. MO

I-21
CAROLINA LEATHER HOUSE INC., Dept. A
P.O. Box 5023
Hickory, NC 28601

Carolina Leather House Inc.—The Finest in Leather Furniture, $2, published annually, illustrated, black and white and color.

Leather furniture in traditional and contemporary styles is the specialty of this company. The exposed wood is solid mahogany, the upholstery top-grain premium leather (color swatches are mailed on request), and the nail-head trim is solid brass with a non-tarnish antique finish. Prices for the chairs, sofas and loveseats range from $204 for ottomans to match a French tufted chair ($521), English club chair or pub chair, to $1195 for a deep, comfortable Concord sofa with loose back and seat cushions. There are also executive office chairs with swivel rocker bases and an amusing Western-style swivel rocker with upholstery that recalls a cowboy's chaps ($585). Each piece of furniture is bench made by only one upholsterer; nothing is mass-produced. MO

I-22
CENTURY FURNITURE COMPANY
P.O. Box 608
Hickory, NC 28601

Eight Furniture Collections, illustrated brochures, black and white and color. Century, 32 pages, illustrated, color. $3 for all literature.

The eight brochures picture and describe traditional and contemporary furniture collections, including Country Classics and the Oriental-style Chin Hua, as well as a line of upholstered furniture and a wide variety of chairs. The 32-page color booklet shows Century furniture photographed in homes and settings. This is handsomely styled furniture, something for every taste. RS

I-23
CHARRETTE
31 Olympia Avenue
Woburn, MA 01888

Charrette Catalog, $2.50, published semiannually, 260 pages, illustrated, black and white.

Charrette's catalogue comes under the high-tech category. While the bulk of the pages show office, drafting, architectural, and art supplies, there's also a furniture section. Here you'll find functional and attractive desk chairs and office stools, desk lamps, desk tops to rest on file cabinets, and a few pieces of good modern design. One is the Boby 3 utility stand designed by Joe Columbo of high density plastic in a wide range of colors. It has a broad top with two 30" wells for drawing and tube storage, three deep storage shelves on one side, and a choice of three, six or nine 2" deep pivoting drawers on the other. Three double nylon casters allow for easy movement, and it can be used as a storage unit for flatware, place mats, and napkins in a modern dining area. The price, according to the number of drawers, ranges from $169 to $210 to $249. Then there's the famous numberless face Museum Clock designed by Nathan George Horwitt, which is battery-operated and has a metal case. This costs around $53 and comes with either a black dial with white case, hands, and 1¾"-diameter hour indicator or a white dial with black case, indicator, and hands. Charrette also sells books on architecture and building construction, some power tools, spray paints, and basswood for model making. MO / RS

I-24
THE CHILDREN'S DESIGN CENTER
RD 4, Geyser Road
Saratoga Springs, NY 12866

The Children's Design Center, free, published annually, 36 pages, illustrated, color.

Everything for children's rooms from furniture to toys, posters, quilts and pillows, plus some outdoor play equipment. The selection is imaginative, colorful, and practical. There is a crib with a three-drawer chest and two huge underdrawers built into the design that can later be converted into a junior bed and free-standing chest ($460), a wicker crib-and-chest combination designed in the same way, and an ingenious highchair with multiple notches on each leg that allow foot and seat levels to be adjusted as the child grows ($64). A delightful dollhouse bunk bed with flower cut-out footholes and picket-fence sides comes either knocked down and ready to roller paint ($655) or knocked down and prepainted ($950). MO

I-25
THE CHILDREN'S ROOM
318 East 45th Street
New York, NY 10017

The Children's Room, $1 (refundable with purchase), 10 pages, illustrated, black and white.

The Children's Room offers flexible systems in children's furniture from Scandinavia in which many items are size-adjustable and the majority come in basic units with varying additions and extensions. An interesting three-position chair in the AG set (1 to 10 years) will seat a child one to two years old at 6" height, a child three to four at 7½" height, and for age five and up it can be

turned over to make a sturdy stool ($30). The Wastl table with two storage drawers and a top that may be used flat or tilted adjusts from child to adult height, as does an accompanying swivel chair on wheels ($239 for the table, $89 for the chair). The systems groups with pleasantly mono-syllabic names like Mur and Var are based on chests and cabinets, desk tops, and shelves for books or records that fit on top. Both groups have a large variety of single beds and double bunks with mattresses and underbed storage drawers. Var beds are made of teak with a choice of teak, polished pine, or red stain. Mur beds are finished in hard-wearing washable plastic, all white or with side panels of red, yellow, or navy. MO / RS

I-26
CONRAN'S MAIL ORDER
145 Huguenot Street
New Rochelle, NY 10805

Conran's, $2.50, published annually, 112 pages, illustrated, color.

This international home-furnishings store puts out a super catalogue of reasonably priced contemporary furniture and furnishings for every part of the house. There are flexible modular seating systems, plump, cushiony overstuffed pieces in modern styles, square-lined sofas and chairs in a choice of monochromatic fabrics, and, for shore or country settings, chunky solid pine furniture with cushions that zip off for dry cleaning, priced from around $175 for an easy chair to around $400 for a sofa bed. Everything you could need to furnish a home is here: clean-cut dining groups; all types of storage units; a wide range of tables in wood, plastic and metal, some with glass tops; dozens of side chairs from Windsor to bentwood to Bauhaus; simple, functional bedroom furniture, and children's bunk beds. Quick Assembly furniture that comes packed in a carton with the elements partly assembled, to be completed at home with a screwdriver or the Allen Key provided, is indicated with a QA symbol. Current prices are in the moderate range, and if you shop carefully it is possible to furnish an apartment very inexpensively. While furniture makes up the major part of the catalogue, there are also bed linens, towels, shower curtains and bathroom accessories, kitchen cabinets and countertops, loads of tableware and kitchenware, tablecloths and napkins, baskets, mirrors, lamps and lighting fixtures, clocks, woven rugs, mats and matting, decorative hardware, fabrics

Country Heart sofa in custom or three standard lengths and choice of leg styles by The Seraph, I-73.

Chippendale-style sofa of button-tufted leather with solid mahogany legs and stretchers by Carolina Leather House, I-21.

Hand painted lacquer oval dining table in choice of twelve colors shown with chrome-framed side chair from Directional's Hayman-Chaffey Collection. I-23.

and wallpapers, frames and posters. Order forms are included in the catalogue and there are clear directions for ordering by mail or phone. Conran's has six stores in the U.S., listed in the catalogue. MO / RS

I-27
LAURA COPENHAVER INDUSTRIES, INC.
P.O. Box 149
Marion, VA 24354

Rosemont, 50 cents, 32 pages, illustrated, black and white.

Originally started by Laura Copenhaver in her family home, Rosemont, to help mountain families during the Depression, this organization is a flourishing source of traditional handcrafts—furniture, quilts, coverlets, and curtains.

Among the pieces of handmade, hand-rubbed furniture copied from old pieces found at Rosemont or in museums, there is an attractive "birdcage" table of solid walnut or cherry (only solid woods are used) with a rotating top, 25" high and 20" in diameter, for $70. Other pieces include an ottoman, Chippendale mirror, shaving mirror, Colonial wing chair, a bedside table with two drawers and leaves on both sides, and a solid

mahogany four-poster canopy bed with reeded posts in twin, double, queen and king sizes, priced from $604 to $750, with canopy frame an extra $75. Chests and coffee tables, not shown in the catalogue, can be made to your specifications. MO

I-28
COUNTRY WORKSHOP, Dept. B
95 Rome Street
Newark, NJ 07105

Catalogue, 50 cents, 16 pages, illustrated, black and white.

This family-operated business makes modern, ready-to-finish hardwood furniture which is sold by mail and through their retail stores. The furniture is modular, made of solid white maple or solid walnut, and comes sanded and ready to oil, stain, varnish, enamel, or what you will. Laminated table tops can be supplied at a small extra charge. The pieces range from chests, bookcases, cabinets, and file cabinets to Parsons tables, butcher-block tables, bunk and storage beds, and storage systems, and are available in a wide range of sizes and prices. Country Workshop also offers the familiar bentwood chairs,

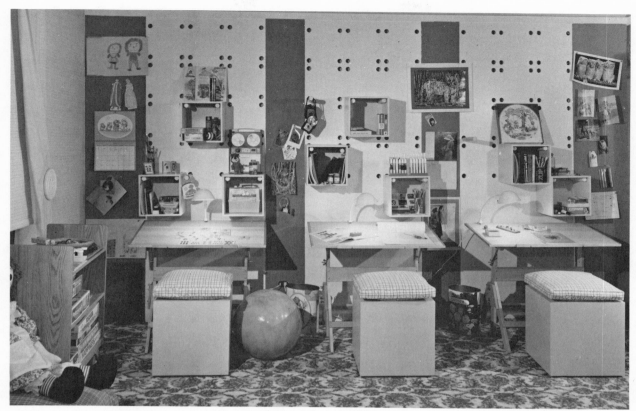

Natural oak drawing tables from Charette double as children's desks in a room by designer Carl Fuchs for Celanese House. I-23.

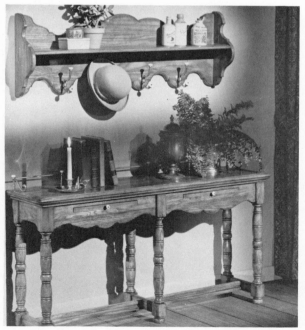

Sofa table with pullout shelves and hanging shelf with brass hooks create a welcoming entrance hall. Riverside, XIV-31.

Reproduction cherrywood Louis XVI desk with 23-karat gold tooled English calfskin leather top from Edward Pashayan, I-68.

Chippendale-style rattan headboard from Deutsch, I-31.

fiberglass chairs, stacking stools, and ceiling poles for storage systems. Prices are reasonable. A Parsons table, 30" x 30" x 29" high, costs $96 in maple. MO / RS

I-29
CUSTOM ART FURNITURE
225 East 24th Street
New York, NY 10010

Catalogue, $2 (refundable with purchase), published every two to three years, 52 pages, illustrated, black and white.

Modular wall systems in every size, shape, style, finish, and price range are the specialty of Custom Art Furniture. The free-standing units are sold either fully installed, assembled in separate upper and lower sections, or in kit form (KD) and come in a choice of wood veneers (birch, oak, walnut, pecan or teak), ready to paint, stained in your choice of colors, or with white plastic laminate facing. All the units are available with contemporary or traditional door treatments. A basic unit chart in the catalogue gives the dimensions of the different units, shown in various combinations in room settings, such as a bedroom storage wall, an asymmetric library wall, a corner arrangement, and a three-section combination bar, stereo, storage and book system. The units are completely portable and can be disassembled in less than an hour and moved flat in a box. Assembly instructions, shown on the inside back cover, come with each kit, and

you need only a regular and a Phillips screwdriver. No price list was included with our catalogue so request one when you write. MO

I-30
DAVIS CABINET COMPANY
Box 60444
Nashville, TN 37206

The Story of Solid Woods, $1, 26 pages, illustrated, black and white and color.

As the title implies, the catalogue provides a step-by-step, illustrated explanation of the making of a fine piece of solid wood furniture, from the raw wood to the finished work. Also included are examples, in full color, of Davis designs in various styles: Italian, English, Oriental, French, and Victorian. A final section has recommendations for furniture care. RS

High-tech wire shelving with chromate finish, used for years in commercial kitchens, from AMCO, I-5.

I-31
DEUTSCH, INC.
196 Lexington Avenue
New York, NY 10016

Catalogues, $2, published annually. 48 pages, illustrated, black and white. 26 pages, illustrated, color.

Deutsch sells what is described as America's largest collection of imported rattan furniture and the catalogues would seem to bear that out. The black-and-white catalogue features chairs, chaises, settees, sofa beds and day beds, storage pieces and bookcases, sofas, loveseats, ottomans, swings, desks and writing tables, cocktail tables, end tables, dining tables, chests and dressers, bar carts, screens, trunks, headboards, plant stands, wine racks, hampers, wastebaskets, display ladders, wall shelves, mirrors, a hanging shade—even a gazebo and a rickshaw. The enormous range of rattan and wicker styles run the gamut from Victorian to campaign furniture to Far Eastern to the squared-off Parsons look. In headboards there are many attractive styles, such as Chippendale, bentwood, trellis, Victorian, Castilian, peacock, sunburst, and arch.

The color catalogue shows some slightly different styles in rattan, including Fijian, which looks like bamboo; burnt rattan pieces; pagoda and Parsons canopy beds; and a marvelous deluxe bamboo armchair, a pure Eastern fantasy. Prices in the two catalogues range from under $100 to just under $3,000. MO / RS / ID

I-32
DIRECTIONAL FURNITURE SHOWROOM
979 Third Avenue
New York, NY 10022

Directional Hayman-Chaffey Collection, free brochure, 6 pages, illustrated, color.

Directional has always been known for exciting and innovative furniture design. In this collection designed by Frederick and Charles Hayman-Chaffey each piece is a stunning work of art, hand-painted and permanently sealed with a unique lacquer bond process that gives an almost gemlike hardness and brilliance of finish. The range of colors is as beautiful as the furniture. RS / ID

Directoire-style X bench with hand-carved details and antique painted finish by Edward Pashayan, I-68.

I-33
DOOR STORE, INC.
3140 M Street, NW
Washington, DC 20007

Brochures, 50 cents, illustrated, black and white.

Door Store is known for its inexpensive contemporary furniture, including butcher-block tables, storage walls, and platform beds as well as line-for-line reproductions of the great classic chair designs. They also have lightweight, attractive outdoor furniture in simple, forthright designs. One is the Harry Bertoia 1952 Italian steel wire chair, with canvas cushion coated with polyvinyl, around $60 for a side chair, $70 for an arm chair. The company sells by mail and from showrooms on the East Coast. MO / RS

I-34
DREXEL–HERITAGE FURNISHINGS
Drexel, NC 28619

Drexel Booklet Collection, $2, and Heritage Booklet Collection, $1, illustrated, black and white and color.

These two series of booklets on the best-selling Drexel and Heritage collections of furniture each contain a room-planning kit with graph paper and stick-on templates of different furniture pieces, with dimensions. There are eleven Drexel booklets, ranging from *Accolade II*, clean-lined contemporary furniture with a fruitwood finish to the French Provincial styles of *Cabernet II*, which features wood carving, deep moldings, and basketweave parquetry panels. Two of the booklets show traditional and contemporary upholstered pieces. The six Heritage booklets range from the traditional styles of *Cameo Classics*, *Brittany*, and *Grand Tour III* to the eclecticism of *Sketchbook*, special designs that fall into no specific category but are concepts from the Heritage designers' sketchbooks. There is also a booklet on upholstered pieces. RS

I-35
EARLY MUSIC STANDS
75 Homer Avenue
P.O. Box 277
Palo Alto, CA 94302

Early Music Stands Catalogue of Chamber Music Furniture, $1 *(refundable with purchase), 30 pages, illustrated, black and white.*

Home musicians can find here a variety of music stands with simple, functional lines, crafted from cherry wood. Included are a solo music stand with fully adjustable three-legged pedestal that moves the desk to different heights ($136), a short-pedestal music stand, stands for stringed instruments, a conductor's stand, stand ensembles for duets, trios, and string quartets as well as accessories—a wall rack for recorders, flutes, and oboes, a footstool for guitar players, a musician's table, and a padded performer's bench. Everything is clearly described with dimensions and keyed to the number on the order form. MO

I-36
EDISON INSTITUTE
20900 Oakwood Boulevard
Dearborn, MI 48124

Reproductions from the Collections of Greenfield Village and the Henry Ford Museum, $2.50, 46 pages, illustrated, black and white and color.*

The Edison Institute has a handsome catalogue of reproductions authorized by Greenfield Village and the Henry Ford Museum, which were founded by Henry Ford, himself an enthusiastic collector of Americana. The furniture reproduc-

Cherry solo music stand, upholstered performer's bench, musician's table, all easily disassembled for convenient carrying, and recorder rack from Early Music Stands, I-35.

tions, which are made by Bartley Collection, Ltd., include a Queen Anne side chair, armchair, drop-leaf table and lowboy, candle table, and joint stool sold in kit form, with instructions, clamps, varnishes, and sandpaper. In addition to furniture, the catalogue also offers clocks, glassware and pewter, hooked rugs, lamps, documentary wallpapers and fabrics, plus wrought-iron pieces, and additional glassware, tinware, pewter, and simple pottery made by the Village craftsmen as part of the crafts program. MO

I-37
FAIRMONT WOODCRAFT
Twiss Hill Road
Waterville, VT 05492

Free brochure, illustrated, black and white.

Fairmont Woodcraft makes a few natural tree-form pieces from Vermont wood cut to follow the grain or show off a knot formation. No two are alike. There's a fireside bench that could double as a coffee table, 16" high, from 12" to 20" wide and from 24" to 60" long, priced at around $20 per foot of length. Larger ones can be made to order. The bench is made of 2" thick Vermont pine. Additional pieces are a lazy Susan, battery-operated pine clock about 14" in diameter, and wall plaques. MO

I-38
FURNITURECRAFT, INC.
Box 285c
Stoneham, MA 02180

FurnitureCraft, Inc. Distinctive Early American Furnishings, 50 cents, published semiannually, 32 pages, illustrated, color.

There are a few pieces of simple, attractive traditional furniture in this catalogue, some of which are offered unfinished and completely sanded in case you wish to match a special color or stain. The finished pieces are hand-rubbed and lacquered and naturally cost a little more. A butterfly tavern table, copied from an eighteenth-century design, made of birch with a dark pine or nutmeg finish, measuring 21" x 26" x 22" high when open is around $80 finished, around $65 unfinished. Also included are ladderback chairs with handwoven fiber rush seats, end and coffee tables, a tilt top table finished in antique black with gold trim (around $65 finished, $56 unfinished), and a charming hand-painted small trunk with interior tray that could be used for sewing or craft supplies. MO

I-39
FURNITURE-IN-THE-RAW
1021 Second Avenue
New York, NY 10022

Catalogue, $2, published semiannually, 36 pages, illustrated, black and white.

This company makes simple modular wood furniture such as cabinets, chests, bookcases, storage/wall units, desks and files, Parsons tables, beds, campaign desks and chests. They are available prefinished, finished or custom-finished in five woodgrain stains or twelve House & Garden colors at no additional charge. There's a one-time fixed charge for color matching to a sample or special color. Prices are medium. A four-drawer chest, 16" deep x 47¼" wide x 18¾" high is around $170; a Parsons dining table, 60" long x 30" wide is around $250 finished or around $330 if covered in laminated plastic. There is a wide range of sizes for all pieces and custom variations will be done on request (inquire about prices for this service). MO / RS

I-40
GOLD MEDAL, INC.
1700 Packard Avenue
Racine, WI 53403

Casual Furniture Collection, $1, published annually, 32 pages, illustrated, color.

Gold Medal originally made a line of folding products for camping, and has since evolved into a leading manufacturer of casual furniture that is attractive, durable, portable, versatile, and reasonably priced. There are several versions of the familiar director's chair in various finishes, child size to barstool height, with seat and back slings of different materials (canvas, nylon, vinyl-coated polyester), some of which are patterned with silk-screened designs. Backs can also be personalized. The Santana chair, a variation of the director's chair, has sled legs and a matching stool. Among other portable or folding wood-frame chairs with canvas covers are the Mojave chair, the officer's chair, the Gull rocker, the circus chair (a type of deck chair), and the cushiony adjustable Hail Ragnar chair. Some of these have matching tables for games or dining. There are also café tables, and tables with folding bases, cylinder bases, and bases that adjust to different heights. Additional pieces include a folding bar, luggage rack, folding stools, divider screens with fabric panels, and a tall unit for holding and hanging plants. In the back of the book is a fabric and finish color selector for frames and chairs. RS

I-41
GUILD OF SHAKER CRAFTS, INC.
401 W. Savidge Street
Spring Lake, MI 49456

Shaker Furniture Reproductions, $2.50 (refundable with purchase), published seasonally, 28 pages, illustrated, black and white and color.

Local craftsmen make for this Guild careful and meticulous copies of Shaker furniture—benches, tables, chairs, chests, beds, and many small items for which the Shakers were known, such as simple oval boxes and baskets, trays, pegboard, and pegshelf. Rockers with spindle or slat backs are $230 with arms, $220 without. They can also be ordered with tape back to match the seat. A simple, beautiful pine double counter or six-drawer chest, noted for its unique top and base molding, is $1,215, but there are many inexpensive pieces, such as a one-slat maple dining chair with tape seat ($94) and butterfly bench ($95). Plain and modest is the keynote of the furniture, accessories, and hand-sewn items in this catalogue. The Guild also offers chair tapes by the yard and a number of paints and stains in traditional Shaker colors such as heavenly blue, ministry green, meetinghouse blue, burnt orange, saffron, and Shaker red. The catalogue lists a number of books on Shaker furniture and shop drawings of the furniture and woodenware. MO

Full-size four-poster canopy bed of solid handcrafted, hand-stained wood by Habersham, I-42.

canopy. The upholstered sofas and chairs, based primarily on Queen Anne and Chippendale styles, come in a choice of fabrics representative of materials woven during the eighteenth century—florals, stripes, flamestitch, and solid-color velvet. Habersham Plantation also has accessories and rugs to complement their furniture and a woven bedspread designed to go with their beds. A sound and helpful glossary at the back of the catalogue explains such furniture terms as carpet cutter (nickname for a rocking chair), sleigh bed (the American version of the Empire sleigh bed, with scrolled ends), and snipe hinge (a wire or staple hinge found on early storage pieces). As all sales are made through Habersham Plantation dealers, request the name of the nearest dealer when writing for the catalogue, which comes with a coupon that enables you to get a refund of the catalogue price of $8.50 on your purchase. RS

I-42
HABERSHAM PLANTATION CORPORATION
P.O. Box 1209
Toccoa, GA 30577

The Habersham Plantation Workbook, $8.50 (refundable with purchase through dealer), published semiannually, 56 pages, illustrated, color.

An impressive catalogue of the superb reproductions of American Colonial country furniture (or, as Habersham calls it, "primitive") with many pieces shown in period settings. This is honest, solid wood furniture in oak, pine, and cherry, handcrafted and hand-stained in a golden honey or darker nutmeg tone. The range is excellent and unusually wide, from major pieces of furniture to such things as a pie safe, pine icebox, quilt rack, coat racks, shelves, towel holders, a spice cabinet, and hand-painted hanging wall cabinets. There are benches, chairs and tables of all types, including an unusual highbacked love settle bench, stools, secretaries and desks, étagères, hutches, cupboards, chests, sleigh and tavern beds, beautifully hand-carved and hand-decorated trunks and wedding chests, mirrors with hand-painted panels, armoires, and a nine-drawer apothecary chest. Among some of the larger pieces are a three-section banquet table with rounded end pieces, a center table with drop leaves, a beautiful Pennsylvania hutch, and a sturdy four-poster bed with scalloped wood

I-43
HARDEN FURNITURE COMPANY
McConnellsville, NY 13401

Harden Furniture, $5, published annually, 160 pages, illustrated, black and white and color.

Harden's traditional handcrafted solid cherry furniture, which comes in distressed finishes, either natural wood or painted, is pictured both in room settings and individually, with dimensions. The table of contents and index group the furniture into categories: upholstered pieces, which have a choice of cushion fillings and skirt treatments; convertible sofas; occasional pieces such as a Pembroke table and a wood, brass, and glass end table; dining room and bedroom furniture. There are also some sectional pieces in the upholstered group. Styles include English Queen Anne, Chippendale, and Sheraton-Hepplewhite, and American Traditional. Among the various collections, the Then and Now collection offers one-of-a-kind accent pieces, such as a planter-server, a wine cabinet, and a cabinet that takes a TV set, derived from eighteenth-century designs that bridge old and new in casual interiors. No prices. RS

I-44
HEKMAN FURNITURE COMPANY
1400 Buchanan Avenue S.W.
Grand Rapids, MI 49507

Hekman Fine Furniture Catalogue, $3, *published annually, 172 pages, illustrated, black and white.*

The catalogue shows the different collections made by this well-known Grand Rapids furniture company. Each one is completely different in design and type. Apart from the chair seats, there is no upholstery. It is the woods that take pride of place. Except for the straight-lined contemporary pieces in the Wind Row collection, most of the furniture is traditional or oriental in persuasion, designed to show off beautiful Mapa burl veneers. One collection consists entirely of hand-decorated pieces. In addition to the major collections, there is a section devoted to chairs and benches, another for multi-purpose pieces that conceal television sets, stereo equipment, and bar supplies. RS

I-45
HENREDON FURNITURE INDUSTRIES, INC.
P.O. Box 70
Morganton, NC 28655

Henredon Upholstered Furniture, $2, *published annually, 64 pages, illustrated, black and white and color.*

Henredon's 5600 Collection enables you to have upholstered furniture made to suit your taste and the dimensions of your rooms. Whether you order a sofa, loveseat, chair, ottoman, or modular unit, you select the design, optional trim details, and fabric. You can choose from four back designs, six arm styles with either square or extended seat cushions, three types of legs, and fourteen flounce styles including various kick pleat, box pleat, shirred, sculptured, and button border treatments. RS

Lightweight, sturdy, impervious-to-elements ABS plastic pieces by Syroco, I-77.

Hand-painted breakfront with chinoiserie decorations has fitted glass shelves and low-voltage spotlights, by Union-National, I-83.

I-46
HICKORY CHAIR COMPANY
P.O. Box 2147
Hickory, NC 28601

Hickory Chair James River Collection, *published annually, 120 pages, illustrated, black and white and color.* ***The Cambridge Collection,*** *24 pages, illustrated, black and white. $3 for the two.*

The James River catalogue illustrates the fine eighteenth-century authenticated reproductions of Hickory's James River Collection, representative of the timeless designs found in American furniture of the Queen Anne period and designs inspired by Chippendale, Sheraton, and Hepplewhite. Recent additions to this historic collection come from three of the most famous of the James River plantations: Shirley, Sherwood Forest, and Berkeley. The less formal country look of the Cambridge Collection interprets Queen Anne, Tudor, and Chippendale styles in oak, olive ash burl, and ash, chosen for their rich graining. This traditional furniture fits easily into contemporary settings. The collection includes a butterfly table, Queen Anne sofa table, Welsh dresser, Windsor chair, rush-seated corner chair, and a variety of dining and seating pieces, cocktail and end tables. RS

I-47
HISTORIC CHARLESTON REPRODUCTIONS
51 Meeting Street
Charleston, SC 29401

Historic Charleston Reproductions, *$3.50 (refundable with $25 purchase), 56 pages, illustrated, black and white and color.*

This treasury of reproductions and adaptations of eighteenth- and nineteenth-century furniture, silver, porcelain, and other home furnishings, commissioned by the Historic Charleston Foundation as part of a fundraising program for preservation and restoration, is one of the most beautiful catalogues we have seen. The excellent photographs are accompanied by informative descriptions of each piece that point out the rare features, furnish background about the original, and give dimensions. The handcrafted furniture reproductions by Baker are shown, in some cases, in historic Charleston houses as well as individually. They include a dramatic eighteenth-century mahogany rice bed with hand-carved rice fronds on the four posts, pointing east, west, north and south to symbolize

Apartment-size prebuilt wine cellar ready to connect to a 120-volt outlet for wine lovers with no cellars, from Viking Sauna, I-84.

Charleston's trade with the four corners of the world; a rare Sheraton inlaid console with serpentine front in mahogany with satinwood veneers; and a graceful mahogany sofa in the manner of the Sheraton "Grecian couch." Also shown are examples of the hand-decorated furniture characteristic of the city, including a "Charleston chair" with chinoiserie scene on the back, a black-and-gold Regency chair, and a Sheraton "fancy" settee in black, gold and terracotta. Prices reflect the quality of the designs and the workmanship. The rice bed is around $3,400; the Charleston chair is $1,133. In addition to furniture, the catalogue shows the Charleston Collection of fabrics—cotton prints and wovens with designs taken from fragments of old wallpapers and fabrics, such as an English-style floral chintz in a pattern from an antebellum quilt, a chinoiserie design, a cotton damask, and a toile. There are also mirrors, lamps, china, silver and crystal, pewter and brassware, needlepoint kits, and a brochure of authentic Charleston paint colors by Devoe. An invaluable catalogue for the collector of American reproduction furnishings. MO / RS

Pine Colonial corner cabinet ready to paint or stain, from Outer Banks, I-67.

I-48
THE HITCHCOCK CHAIR COMPANY
Riverton, CT 06065

Hitchcock Consumer Catalogue, *$4, 64 pages, illustrated, black and white and color.*

Handcrafted traditional American furniture is the specialty of the Hitchcock Chair Company, which restored the long abandoned factory of Lambert Hitchcock, maker of the famous stenciled Hitchcock chair. All processes are done by hand, down to the weaving of rush chair seats and staining, stenciling, banding, and striping. There are reproductions of the Hitchcock chair, with wood or upholstered seats as well as the traditional rush, rockers, many other types of chairs, benches, bedroom and dining furniture, cabinets, mirrors, and occasional pieces such as bookcases, end and console tables, desks, and a cabinet bar. All are shown in color and in sketches with dimensions. A recent addition is the Connecticut House Cherry Collection, unadorned wood furniture in classic eighteenth-century styling.

If you are interested in the history of American

Mahogany bar cabinet adapted from a Korean stacked chest has heat- and alcohol-resistant pullout shelf and deck. Henredon, I-45.

Handwoven Mayan Indian design hammock from Lyon Hammocks, I-59.

furniture, the company also sells for $5 *The Hitchcock Chair*, a 340-page softcover book written by retired president John Tarrant Kenney, which tells the story of Lambert Hitchcock and the restoration of his nineteenth-century manufactory. It is fascinating reading and is lavishly illustrated with 400 black-and-white photographs and 8 color plates, many of which show examples of painted and stenciled furniture. RS

I-49
MARTHA M. HOUSE
1022 South Decatur Street
Montgomery, AL 36104

Southern Heirlooms from Martha M. House, $1, published annually, 48 pages, illustrated, black and white and color.

Reproductions of the kind of Victorian furniture that at one time graced the mansions of the South. Each piece is handcrafted of Honduras mahogany, with a choice of finishes—mahogany, walnut, fruitwood, and white with brushed gold trim. Upholstery is velvet, brocade, tapestry, and brocatelle (fabric swatches will be sent on request). Among the pieces are lyre-base tables, marble-topped tables, a camel-back sofa, duchess benches, a Lincoln rocker, and both four-poster and solid brass beds. The latter are especially attractive and include a brass-frame sofa bed. Prices on request. MO

I-50
HOUSE OF HAMMOCKS
P.O. Box 304
Barnstable, MA 02630

House of Hammocks, free brochure, published annually, illustrated, black and white.

Four really beautiful imported hammocks are illustrated in this exceptionally clear and simple brochure: The Mayan, The Guatemalan, The Brazilian, and The Rio. They come in cotton string or close-woven cotton with fringed sides and in a large variety of color combinations and lengths from 10 to 14 feet. In the Mayan model there are three sizes: individual, matrimonial (for two), and family size (for more than two). Prices range from $33 to $61. How do you use a hammock? As an extra bed, in playrooms, on patios, on boats, on camping trips, or for children's naps. MO

I-51
H.U.D.D.L.E.
3416 Wesley Street
Culver City, CA 90230

H.U.D.D.L.E., $2, folder with 7 color pages, descriptive price lists, published annually.

Jim and Penny Hull, founders of H.U.D.D.L.E. (Hull Urban Design Development Laboratory, Etcetera), design and manufacture a small, unconventional assortment of furniture for children and adults, fabric graphics, and accessories indicative of their very individual approach to home furnishings that fit a young and active lifestyle. The emphasis is on comfort, informality, and designs that suggest togetherness and freedom of communication while solving seating and sleeping problems. Since they started their small business in 1970 it has grown to include retail showrooms in Southern California, as well as mail order sales, which proves that builders of better mousetraps often do succeed.

The Toobline system of children's furniture consists of beds and bunks made of rigid "toobs" with bright vinyl surfaces and solid wood plus matching desk, chair, dresser, shelves, stool, shelving, and toy box, most of which comes KD (knocked down) and can be assembled with a screwdriver. The Sideline series, for rather older children, is made of pressed wood with white lacquered endboards and side panels laminated with brightly colored vinyl to mix and match with the drawer fronts on the dressers. Big Toobs are bunks and beds that look like space capsules, with matching table, stools, bookcase, and dresser. Adults can loll on the cushiony, comfortable Huddlecouch, which has a frame with four, three, or two sides, so it can double as a bed. Penny Huddle's Fabric Graphics, bold, colorful designs hand-silk-screened on 100 percent cotton, are sold as yardage, stretching kits, pillows, and comforters.

For kitchen and bath there are small "toobs"

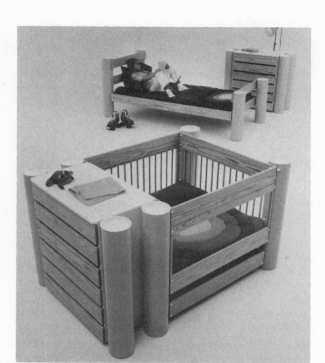

Baby bed of vinyl-laminated support "toobs" converts to a twin bed. From a component furniture system that grows with your child by H.U.D.D.L.E., I-51.

that act as towel bars or rings, shelves, handles, holders, and hooks, made from metal tubing, chrome, solid brass, or steel with a plastic coating in white or brilliant colors. Plantoobs, in sizes from 9″ to 41″ high and different diameters, are made of laminated fiberply with a covering of plastic-coated natural cane or mirror-like mylar with chrome or brass finish, and can be used as planters for flowers or trees, or as wastebaskets. The prices for these fresh, simple, functional designs are extremely reasonable. The queen-size Huddlecouch frame with four canvas side panels costs under $200, a Big Toob table with white base and vinyl-laminated round top is around $70, Plantoobs range from $14 to $39, and fixtures from $12 to $36, according to type and material. MO

I-52
ISABEL BRASS FURNITURE, INC.
120 East 32nd Street
New York, NY 10016

Isabel Selections, $3 (refundable with purchase), published annually, 20 pages, illustrated, color.

These custom designers and manufacturers produce some of the most glorious brass beds and

sofa beds we have seen, from the romantic and traditional to the sleekly contemporary. There is even a brass platform bed. It would be impossible to describe the two dozen designs featured in the color catalogue, but each is superbly detailed and crafted. No information or dimensions are given. Presumably these are included with the price list, which we did not receive. Be sure to request it when writing. MO

I-53
JENSEN–LEWIS COMPANY, INC.
156 Seventh Avenue
New York, NY 10014

Jensen-Lewis Canvas, $1, published annually, 16 pages, illustrated, black and white.

The major offerings in this catalogue are seating pieces with canvas covers. There are director's chairs, officer's chairs, deck chairs, the Gull rocker, the circus chair, an upholstered chair, a sofa/sleeper, and modular seating and sleeping units upholstered in canvas. In addition, canvas is used for a three-panel screen, drawers in wood-and-metal stacking storage units, a magazine rack, and a folding cot. Non-canvas pieces in the catalogue include chairs with wood frames and hemp-rope seats and backs, a sofa and ottoman upholstered in tufted leather or natural Belgian linen, wood tables, chairs with rush or cane seats, a table that adjusts from coffee to dining height, open-shelf systems in unfinished pine, and some simple, functional lighting fixtures and lamps. Prices are reasonable. MO

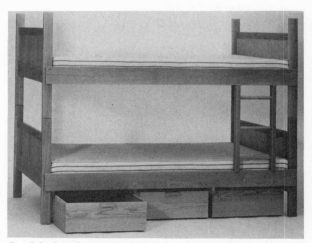

Bunk bed with underbed drawers, handmade of oak, can convert to two twins. Charles Webb, I-86.

I-54
KINDEL FURNITURE COMPANY
100 Garden Street, S.E.
Grand Rapids, MI 49507

Kindel Furniture China Trade Collection,
*$1, published periodically, 30 pages,
illustrated, black and white and color.*

The Chinese developed timeless forms of great functional and aesthetic appeal, a serenity of design that is the inspiration for Kindel's China Trade Collection of living room, dining room, and bedroom furniture. Cherry veneers and solids combined with highly figured walnut veneers are enhanced by hand-rubbed finishes, and several patterns offer the option of chinoiserie hand decoration, with a choice of lacquer background colors. Hardware is solid brass, hand-buffed, in traditional oriental designs. The upholstered chaises and sofa have a straight-lined simplicity that harmonizes with the wood furniture. Among the more unusual and versatile pieces are the stacking components. You can put together your own "collector's wall," using drop-front and tambour cabinets, china-top units with fretwork grille over glass and faux bamboo trim, three-drawer, open-shelf, and base units. An interesting collection of handsome furniture that would look well in traditional or eclectic rooms. RS

I-55
KITTINGER COMPANY
1893 Elmwood Avenue
Buffalo, NY 14207

***A Library of 18th-Century English and
American Designs,*** *$7, published every two
years, 180 pages, illustrated, color.*

Kittinger's appointment as exclusive maker of Williamsburg Furniture Reproductions and Historic Newport Furniture Reproductions attests to the high quality of craftsmanship employed in its furniture manufacture. The weighty catalogue includes tables, chairs, sideboards, desks, beds, and sofas, mostly fashioned after eighteenth-century English and American designs. There are, however, a number of modern sofas and upholstered chairs and benches. In addition to the furniture, the catalogue has a design dictionary, and a listing of showrooms and sales representatives throughout the country. RS / ID

I-56
KNIGHT'S SPIDER WEB FARM
AND GIFT SHOP
Cliff Place
Williamstown, VT 05679

Knight's, *no charge, published annually, 6
pages, illustrated, black and white.*

The booklet sent out by Knight's Small Cabinet Store, a family business, shows the hand-crafted pine miniature furniture, small cupboards, lap desk, lap board, whatnot shelves, and other simple things they make. They finish the pieces with a medium-tone stain that blends well with dark or light woods and a fine furniture lacquer, with a few extra coats added for that "piano" finish. Their trademark, made only on request, is a small reproduction Governor Winthrop desk that could hold jewelry or silverware. It is 18" high x 17" wide x 11" deep, with three drawers and a brass-hinged drop-leaf front ($150). Also included are miniature two-, three-, and four-drawer chests with porcelain knobs, the drawers unlined or lined with calico, at prices ranging from $26 to around $39 as well as two cupboards, one a Shaker-style wall cupboard, 15" high x 10½" wide x 5½" deep, that could be used in a bathroom or kitchen, to house small collections, or on a porch as a mail box. This is around $26, or $21.95 unfinished, in case you want to paint or stencil it. The whatnot shelves, about 30" high with two drawers at the bottom, would be good in almost any room for storage and display of small objects. The lap board, an old-fashioned idea that bears reviving, is 33" long x 17" deep and could be used for playing cards or doing crossword puzzles while you sit in your easy chair. MO

I-57
LEATHERCRAFTER
303 East 51st Street
New York, NY 10022

Leathercrafter, *$1 (refundable with
purchase), published annually, 32 pages,
illustrated, black and white.*

With the neat little catalogue comes an envelope filled with color samples of the heavy saddle leather used on the chairs shown. They will also send, on request, color samples of bucksuede, soft cowhide, and glove leather. The chairs are a variety of modern designs, and the techniques used are the same as those that made early American saddlers and leather craftsmen famous for fine workmanship. Leathercrafters offers versions of some of the most famous chair designs of this century and seems to have a chair or stool to suit every taste at prices ranging from around $65 to $480. Price list and order form are included, as well as a leaflet advertising their recommended suede and leather cleaners. MO

I-58
A. LISS & CO., INC.
35-03 Bradley Avenue
Long Island City, NY 11101

Materials Handling, Safety & Industrial Equipment, no charge, published semiannually, illustrated, black and white.

This catalogue from a wholesaler of industrial equipment would be of interest to anyone with a fancy for high-tech decoration. Everything here is strictly functional—work and folding tables, stacking boxes, desks, desk chairs and stacking chairs, steel-topped and modular work benches, tray-type stock carts, mobile wire carts, ceiling fans and lots of multiple-drawer units, lockers, open-bin storage units, and shelving. The library and modular wire shelving would be extremely useful in storage areas or a kitchen, and the colored polyethylene stacking containers in a steel frame would make good toy, craft, or canned goods storage units. While this is not strictly a consumer catalogue, browsing through will give you some idea about what is available in and what can be done with industrial equipment, which is invariably sturdy and a good buy. Prices are reasonable. MO

I-59
THE LYON HAMMOCK COMPANY
41 Galen Street
Watertown, MA 02172

Lyon Hammocks, 25 cents (refundable with purchase), published annually, 12 pages, illustrated, black and white.

The Mayan Indians invented the hammock thousands of years ago, weaving it from hamack tree bark fiber, which gave the hammock its name. The design has not altered, although Mayan hammocks are now made in softer, stronger cotton; they are woven by hand on long wooden racks, a process that takes weeks of work. Lyon not only sells these wide, comfortable hammocks but tells you how to hang them indoors or out (the cotton handles should be first hitched to rope, not hung directly on metal hooks that would chafe and wear them out), lie in them (crosswise, not lengthwise), fold them, and wash them. The hammocks come in natural beige, rainbow colors, or combinations of white and a solid color and regular, large, and extra-large sizes at prices from $38.95 to $58.95. A hanging kit is $3. MO

I-60
MAGNOLIA HALL
726 Andover
Atlanta, GA 30327

Yesteryear Furniture, $1, published semiannually, 80 pages, illustrated, black and white.

If you like Victoriana, you'll be delighted by the selection in this catalogue. A charming mirror-back hand-carved mahogany love seat is around $560, a "fancy" chair with elaborately carved back rail, $189.95. You can buy a complete parlor set with mahogany triple-crested sofa, two armchairs, two double-drawer, lyre-base lamp tables, and a pedestal coffee table for around $2,000. A spring-seat folding rocker with carved wood top, turned spool stretchers, and Victorian tapestry upholstery is around $80. Each piece is illustrated and fully described, with dimensions. MO

I-61
MALLORY'S LTD.
P.O. Box 1150
Jacksonville, NC 28540

Flyer, no charge, illustrated, black and white.

Mallory's sells furniture collections by major American manufacturers including Henredon, Heritage, and Drexel at discount prices and will also give you quotes on a wide selection of home furnishings such as furniture, lamps, accessories, clocks, Oriental rugs, bedding, and bedspreads from other leading manufacturers whose names are listed in the flyer. You can call their toll-free number for quotes or to place orders. In the flyer there is an order form for the manufacturers' booklets on the various collections showing the pieces and giving specifications, at prices from 50 cents up. When you order and receive a booklet you also get Mallory's discounted price list for the furniture, and fabric samples will be sent on request. Their sales representatives will take orders and answer questions over the phone and as they handle all the details of ordering and shipping, you save time and trouble as well as money. MO

I-62
MARJON WOODCRAFT
Box 41, Mountain Falls Route
Winchester, VA 22601

Cobbler's Bench, free leaflet, illustrated,
black and white.

This reproduction cobbler's bench is handmade of Ponderosa pine, sanded, stained, and given an oil finish, with some tool marks and distress, as typical in the originals. The bench has five hand-fitted drawers with porcelain knobs and a "dished out" seat. For those with Early American furnishings, it makes a nice end table. The price is $125, shipped collect. MO

I-63
EPHRAIM MARSH COMPANY, Dept. 753
P.O. Box 226
Concord, NC 28025

Ephraim Marsh—Distinctive Furniture, $1,
published semiannually, 140 pages,
illustrated, black and white and color.

Traditional furniture for home and office in American Colonial, Queen Anne, and Georgian styles. There is a wide variety of dining room and bedroom furniture, upholstered pieces, desks, occasional pieces, and cocktail or coffee tables. Price lists, order forms, descriptions, and specifications are included and fabric swatches will be sent on request. Prices range from under $100 to under $2000. MO

I-64
THOMAS MOSER
5 Cobb's Bridge Road
New Gloucester, ME 04260

Thomas Moser, Cabinet Makers, $2,
published annually, 44 pages, illustrated,
black and white.

The superb handcrafted pieces made by Thomas Moser and his band of craftsmen are squarely rooted in Shaker and other American traditional forms; however, one can see a subtle drift toward the contemporary clearly evidenced in the beautiful furniture shown in this catalogue. The predominant wood is American cherry, selected for its color and clarity of grain. No stains are used; the wood is first aged to a dark crimson brown and then given a rubbed oil and natural finish. Each piece of furniture is built entirely by one man, using traditional methods of joinery, and is signed and dated by him. Among the pieces

shown are a harvest table, trestle table, extension tables, cabinets and cupboards, sideboards, desks, headboards, a pencil-post bed, clocks, and a variety of chairs, benches, and settees. Especially striking are the continuous arm chairs, derived from the Windsor chair, and the graceful Rogers "alienation" bench, which has seats on either side, separated by a curving back rail. There are also bowback, fanback, barrel back, and ladderback chairs. Prices range from $300 to $2000. Moser will do custom work to your specification from a photograph or measured drawing, or based on their own designs; these can be either strict period reproductions or contemporary styles. MO

I-65
NICHOLS & STONE COMPANY
232 Sherman Street
Gardner, MA 01440

The Colonial Chair, $1, published annually,
32 pages, illustrated, black and white and
color.

This century-old company is known for making Early American chairs including Boston rockers, Windsor rockers, Windsor side and arm chairs with bow backs, comb backs, and fan backs, and the classic Hitchcock chair. There are also settees and benches, a table collection, and, in the Declaration Americana line, traditional buffets with or without china deck.

Finishes for the chairs range from natural wood tones to traditional colors like barn red and Colonial green, and some have hand-painted or stenciled decorations. The company will send, on request, the name of a dealer in your area. RS

I-66
ORLEANS CARPENTERS
Box 107-C, Rock Harbor Road
Orleans, MA 02653

Colonial and Shaker Reproductions, 25
cents, published annually, 12 pages,
illustrated, black and white and color.

Dick Soule, a former builder and carpentry teacher, and his wife, Phoebe, make the reproductions of Shaker and Colonial pieces, which range from cutting boards and an attractive wood bread-cooling rack to a hutch or chair table with tilt-back round table top and seating space with a storage compartment underneath copied from one in Sturbridge Village, $175 stained and finished. There are also a cedar chest, 43" x 19" x

19½" high ($200), a Colonial mirror with hand-crafted molding, a Shaker stepstool, Shaker peg boards, trays, and boxes, a tavern wall rack, and Shaker bonnet rack or clothes tree made of pine with six birch pegs. Prices are subject to change. MO

I-67
OUTER BANKS PINE PRODUCTS
P.O. Box 9003
Lester, PA 19113

Colonial Corner Cupboards, *brochure, 25 cents, illustrated, black and white.*

A collection of attractive and reasonably priced corner cabinets in eight Colonial styles, available either knocked down or fully assembled. The cabinets are of Ponderosa pine, sanded smooth and ready to stain or paint, with such details as raised panel doors, scalloped-edge shelves, fluted pilasters, finished backs, and bonnet tops. Prices range from under $200 to around $300. The kits, of course, cost less than the assembled pieces. MO

For an office at home (bottom) or a studio workshop (top), Ethan Allen's matching modular wall units offer an open stock plan for solving storage problems. I-4.

I-68
EDWARD PASHAYAN & CO., INC.
305 East 63rd Street
New York, NY 10021

Quality French Furniture, $10, published
semiannually, 50 pages, illustrated, color.

Pashayan is famous for superbly crafted authentic reproductions of eighteenth-century French furniture. The beautifully illustrated catalogue contains armoires and benches, breakfronts, buffets and sideboards, cabinets, commodes, consoles, desks and writing tables, headboards, mirrors and chandeliers, and many different chairs—bergères, fauteuils, desk chairs, dining chairs—shown alone and in handsome room settings. Pieces of modern vintage, such as a glorious Art Deco-style wall unit in Carpathian burl elm with pilasters in burnished gold leaf, coffee tables in Chinese Chippendale style, or polished brass, or brass and steel are equally fine. Many models can be made with variations of size, color, and finish. One of our favorite pieces in this catalogue is a Louis XVI settee copied from one in the Villa D'Este, made deeper and more comfortable with lower back and arms, in a painted finish with a heavenly shade of flame-colored velvet upholstery. RS / ID

I-69
PENNSYLVANIA HOUSE
137 North 11th Street
Lewisburg, PA 17837

The Collector's Book, $7.50, published
annually, 224 pages, illustrated, color.

Pennsylvania House's lavishly illustrated and informative color catalogue shows their four major design collections—Upholstery, Independence Hall Cherry Collection, Stone House Oak Collection, and Bucks County Pine Collection—both as individual pieces with dimensions and in room settings. Some of the room settings show how to switch furniture and room from a winter to a summer color scheme by using Pennsylvania House custom slipcovers; others concentrate on ideas for decorating apartments, on transforming walls or on creating different looks in a room. At the end of the catalogue is a valuable section of consumer information. You are shown how the pieces are made and upholstered. A chart of fabric fibers rates the qualities of each in terms of color fastness, strength, resistance to sun, abrasion, and wrinkling, with cleaning recommendations. There are also pages on color schemes

and the color wheel, wood finishes, the care and cleaning of wood and upholstery, and a floor plan graph with furniture cutouts that enable you to plan a living room, bedroom, or dining room on paper. A list of stores, by state, that sell Pennsylvania House furniture, is included. RS

I-70
LEW RAYNES, INC.
40 East 34th Street
New York, NY 10016

Murphy Beds in Cabinets, leaflets and
brochures, 50 cents.

Shown in the leaflets and brochures are seven different styles of wall cabinets, from modern to traditional to oriental, with the familiar tucked-away Murphy bed in single, double, and queen sizes. The beds are also sold without cabinets. MO

I-71
ROCHE–BOBOIS
200 Madison Avenue
New York, NY 10016

Roche-Bobois, $5 (refundable with
*purchase), published every 18 months, 148
pages, color, illustrated, with illustrated
price list.*

Handsome international designs in contemporary furniture, shown individually and in room settings, make up most of this beautiful, lavishly illustrated catalogue from a company that has showrooms throughout the world. The Roche–Bobois collection is exclusive, with a few exceptions, and all the merchandise has undergone strict selection. In the current catalogue, there are some stunning contemporary versions of Chinese styles, such as a black-lacquered dining suite; a fascinating octagonal dining table in shiny black and red lacquer with a geometric design on the top; a great variety of modern beds, including an oversized "Las Vegas" bed upholstered in velvet or velours; a large 6-seat sofa, and two seating units that can be combined to make an elegant, cushiony daybed. They also have some extremely good-looking wall storage systems, one very avant-garde in dark smoked glass and aluminum, another in amber lacquered wood that looks like tortoiseshell, children's furniture, modern desks and chairs and lots of modular seating units that can be grouped in different ways. The price range is wide, from under $100 for a simple lacquered metal and canvas seating unit to over $6000 for a fabulous sycamore veneer wall unit with inlays of 24-karat gold gilded metal. Roche–Bobois offer a customer advice decorating service in their showrooms. MO / RS

I-72
SELIG MANUFACTURING COMPANY, INC.
54 Green Street
Leominster, MA 01453

Design Folio, $2, published annually, 36 pages, illustrated, black and white and color.

Selig is a specialist in contemporary seating and their product lines are the work of a number of designers both in this country and in Europe, although the furniture is manufactured in the United States. They also import chrome, steel, and glass furniture from Italy, Scandinavia, and other countries. The Design Folio shows two categories of their upholstered furniture—the Monroe Collection in the medium price range, and the more expensive custom Imperial Collection. The groups encompass modular seating, sofas and chairs of different types including convertible sofas, coffee tables, end tables, console tables, and dining tables with bases of wicker, rattan and metal, and glass tops. Unusual wedge-shaped tables designed to match and curve around one of the modular seating groups are included, as is the marvelous contemporary steel-and-leather Franco rocker with a curving

Pacific Silvercloth liners in the four drawers of this cherry silver chest keep the silver bright. Both from Ephraim Marsh, I-63.

frame. Selig designs are sold in department and furniture stores across the country and they will send you, on request, the name of the closest outlet, where you can also see the extensive collection of Selig fabrics. RS / ID

I-73
THE SERAPH, Dept. HDC
Route 148
Brookfield, MA 01506

Brochures, 95 cents, illustrated, black and white.

The Seraph is a family business making reproductions and custom designs developed by architect Valentin Dzelzitis. The sofas, chairs, and chandelier shown in one brochure were originally designed for the restoration of the eighteenth-century restored house adjoining their shop. There are Queen Anne- and Hepplewhite-style wing chairs, and country sofas of the kind made by regional craftsmen in the eighteenth and nineteenth centuries who adapted the popular styles of the day, such as Sheraton and Chippendale, to rural households. The sofas come 54", 66" or 72" long, with straight, rounded, or chamfered legs, upholstered either in their fabrics (samples are sent to you) or, at slight extra cost, in Waverly, Greeff, or Schumacher fabrics. They also do custom work and will design reproduction furniture and accessories from measured drawings. The Seraph reproduction chandeliers of wood and iron and a black iron standing chandelier are each $65. Prices for the country sofas

Hand-carved shell-design blockfront desk is a handsome adaptation.

are from around $465 to $600, according to length and fabric; chairs from $360. MO

I-74
VICTOR STANLEY, INC.
P.O. Box 144
Dunkirk, MD 20754

Slumber/Seat Convertible Chair, free folder, 5 pages and fabric samples, illustrated, color.

Slumber/Seat chairs open into beds of different widths. Enclosed samples show the choice of upholstery materials and colors, among them Herculon velvet olefin fiber, cotton velvet, tweedy patterns in olefin fiber, and solid-color Naugahyde. Also featured are a love seat that opens to a 62" wide bed and a three-section pad that can be folded to make a hassock, lounger, or mattress. Recommended retail prices are included in the folder. RS

I-75
STANLEY FURNITURE
Stanleytown, VA 24168

Showcase Portfolio, $3, published seasonally, illustrated, color.

Five folders comprise the portfolio showing different collections of Stanley's bedroom, dining room, and living room furniture. Vision III, designed by John Mascheroni, features contemporary modular furniture that makes good use of wall space in conjunction with beds, tables, and chairs. Colleen bedroom furniture for a teenage girl comes in soft painted finishes. The other three collections—Simplicity I, Second Edition, and Timbermist—are contemporary styles from elegant to casual. The portfolio also includes graph paper and furniture cutouts for room planning. RS / ID

I-76
SUGAR HILL FURNITURE CORPORATION
Main Street
Lisbon, NH 03585

Brochure, free, 12 pages, illustrated, sepia.

The brochure shows the pieces in this manufacturer's Dartmouth Collection, a line of prefinished, ready-to-assemble furniture that comes individually boxed through dealers with step-by-step assembly instructions and an "Allen wrench" for chair assembly. The collection, made with New Hampshire woods by country craftsmen, includes beds, chairs, tables, wall storage units, sofa units, desks, cabinets, and blanket desk in simple, sturdy contemporary styling and comes with natural finishes or pre-applied dark patina. No prices, but the name of a dealer in your area is supplied on request. Sugar Hill also makes a line of traditional pine furniture. RS

I-77
SYROCO
P.O. Box 4875
Syracuse, NY 13221

Syroco Decorative Accessories Catalogue, free, published annually, 42 pages, illustrated, color.

Although primarily devoted to decorative accessories, this catalogue has a few pages of inexpensive indoor-outdoor furniture made of high impact thermoplastic in white and yellow that could fit many contemporary settings. There are simple game and dining tables with glass or laminated plastic tops and matching chairs, and modular seating systems that can be grouped as sofas, loveseats, or sectionals with plastic frames styled like bamboo and a choice of manmade or natural fabrics for cushions. No prices are given. RS

I-78
TELL CITY CHAIR COMPANY
P.O. Box 329
Tell City, IN 47586

Tell City Primer of Early American Home Decorating, $4, published annually, 124 pages, illustrated, black and white and color.

This hardbound book is both a catalogue of the company's traditional furniture and an introduction to Early American styles and backgrounds, from the Jamestown colonists through the sophisticated design influences of the eighteenth century. The first pages show you how to create a setting with paint, wallpaper, paneling and planking, moldings and beams; give you ideas for dining rooms, window treatments and floors, and lighting; and supply you with pointers on furniture construction. There's also a room-planning kit in the back with furniture cutouts and a graph sheet. The rest of the book shows the different groups of dining room, bedroom, and living room furniture, individually and in room settings; a variety of American rockers,

Robert Whitley designed his rocker twenty-five years ago; each is an original, signed by the creator. I-89.

Thomas Moser's continuous arm chair derived from the traditional Windsor design combines maple, ash, and cherry for strength and beauty. I-64.

chairs, and settles; and accessories from lamps to mirrors to hanging shelves and racks for coats, hats, quilts, and magazines. No prices. RS

I-79
THINLINE
P.O. Box 5688
El Monte, CA 91734

Thinline Outdoor Furniture, free, 8 pages, illustrated, color.

Thinline's La Costa, Rancho, and Casita Diagonal—groups of lightweight, rugged furniture with polyester enamel finish on tubular aluminum frames and vinyl strap or mesh seats and backs—are shown. Table tops are made of clear or smooth-rough tempered glass. The groups include chairs, tables, lounges, ottomans, a bar and bar stools and come in a choice of solid colors. No prices, but a list of showrooms and representatives is given in the catalogue. RS / ID

I-80
THOMASVILLE FURNITURE INDUSTRIES
P.O. Box 339
Thomasville, NC 27360

The Mahogany Collection, $2.50, 50 pages, illustrated, color.

A collection of fine traditional furniture in eighteenth-century styles executed in rich, glowing Honduras mahogany, the wood originally exported to England for cabinetry and used in the Chippendale, Sheraton, and Hepplewhite workshops. Every piece is a treasure, meticulously detailed and designed to express the heritage of

Robert Barrow has faithfully reproduced the Windsor continuous arm settee. I-8.

Colonial America. Included are an oval Queen Anne dining table and chairs, a Sheraton sideboard, an impressive Chippendale buffet and closed deck, and a Hepplewhite console as well as some uniquely American pieces such as the Philadelphia highboy, Charleston tallboy with shell carving and bonnet top, Goddard block-front chest, and a rice poster bed in the Southern plantation style with elaborate rice-leaf carvings and fluted columns. The furniture is shown in room settings in color and in sketches with dimensions. The text that accompanies the photographs is well written and is also packed with information about mahogany, eighteenth-century design, and Colonial America. At the back of the catalogue is a room-planning kit with graph paper and furniture templates. RS

I-81
TOMLINSON FURNITURE
305 High Avenue West
High Point, NC 27261

French from the Provinces, $3.50, 20 pages, illustrated, black and white and color.

This distinctive collection of furniture in the French Provincial style from a leading manufacturer is characterized by attention to detail, elaborate carvings, and selected hardwoods blended with handsome ash and ash burl veneers. There are some truly striking pieces including a handsome refectory dining table with intricate bold relief carvings, a display cabinet, 90″ high x 82″ wide, with rococo carvings, and a magnificent armoire. The entire assemblage of dining and occasional pieces is available in a variety of finishes. RS / ID

I-82
TROPITONE FURNITURE COMPANY, INC.
P.O. Box 3197
Sarasota, FL 33578

Tropitone Casual Furniture, $3, published annually, 48 pages, illustrated, color.

Tropitone's furniture is the kind that takes naturally to the outdoors—by the pool or on the patio. Frames are of heavy-duty aluminum tubing with a durable plastic coating, table tops are of cast acrylic that looks like rough-smooth hammered glass but has seventeen times the impact strength, and the lacing on the seating pieces is of heavy-duty vinyl in a wide variety of colors to mix or match with the frames. Within the different style groups there are dining tables and chairs, sun chaises, lounge chairs with ottomans, side tables, lounging cots, loveseats, umbrella tables, sand or pool chairs, bar stools and a buffet bar, a circular sun lounger, even a drying rack for swimsuits. No price list comes with the catalogue. RS / ID

I-83
UNION–NATIONAL, INC.
226 Crescent Street
Jamestown, NY 14701

Furniture Designed for Gracious Living, $3, 40 pages, illustrated, color.

The catalogue shows the different lines of Union–National's traditional dining and bedroom furniture, available in standard and custom wood finishes or standard and custom painted finishes. The outstanding feature of this furniture is the hand-painted decoration in chinoiserie and floral designs. RS

I-84
THE VIKING SAUNA COMPANY
P.O. Box 6298
San Jose, CA 95150

The Wine Vault, free brochure, 6 pages, illustrated, color.

The ultimate for wine lovers with no cellar to call their own is Viking's Wine Vault, a prebuilt unit that need only be connected to a standard 120-volt outlet. A cooling unit keeps the temperature at a cellar range of 53°F to 57°F in a dark, quiet, vibration-free atmosphere conducive to wine aging, with regulated humidity. The redwood racks are designed to assure proper air circulation around the bottles. The Wine Vault comes in a range of sizes; the Demi Petit, suitable for an apartment, holds 156 bottles (13 cases) and measures 6′ 8″ high x 22½″ deep x 4′ wide ($2,250); the Cellar Master is large enough for almost 2,000 bottles, at a costly $7,250. Custom models can also be made to order. RS

I-85
WALPOLE WOODWORKERS, INC.
767 East Street
Walpole, MA 02081

Walpole Woodworkers. The Distinctive World of Cedar, $1, published annually, 10 pages with order form and price list, illustrated, black and white.

Cedar was one of the first woods harvested and used by the early settlers and one of the earliest sawmills was located in Walpole, where the Walpole Woodworkers have their white cedar fence and furniture plant. Cedar weathers beautifully outdoors, so these simple, rugged chairs, tables, and benches in traditional New England designs —including the Bangor chair, Boothbay rocker, Darien stool, and Aroostock bench—can be used in the garden, in a family room or on a porch. There are also chaises and an old-fashioned porch swing. The furniture, made by local craftsmen, is KD (knocked down) and shipped partially assembled with directions for completing the assembly. Polyfoam pads for chairs are covered with duck cloth in green, blue, tangerine, brown, or yellow. The furniture is carefully crafted for long life, with joints that are mortised and tenoned, pinned, and then waterproof-glued. You'll also find bird feeders and a cracker barrel or cranberry scoop planter on the order form. The prices are very reasonable; around $70 for the Bangor arm chair, plus $19.95 for the seat pad; $96 for the Penobscot settee, 48″ wide x 24″ deep x 35″ high; around $8 and $9 for the planters. MO

I-86
CHARLES WEBB DESIGNER/WOODWORKER
28 Church Street
Cambridge, MA 02138

Catalogue, $2 (refundable with purchase), published annually, 29 pages, black and white.

From a one-man shop, Charles Webb's workshop has grown over almost twenty years to a group of twenty-five cabinetmakers from different countries, so all the furniture is handmade by craftsmen who know their trade. Exceptionally durable and designed in a forthright contemporary way that follows no set style, it has a timeless quality that mixes well with other furniture. Among the pieces shown is the freestanding Shelf System, an assembled-to-order collection of cabinets, drawers, desk, and shelves that may be combined in many different ways, with additional units added as required. It is made of white oak in a natural finish, protected by a film of low-sheen vinyl. Units in cherry, walnut, and stained oak are available on special order. There are various sofa beds, bunk beds, a platform bed cantilevered out from "sled runner" legs with a plain plank or a framed headboard ($330 in queen size with framed headboard), and a plain bed with trundle bed underneath. Other pieces include dining tables, chairs, a slat bench, sofa, sideboard, desks, file cabinets, chests, an armoire, and library steps as well as a planter with slatted sides, bookshelves, a cart, a crib, a pegged board for hanging coats, and a towel bar—a rather amazing collection. The prices are very reasonable for handmade furniture. The library steps cost $85 in oak, $105 in walnut; a four-drawer chest is $310. The sideboard and armoire, each slightly over $800, are the most expensive pieces. MO

Huddlebed, designed by Jim Hull for sleeping or sitting comfort, has three chrome and canvas side frames, a queen-size mattress, and eight plump polyester-filled pillows. I-51.

I-87
WEST END SHOP

P.O. Box 3216
632 South Peters Street
New Orleans, LA 70177

Brochure, 25 cents.

West End Shop started when a group of designers built pieces of furniture for themselves. Friends and visitors saw and liked them, orders came in, and the business started. Their objective is to produce high quality in design, craftsmanship, and materials at a low price, which the brochure would seem to bear out. For instance, the Taj table of solid mahogany with brass ornamentation, a marriage of East and West in style and detail, is just $40 for the cocktail size (18" x 36" x 16" high) and $33 for the end table. The sleekly handsome wood-and-cane Stockholm table is $46 in cocktail size, $41 for the end table. A handsome solid mahogany bar cart with removable tray top and brass corners is around $50. A $2 catalogue currently in preparation was not ready in time for us to review it. MO

I-88
WHITE FURNITURE COMPANY

P.O. Box 367
Mebane, NC 27302

Lorraine V, and Living with Tradition, $1 for the two catalogues, 36 and 14 pages, illustrated, black and white and color.

The 36-page *Lorraine V* catalogue shows the company's dining room and bedroom groups in French Provincial styling and warm fruitwood tones or handpainted antique white finishes. The woods are solid cherry and walnut veneers which are matched to create unique patterns in table tops. There are numerous pieces in the collection—tables and chairs, buffets with china tops, china cabinets, cabinet servers, chests, armoires, beds, dressers, night tables, dressing tables, benches, and matching mirrors—shown both in room settings and individually sketched pieces, with specifications. *Living with Tradition* shows the same style of chests, armoires, and buffets with delicate painted floral and chinoiserie decoration on the antique white finish or raised gesso chinoiserie decoration on wood finish, plus headboards and glass-topped tables with bases of cast aluminum finished in gold metal leaf. A small booklet included with the catalogues tells how the furniture is made—the selection, conditioning, and working of the wood, the construction, hand finishing, and hardware—and how to care for and maintain it, with useful tips on removal of burns, alcohol spots, paint, scratches, nail polish, and spilled liquids. RS

I-89
ROBERT WHITLEY STUDIO

Laurel Road
Solebury, PA 18963

The Whitley Rocker, $4 (refundable with purchase), published annually, 16 pages, illustrated, black and white and color.

Robert Whitley is a master craftsman who restores antiques and makes antique reproductions, mostly for local or special orders; however, he also sells by mail a bent-back rocker in American black walnut (cherry and ash are alternate choices) which he describes as "a contemporary statement rooted in the furniture of the past." The rocker, while hardly inexpensive ($1400), is a unique work of art in which the grain of the wood and sculptural lines combine to make a beautiful object that is also strong and functional. As Mr. Whitley says, "The rocker is designed for utmost comfort and comes alive when it is used . . . the curve and slant force you to sit back until you are almost cradled in it." Anyone who loves rockers or, for that matter, superbly handcrafted furniture, could not fail to fall in love with it. The handsomely illustrated and well-written brochure shows steps in the hand manufacture, from turning to spoke shaving to steam bending to finish sanding and assembly (each angle and joint of the rocker is designed and constructed to interlock) and makes fascinating reading. The rocker and other pieces of Mr. Whitley's fine contemporary sculptural furniture may be seen at his studio, which is outside New Hope in Bucks County. A map is shown on the order form. MO

I-90
THE WICKER WORKS

650 Potero Avenue
San Francisco, CA 94110

Wicker Works, $1, published seasonally, 12-page brochure, illustrated, black and white.

Handsome, contemporary wicker seating and dining pieces for indoors and out—chairs, sofas, loveseats; daybeds and ottomans with loose, reversible cushions; bar stools; and table bases with glass tops in various styles and sizes, from end tables to coffee tables to dining tables—are

Le Corbusier's highly personal, simplified twentieth-century designs, reproduced by Atelier International, I-7, contrast sharply with the fussier lines of the Victorian reproductions from Martha M. House, I-49.

Oak flat office files can be used at home for storage of flatware, place mats, and napkins. Charette, I-23.

the main focus of this brochure. The Wicker Works also shows pieces from other collections, such as Provincial chairs with wood frames and upholstery, or cane backs, or rush seats; a glass-topped rattan table; and a stone garden seat that simulates wood. No prices are given. RS / ID

I-91
LEE L. WOODARD & SONS, INC.
P.O. Box 001, Elm Street
Owosso, MI 48867

The Worth of Woodard, *$3, published annually, 80 pages, illustrated, color.*

An attractively produced catalogue of Woodard's collections of hand-forged iron indoor-outdoor furniture, available in a choice of 21 color finishes. The design details in the different collections are shown in close-up and in settings outside and inside. Some of the pieces have vinyl strapping, others have vinyl cushions; tables have glass or mesh tops. There are engaging versions of bentwood, traditional, and sleekly contemporary designs. In addition to seating pieces and tables, Woodard has matching serving carts, baker's racks, and plant stands. RS / ID

I-92
WORKBENCH
470 Park Avenue South
New York, NY 10016

Workbench, *$2, published every two years, 44 pages, illustrated, color.*

Good design and workmanship at a reasonable price have been the concerns of Workbench. Their clean-lined, functional contemporary furniture, from the modern classics to trend-setting new designs, much imported from Europe or designed exclusively for Workbench, covers everything imaginable from upholstered pieces to children's furniture to Italian plastic stacking modules, nesting tables and chairs, wastebaskets, and stackable mesh baskets. In upholstered furniture you can have stock or custom upholstery and seating pieces with KD (knocked down) construction that can be assembled without tools. There are sectionals, seating pieces that open into beds, upholstered chairs, butcher-block tables, dining tables in wood and plastic, wood and Swedish white-lacquered stacking storage units, desks, desk chairs, filing cabinets, end and coffee tables, and eighteen kinds of dining chairs, from Windsors to cane and tubular chrome. Workbench has bedroom furniture, leisure furniture, and an ingenious cooking center or desk combination by Palaset that combines eight cubes with drawers, shelves, cabinets, and vertical storage space plus a butcher-block top. One especially attractive piece of children's furniture is the Italian bunk bed with white metal tube frame and ladder, snap-on canvas end panels and a crib that converts to a desk, designed to coordinate with white-lacquered Finnish modular storage units. MO

I-93
YIELD HOUSE, INC.
Route 16
North Conway, NH 03860

Yield House, free, published quarterly, 74 pages, illustrated, color.

Yield House is most famous for furniture kits that come ready-to-assemble and finish, although a few pieces of furniture shown in the catalogue are not available in kit form. These include an Oriental cabinet with handpainted chinoiserie decoration, signed by the artist, around $450, and a Queen Anne-style desk with black-and-gold drawers, hand-stenciled in the Hitchcock manner. The furniture sold either in an Easy Kit or finished is varied in style. There's a tall curio cabinet (around $120 in kit form, $180 finished), a Rutherford Hayes rolltop desk, a rolling buffet, a sewing/hobby center, bookcases, file cabinets, hutches and other storage pieces, and all kinds of tables and chairs. MO

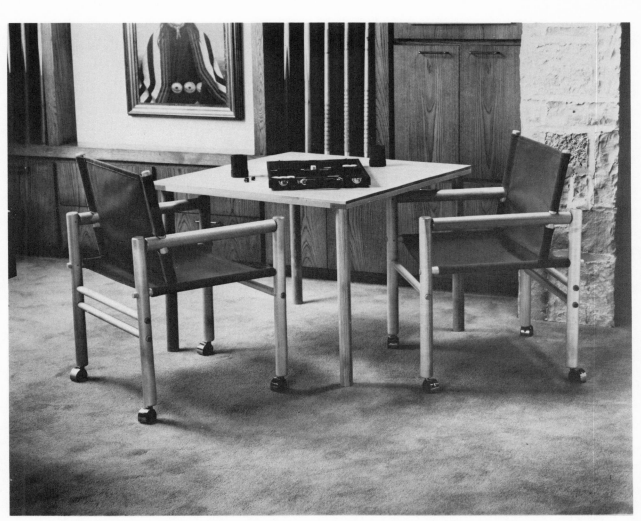

Hardwood table and chairs with canvas covers can double for games or dining, come KD from Gold Medal, I-40.

II

Floor, Wall, and Ceiling Coverings

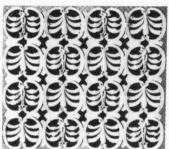

II-1
AA–ABBINGDON CEILING CO., INC.
2149 Utica Avenue
Brooklyn, NY 11234

Return with Us to Yesteryear, free brochure, illustrated, black and white.

This company makes the pressed metal ceilings that are back in vogue. They have about twenty patterns, some like the old-fashioned tin ceilings, others more contemporary, with cornices to match or harmonize. Installation is easy and can be done by an amateur. Instructions on the back tell you how to do it yourself. The metal can either be painted with an oil-based paint or coated with clear polyurethane to retain the natural color. Request the price list when sending for the booklet. MO

II-2
ALEXANDER WALLPAPER
12221 Nebel Street
Rockville, MD 20852

Arirang Oriental Grasscloths, $2.25, swatches and order form.

The beautiful handmade grasscloths in the swatch book range from solid colors to delicately shaded neutrals on colored or metallic backgrounds. There are also two very interesting cork designs. Prices for a single roll range from $8.90 to $15.90; however, grasscloth is sold by the double roll only—3' wide x 24' long or 72 square feet. The order form explains a simple way of estimating how much you will need. MO

II-3
ETHAN ALLEN, INC.
Ethan Allen Drive
Danbury, CT 06810

The Ethan Allen Treasury of American Traditional Interiors, $7.95, published every two years, 394 pages, illustrated, color.

A few pages in this huge catalogue from a major home-furnishings manufacturer are devoted to broadloom carpet. A wide range of colors, textures and fibers, rugs of Oriental inspiration, and braided, Berber weave and alpaca fur accent rugs are featured, all designed to harmonize and coordinate with Ethan Allen furniture. RS

II-4
AMERICAN DISCOUNT WALLCOVERINGS
1411 Fifth Avenue
Pittsburgh, PA 15219

Order form, no charge.

This company will give you a quotation on wallcoverings if you write or call them with the pattern number and name of the book, and you buy at a discount. We suggest you write for the order form, as it gives a lot of pertinent information; however, if you know the wallpaper pattern and amount you need, call their toll-free number, 1–800–245–1768. Orders may be charged to MasterCard or Visa. MO

II-5
AMERICAN OLEAN TILE COMPANY
1000 Cannon Avenue
Lansdale, PA 19446

American Olean is Ceramic Tile, *free catalogue, published annually, 36 pages, illustrated, color, and* **Real Ceramic Tile,** *free brochure, illustrated, color.*

The catalogue shows the various patterns, colors, finishes, and shapes of American Olean's glazed tile, ceramic mosaics, and quarry tile, in installations and individually. The tiles are described in detail with color names and sizes, recommendations for application, trim, and harmonizing bathroom accessories to be set into the tiled wall. There are also photographs of installing pre-grouted and back-mounted sheets of tile. A list of sales representatives, sales service centers, and distributors is given. A handy reference if you are considering tiling a floor, wall, or countertop. The brochure on ceramic tile depicts its use in kitchens and bathrooms and rates its practicality and serviceability against that of other materials. RS

Windowless wall in a city apartment is opened up with a forest scene photomural from Naturescapes, II-23.

II-6
ARIUS TILE COMPANY
P.O. Box 5497
Santa Fe, NM 87502

Arius Tile, $3 *(refundable with purchase), published semiannually, 26 pages, illustrated, color.*

Arius buys unglazed floor tile, machine-made in the U.S. and handmade in Mexico, and the designs and glazes are applied by their own artisans. The tiles are compatible with American quarry tile in 6″ square, 6″ hexagonal, and 4″ x 8″ sizes, and with the Mexican terra-cotta tile in 4″, 8″ and 10″ squares. These unusual and distinctive art tiles, many with American Indian and Southwestern motifs, can be used in bathrooms, around pools, and around fireplaces, hearths, and ranges. You can also have wallpaper designs duplicated on tile for bath or kitchen. Shown in the catalogue are some striking designs by Santa Fe artist Ford Ruthling, zodiac designs by Karen Moffitt, natural motifs, and pictorial designs. There are also tile murals, backgammon and cheeseboards with tile inserts, and tables of oiled

Floor patterned with traditional floral and geometric designs of Karastan's Oriental rug shows off Chinese-style dining pieces. II-19.

Walls paneled with redwood create a contemporary and natural-looking bath. California Redwood, XIII-5.

Ceiling and walls covered in allover print vinyl contrast with stainless steel, clear acrylic, white tile, and jet black Naugahyde in this sophisticated dining kitchen designed by Judith Ross and Nina Saunders. Uniroyal, III-30.

Western alder wood topped with arrangements of tile with pre-Columbian motifs (you can, if you prefer, make up your own arrangement using examples in the catalogue). You can also order framed tiles bearing name, address, and house number. Prices for individual tiles range from $5 to $27.50, according to size and design. Shipping weights are given and there's a UPS rate chart for weights from one to 50 pounds. Shipping, packing, and crating charges are extra.

In addition to the decorative tiles, Arius offers two lines of floor tiles. A selection of glazed tile designs can be used in conjunction with standard quarry tile to give a floor a custom look in a small number of stock designs. (You can select your own color combinations or submit your own designs.) The second line, Tiles of Santa Fe, consists of handcrafted tiles with the look of terra-cotta, flat and presealed for easy installation, but as no two tiles are exactly alike they have an individuality you don't get in standard tile. All the traditional shapes are available in antique leather finish. Literature on the floor tiles is free. MO

II-7
LAURA ASHLEY
Mail Order Department
Building 296, Radar Street
Port Newark, NJ 07114

Laura Ashley by Mail, $2, 22 pages, illustrated, color.

Among the color and pattern coordinated home furnishings in the Laura Ashley mail-order catalogue are some charming ceramic wall and floor tiles made in Italy, approximately 7¾" x 7¾" square, in 23 patterns and matching plain colors. Like the fabrics they complement, the patterns have a country air—sprigged, leaf and flower, or simple geometrics in fresh bright colors on a white or cream background. They run around $3 a tile, or $56 per square meter. MO

II-8
BARNEY BRAINUM–SHANKER STEEL COMPANY, INC.
70–32 83rd Street
Glendale, NY 11385

Decorative Metal Ceilings, no charge, 8 pages, illustrated, black and white.

"Tin ceilings" were all the rage in the nineteenth century and have been enjoying a revival over the last few years. This company copies them in decorative repoussé plates of sheet steel made on huge power presses. The plates come in 3″, 6″, 12″ and 24″ multiples measuring 24″ x 96″ and in many different patterns, and can be used on walls as well as on ceilings. There are also cornice strips 4′ long to combine with the plates. One page of the booklet has installation instructions and photographs showing how to assemble the ceiling, which should be painted with an oil-base paint. Prices on request. MO / ID

II-9
BLACKWELDER FURNITURE COMPANY
Highway 21 North
Statesville, NC 28634

Blackwelder's Fine Home Furnishings, $3, published annually, 108 pages, illustrated, color.

Among the other home furnishings Blackwelder sells at below-retail prices are reproduction Oriental rugs by Pande Cameron. For details of their pricing and ordering operation, see page 19. MO

II-10
CONRAN'S MAIL ORDER
145 Huguenot Street
New Rochelle, NY 10805

Conran's, $2.50, published annually, 112 pages, illustrated, color.

Tough, durable, inexpensive mats and matting are part of Conran's mail-order merchandise (handwoven rugs are mainly obtainable through the stores). A circular plaited grass mat from China, 48″ in diameter, is $12.50; a Panama mat of coir tightly interwoven with aloe in a checkered effect, 4′ x 7′, is $36; another from India in

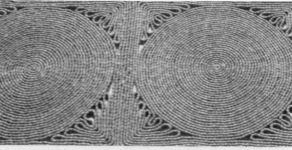
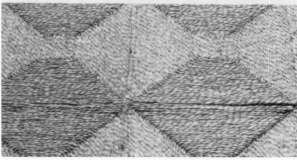

Bullseye and Chinese rush tile matting from Conran's, II-10.

a chevron weave, 4′ x 6′, is $55. There is also a collection of good-looking coordinated contemporary wallpapers and fabrics: some of the papers are vinyl-coated, others have spongeable surfaces, many are prepasted; the fabrics are 100 percent cotton. Prices are reasonable. Conran's also offers a curtain-making service. You will also find in the catalogue bed linens in solid colors or crisp patterns with matching covers for the duvets (comforters) they sell. MO / RS

II-11
COUNTRY FLOORS
300 East 61st Street
New York, NY 10021

Ceramic Tiles for Floors and Walls, $5 (refundable with purchase), published annually, 34 pages in folder, illustrated, color.

A handsome and varied collection of imported tiles. The incomparable traditional terra-cotta floor tiles of Provence in a variety of shapes, also available in deep, transparent colors; handmade terra-cotta floor tiles from Mexico; from Italy, most unusual Perspettiva graphic floor tiles, modules that combine into three-dimensional patterns, and wall tiles in both traditional and chic contemporary designs; hand-painted wall relief tiles from Spain with traditional Moorish, chevron, and checkerboard designs; Portugal,

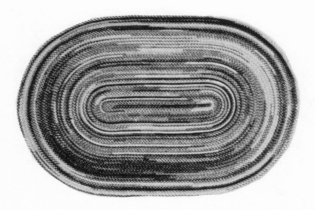

Oval braided rug in many colors from Habersham, II-16.

the country most deeply rooted in ceramic tile decoration, provides beautiful traditional patterns; the Royal Makuum Dutch tiles with seventeenth- and eighteenth-century designs; and a riot of highly decorative and rustic Mexican tiles. Tile fanciers can have a field day. While mail order is hardly the ideal way to buy heavy items like tiles, it is the only answer if you live in a part of the country where the choice is limited. Price lists and installation instructions are available on request. MO / RS / ID

II-12
EDISON INSTITUTE
20900 Oakwood Boulevard
Dearborn, MI 48124

Reproductions from the Collections of Greenfield Village and the Henry Ford Museum, $2.50, 46 pages, illustrated, black and white and color.

The Edison Institute's reproductions include documentary wallpapers and fabrics by the S. M. Hexter Company, ranging from a pattern used to line an eighteenth-century hatbox to the crewel work found on a Queen Anne wing chair to a chariot wheel design from a coverlet. The Greenfield Collection of wallcoverings comes in 94 colors; prepasted, pretrimmed papers, and strippable and washable acrylic vinyl. Some have matching fabrics. The fabrics are 54"-wide cotton sailcloth or 50"-wide cotton and polyester chintz; the designs are taken from printed textiles, books, engravings, china, paintings, and antique quilts and coverlets in the Edison Institute's collection. There are also some fine hooked rugs made by Mountain Rug Mills of North Carolina; you'll find original stenciled designs from the Edward Sands Frost catalogue as well as exact copies of hooked rugs used in the historic houses of the Village. MO

II-13
ELON, INCORPORATED
198 Saw Mill River Road
Elmsford, NY 10523

Elon Tiles, $1, 16 pages, illustrated, color.

Contemporary handmade tiles from Mexico in a wonderful range of sizes and types. There are the familiar unglazed terra-cotta tiles, finished with a clear penetrating oil-base sealer to enhance the natural look, some with decorative blue-and-white tile inserts that can be combined with the square, rectangular, or hexagonal tiles. Also in-

cluded are solid glazed square tiles for walls, floors, bathtubs, countertops, and backsplashes in seventeen different colors, decorative tiles with traditional provincial and geometric motifs, and others with designs of fruit, flowers, birds, and vegetables that would look great in a kitchen. A unique group features lava-stone tiles for interior or exterior walls, marble tiles with pink or gray tones, and relief tiles available in all glazed colors or unglazed tones. Standard or custom trim is available to coordinate with the tiles. Elon also has a line of handmade sinks and accessories to match the tiles. Request price list when writing. MO / RS / ID

II-14
FLOORCLOTHS INCORPORATED
P.O. Box 812
Severna Park, MD 21146

Brochure, $2, published annually, 9 pages, illustrated, black and white and color, with color swatches on canvas chips.

This company was formed about ten years ago to reproduce floorcloths, the hand-painted patterned canvas floor coverings used in the eighteenth and nineteenth centuries instead of expensive imported rugs and carpets. One of the earliest references to them is in a 1729 inventory of William Burnet, once the governor of New York, Massachusetts, and New Jersey, who listed "two old checquered canvases to lay under the table" and "a large painted canvas square as the room." Painted floorcloths continued to be used until the third quarter of the nineteenth century, sometimes as a summer replacement for heavy carpets, sometimes as hall and stair runners. Patterns were plentiful and ranged from plain colors to complicated geometrics to elegant florals.

Floorcloths Incorporated chooses designs from documented patterns taken from eighteenth- and nineteenth-century designers, period paintings, museum archives, or from original orders. One, a trompe l'oeil pattern that looks like squares of marble, was taken from an American primitive painting that hangs in the Abby Aldrich Rockefeller Folk Art Museum, dated about 1800; another came from a Pennsylvania Dutch blanket chest. The floorcloths are made of specially milled canvas and painted with oil-base paints in a hard-gloss or semigloss finish. In addition to the standard colors shown on the chart, custom colors can be mixed from paint chips, wallpaper, fabric, etc., at an extra charge of from $50 to $75, according to size. Prices range from $150 for a 3' x 5' to $1400 for a 10' x 14' floorcloth. Through the customer design service, the designers will create motifs or a personal design to your order. Floorcloths come with instructions for care and cleaning. MO

II-15
FURNITURECRAFT, INC.
Box 285c
Stoneham, MA 02180

FurnitureCraft, Inc. Distinctive Early American Furnishings, 50 cents, published semiannually, 32 pages, illustrated, color.

Among the traditional American furnishings shown in this nifty little catalogue are braided rugs, with or without fringed borders, and matching unfringed stair treads, thirteen to a set, made of a soft but durable nylon-acrylic mixture. Background colors are rust, brown, or bronze. You can also get matching fringed or unfringed seat pads for chairs ($17 for a set of four). The rugs come in full sizes from 6' x 9' to 9' x 12', and in three scatter sizes. They range in price from $18.35 for a 22" x 44" scatter rug to around $185 for a 9' x 12' room-size rug. A reversible flat-braid half rug, 36" wide x 18" deep in red, gold, or yellow, perfect in front of a sink, hearth, or front door, is around $23. MO

Cool ceramic tiles for the floor, walls, and countertops combine with wood-paneled ceiling and cabinets in this very contemporary kitchen by American Olean, II-5.

Warm wood tones of parquet squares add richness to a library/sitting room. Harris, II-17.

II-16
HABERSHAM PLANTATION CORPORATION
P.O. Box 1209
Toccoa, GA 30577

The Habersham Plantation Workbook, $8.50 (refundable with purchase through dealer), published semiannually, 56 pages, illustrated, color.

The beautiful catalogue put out by Habersham Plantation includes a small number of rugs compatible with their American country furniture. The rugs come in oval, round, and rectangular shapes, some with floral designs, others with simple, contemporary motifs that work well with period furniture. Quite a few are the traditional braided rugs. RS

II-17
HARRIS MANUFACTURING COMPANY
P.O. Box 300
Johnson City, TN 37601

Harris Hardwood Flooring, 50 cents, published annually, 12 pages, illustrated, color.

Harris parquet floorings come in different wood species such as red oak, white oak, walnut, maple, and angelique teak, and in patterns from simple to intricate, all of which are shown in close-up in the color catalogue. They also have ¾"-thick traditional random width plank flooring in teak and oak with tongue and grooved sides and ends and beveled or square edges that can be used to panel walls. A specification data chart is given in the back of the catalogue. RS

II-18
HOBOKEN WOOD FLOORS CORPORATION
100 Willow Street
East Rutherford, NJ 07073

Hoboken Wood Floors, $1, published annually, 10 pages, illustrated, color.

The different styles of Hoboken's flooring— among them plank flooring, custom designs in parquet, and a white-stained hardwood parquet with polyurethane finish that looks like handlaid stone—are shown in colorful room settings in this catalogue. There's also a natural cork flooring bonded between a vinyl backing and transparent surface and a vinyl-bonded flooring made with real wood veneers that can be cleaned with a damp mop. For do-it-yourselfers, Hoboken will supply instructions for installing many of their floors and give advice on the proper tools and adhesives. Most wooden floors can be installed over any subfloor including concrete, vinyl, and plywood, as well as over radiant heat. RS

II-19
KARASTAN RUG MILLS
919 Third Avenue
New York, NY 10022

Rug Collections of Karastan, $1.50, published semiannually, 36 pages, illustrated, color.

This is basically a handbook designed to give consumers quite detailed information about Karastan's collection of Oriental design area rugs, some of which are adaptations of treasured historic rugs from great art museums. It contains fascinating background material on Oriental rug designs and on the making of the Karastan rugs, woven on special Axminster looms that can reproduce a virtually unlimited number of colors in a pattern (computers control the feeding of the different colored dyed-in-the-wool yarns into the machinery), with color photographs of the different patterns in a variety of room settings.

The catalogue also shows contemporary "carved rugs" in solid colors with a sculptured look, for which patterns are hand-carved with electric shears into the surface of luxurious plush wool broadloom. Besides the forty standard patterns, Karastan will also custom-carve a rug to your own design and size specifications, for an additional charge. Karastan rugs are sold through retail sources. RS / ID

II-20
MAYFLOWER WALLPAPER COMPANY
363 Mamaroneck Avenue
White Plains, NY 10605

Swatches of grasscloth wallpapers, $2, refundable with purchase.

There are fifty-eight 3" x 4" swatches of grasscloth wallpaper in the samples sent by Mayflower, both solids and color combinations, in close or open weaves. Prices for a single roll (36" x 12') range from $9.95 to $15.50. MO

II-21
MILL HOUSE
Scotts Corners
Pound Ridge, NY 10576

Free catalogue, 6 pages with price lists, illustrated, color.

The Mill House catalogue of imported faience features some delightful "culinarios"—hand-painted tiles from Portugal depicting such natural motifs as fruits, nuts, vegetables, birds, and animals—that would be perfect for a kitchen wall, a countertop, a hearth, or a table top. They have 75 different designs (about 39 are shown) that can be combined with blank and border tiles. Culinarios are 5½" square and cost $5.95, blank tiles are $2.95. A 10 percent discount is given on 50 or more tiles. MO

II-22
MUSSALLEM ORIENTAL RUGS, INC.
1922 Phoenix Avenue
Jacksonville, FL 32206

Mussallem, $3.50, 24 pages, illustrated, color.

A lavishly illustrated booklet containing information about authentic Oriental rugs and a short history of the Mussallem family business. Illustrated in color are examples of various rugs: Antique Sarouk, Tienstien Chinese, prayer design Tabriz, Abade Persian, Ardebil, and Antique Heriz, plus photographs of Oriental rugs in room

Coordinated patterns in wall coverings and fabrics give this tiny bedroom a fresh, cozy look. Van Luit, II-30.

Exact copies of early hand-hooked American rugs from the homes of Greenfield Village are reproduced by Mountain Rug Mills for Edison Institute, II-12.

settings with traditional and modern furniture. Mussallem also has a reweaving and cleaning service for these precious handmade works of art. RS

II-23
NATURESCAPES, INC.
Brenton Cove
Newport, RI 02840

Naturescapes, free, published annually, 24 pages, illustrated, color.

A range of dramatic color photo murals reproduced on a smooth, matte finish synthetic paper that can be installed with liquid vinyl wallpaper paste in a couple of hours. As the material won't stretch or tear when wet it can be applied, moved, and pulled off the wall until properly aligned. The panels are pretrimmed for overlap in any direction. The murals are completely dry strippable, so they can be peeled off a wall and rehung in another location. These works by fine photographer/naturalists include woodland scenes, a flowering desert, rippling streams, lakes and mountains, sand dunes and seascapes, and are so realistic and beautiful that they give a room a totally new dimension, like opening a window on nature. No prices are given, but a list of distributors is included. Naturescapes also sells for $20, direct or from distributors, a hardcover 16″ x 20″ book showing the whole design collection. Write for the name of your nearest retail source. RS

II-24
OLD WORLD MOULDING & FINISHING COMPANY, INC.
115 Allen Boulevard
Farmingdale, NY 11735

Design Style Book of Genuine Hardwood, Modular Paneling, Cabinetry and Fine Mouldings, $1, 24 pages, published annually, illustrated, black and white and color.

Cost and the scarcity of craftsmen has restricted the manufacture of fine woodwork with carved trim and antique finishes, but Old World Moulding, through a patented system for the modular fabrication of complete interiors and the development of new woodworking methods, has found a way to recreate ornamental woodwork in period styles. The company can handle all aspects of architectural woodworking, such as paneling, cabinetry, mantels, stairways, carved beams, and mouldings of all kinds and will undertake custom work. The catalogue shows some interior installations in color and the individual elements in black and white with sizes and prices. Prices for trim start at 45 cents per foot, reasonable for this quality work. MO / ID

II-25
ORIENTAL RUG RETAILERS OF AMERICA
P.O. Box 5337
Jacksonville, FL 32207

Romance of Oriental Rugs, $1, 20 pages, illustrated, color.

A booklet that will answer many of your questions about Oriental rugs. First it defines a genuine Oriental rug as one made of wool (or perhaps silk) entirely hand-woven by native craftsmen in areas from the shores of the Persian Gulf to India, China, and Japan, and gives history and background information. One sketch shows the famous weaving centers; also illustrated are the Persian or sehna knot and the Turkish or ghiordes knot. There's a discussion of patterns and a definition of the different types of rugs from Persian to Chinese. Rugs are shown in room settings and a final section has advice on care and buying. MO

II-26
ROLLERWALL, INC.
P.O. Box 757
Silver Spring, MD 20901

Free brochure, published annually, illustrated, black and white.

This company has come up with a new, easy-to-use two-part roller to paint patterns on walls, floors, ceilings, furniture, or fabric. One part is a 6″ wide rubber roller with a pattern embossed on the surface, the other an applicator with frame, handle, and a sponge feeder roller that you first dip in the paint; snap on the design roller and you're ready to go. The patterned roller picks up just enough paint to print a perfect pattern on the surface and you renew the paint after every fourth stroke. The 170 patterns shown, ranging from floral to woodgrain to scenic, have an all-over repeat; all you do is paint each stroke alongside the previous one so the patterns touch or slightly overlap. Any type of paint can be used, and you can erase a pattern by painting over it. There are two types of applicator. Model A has the feeder roller ($12.95); Model B has a feeder roller plus paint tank, which will hold enough to paint a whole room ($24.95). The design rollers are sold separately at $9.95 each, or with a 20 percent discount on 18 or more design rollers. MO

II-27
SHIBUI WALLCOVERINGS
P.O. Box 1638
Rohnert Park, CA 94928

Handcrafted Wallcoverings, and Genuine Cork Wallcoverings, $2 (refundable with purchase), brochure and samples, illustrated, color.

Shibui's selection of wallcoverings, samples of which are sent with the brochure and order sheet, includes cork, jute-fiber grasscloth, rush-cloth, bamboo-like split reed on a paper backing, bamboo-design linen, and various textured fiber weaves. They also sell split bamboo molding with predrilled holes and matching color nails, as well as all the tools and accessories you need to hang the wallcoverings yourself, such as a paper-hanging kit, adhesive, and a spray-on protective coating (if you prefer, the company will apply the coating before sending your order). Shibui claims that their handmade wall-coverings sell for about half the retail price and certainly they are most reasonable, starting from around $11 to $20 for a single 36" x 12' roll. Wallcoverings are packaged in double and triple roll bolts, cork in double rolls 30" wide x 30' long. The company will estimate the number of rolls you need if you send them the dimensions of your room. MO

II-28
SMALL FRY SHOPS
Box 76303
Los Angeles, CA 90005

Children's Decorative Items, free, published annually, 16 pages, illustrated, color.

Small Fry Shops has a full line of cut-out and paste-on wall decorations for children's rooms, starting with nursery rhymes and working up to space ships. Included are giant 2'-tall circus animal cutouts for nursery or bulletin board (48-piece set is around $5); a set of 24 butterflies; an amusing mock fireplace with alphabet tiles, clock, doll, piggy bank, and candlestick on the mantel, with a wood basket and hearth broom. The sets of bright letters and numbers make learning into a game. MO

Rustic Portuguese wall tiles, still handmade in the 400-year-old tradition, charmingly enliven this powder room. Country Floors, II-11.

II-29
ERNEST TREGOWAN, INC.
306 East 61st Street
New York, NY 10021

Tregowan Moroccan Rugs, and New England Guild Tregmaid Rugs, free color brochures.

One brochure shows a few examples of rugs hand-knotted in Morocco, of which there are over 90 patterns with a choice of 103 stock colors. The other features handcrafted Tregmaid wool rugs in a variety of motifs, ranging from a reproduction of an eighteenth-century Agra rug to traditional American quilt and floral designs to needlepoint and contemporary patterns. RS / ID

II-30
VAN LUIT & COMPANY
4000 Chevy Chase Drive
Los Angeles, CA 90039

Wallcoverings brochure, $1, and sample, 50 cents, published quarterly, 16 pages, illustrated, color.

Van Luit is one of the leading names in beautiful wallcoverings and the Environs Collection brochure we received shows 17 of their designs, each of which is available in different color combinations, in some cases with related fabrics. A few of the papers have shimmering metallic backgrounds, while others are inspired by tea-chest papers, Dutch tile, and damask. RS / ID

II-31
SHERLE WAGNER INTERNATIONAL, INC.
60 East 57th Street
New York, NY 10021

Sherle Wagner Catalogue, $5, 82 pages, illustrated, color, and **The Sherle Wagner Tile Collection** *supplement, 8 pages, illustrated, color.*

The tile collection supplement to this fabulous catalogue of bathroom fittings and accessories shows the beautiful limited-edition, hand-painted wall tiles that match or harmonize with the bowls, faucets, and accessories. The tiles, 8″ square, are ingeniously designed to form linking patterns that can be combined in different ways to make a series of wall murals. One of the most gorgeous is the water lily pattern—lily pads,

flowers, and butterflies on a deep blue ground. There are also sculptured and plain tiles coated with gold or platinum. MO / RS / ID

II-32
WINFIELD DESIGN ASSOCIATES, INC.
P.O. Box 3711
San Francisco, CA 94119

Brochure 7, free, 20 pages, illustrated, color.

Winfield manufactures wall coverings and this brochure shows fourteen of their very striking modern patterns, which range from geometrics to mural panels, many in colors combined with metallics. One very interesting concept is "Alluvia," a design system of stripe panels and round corners that can be combined in many different ways for various effects. If you are looking for out-of-the-ordinary wall coverings, this company has them. While this is the only brochure they mail out, they do have many other wall coverings that are sold through retail stores. RS / ID

Alluvia, the design system that combines two patterns to create variations of custom wall treatments, from Winfield, II-32.

III

Bedding, Curtains, Shades, Blinds, and Fabrics

III-1
LAURA ASHLEY
Mail Order Department
Building 296, Radar Street
Port Newark, NJ 07114

Laura Ashley by Mail, $2, 22 pages, illustrated, color.

The mail-order catalogue of this British-based company, which has stores in the U.S. and Canada, shows the various patterns and color choices in the comprehensive collection of coordinated home furnishings and accessories for the table, desk, and bedroom designed by Laura Ashley. The prints have a fresh, crisp, country charm and would be delightful in a bedroom, living room, guest room, and bathroom. The collection includes 48"-wide country cotton in sprigged floral patterns with matching solid colors and 90"- to 95"-wide cotton for curtains, draperies, and slipcovers or upholstery; 48"-wide plasticized cotton and double-sided quilted cotton; cushion covers; tablecloths, napkins, and quilted place mats. These, plus matching wallpapers with border prints, ceramic floor or wall tiles, and flat or gloss vinyl paint in twenty-one colors, make it simple to create a total effect in a room. There are even fabric-covered accessories, including cosmetic and lingerie bags, a picture frame, desk pad, diary, engagement book, photo album, and sewing or jewelry box. Wallpaper is around $15 a roll. Cottons range in price, according to width and type, from $8.50 to $21 a yard, with a lining cotton in white or cream at $8.50 a yard. MO / RS

III-2
CAROL BROWN
Putney, VT 05346

Free brochure, with stamped, self-addressed envelope.

Carol Brown, over ninety and still going strong, runs a very personal family business with her nephew, Lawrie, stocking and selling Irish products and various fabrics. The brochure describes the kinds of things they have, such as hand- and machine-woven Irish tweeds of varying weights, textures, patterns, and colors for clothes, upholstery, curtains, or hangings; handwoven Irish wool bedspreads; Irish blankets; and lots of cottons, by the yard, for bedspreads and panels. There are a few wall hangings listed and priced. One is a colorful, washable Dutch/African batik print on cotton, 47" x 70" ($16.50 ppd.). Unless you can stop by the Browns' cottage-cum-store in Vermont, the thing to do if you have a very specific request is to write listing purpose, quantity, color, etc., and ask for samples. MO / RS

III-3
CAROLINA STUDIOS
P.O. Box 191
Southern Pines, NC 28387

Carolina Studios Custom Bedspreads, $1, 12 pages, illustrated, black and white and color.

Carolina Studios offers a fabric quilting service, either in your own or one of their hundreds of fabrics, samples of which will be sent on request. The catalogue shows a selection of styles from which you can choose. In addition to quilted bedspreads and valances, they also make draperies, pillows, tiebacks, bolsters, and table covers. A measuring guide is given in the back of the catalogue. Prices for a bedspread made up in your own fabric run from around $50 for twin size to just under $100 for king size. Valances, 20″ deep, are $3.50 a foot. MO

III-4
CENTENNIAL CURTAINS
P.O. Box 223
Englishtown, NJ 07726

Classical Grace from Centennial Curtains,
free brochure.

Centennial Curtains offers four traditional styles, some with matching quilted bedspreads and pillow shams. Among them are tier curtains, tiebacks with valances, and natural-color tab curtains of permanent-press polyester cotton with a border print trim. The tab curtains are priced from $11 to $22 a pair, plus $1.50 for tiebacks. MO

III-5
CENTRAL SHIPPEE, INC., THE FELT PEOPLE
Bloomingdale, NJ 07403

Colors in Felt, and *Hushalon/Tempora, free*
leaflets of felt swatches.

Rightly named the Felt People, Central Shippee has a fabulous selection. There is 12-ounce mead felt and 9-ounce craft felt of 40 percent wool and 60 percent viscose rayon, both 72″ wide, in 72 colors. Hushalon, a heavier 100 percent wool felt for wallcoverings, colorfast, soil- and flame-resistant, and easy to apply, is preshrunk to 54″ and available in 39 colors. Tempora, a 60″-wide drapery and upholstery felt available in 45 colors, is flame- and fade-resistant and permanently mothproofed. There's also specially woven extra-heavy Willi-Cloth of 75 percent wool and 25 percent nylon for billiard and pool tables, and flameproofed Showfelt, 72″ wide in 36 colors. Prices on request. MO

III-6
CHURCHILL WEAVERS
P.O. Box 30
Berea, KY 40403

Churchill Weavers, $1, published annually, 4
folders of loose color pages, illustrated.

Two of the brochures show throws, baby blankets, and shawls; the others show clothing.

There are handwoven all-wool throws in solid colors, plaids, overplaids, stripes, twill and striated plain weaves, solid colors with border accents, houndstooth, and a design adapted from the traditional Weaver Rose pattern, measuring 50″ x 72″. A thermal-weave crib blanket in orlon acrylic with nylon-bound ends comes in white or yellow and measures 39″ x 60″. Prices on request. MO

III-7
COLONIAL MAID CURTAINS
Depot Plaza
Mamaroneck, NY 10543

Colonial Maid Curtains, 50 cents, published
biannually, 48 pages, illustrated, black and
white and color.

The catalogue shows all types of curtains—tiered or full length, tailored, gathered, smocked, tabbed, ruffled, ball-fringed, eyelet- or lace-trimmed, with some delicate embroidered polyester voile panels in a sprigged pattern. Many of the curtain styles are available with matching bedspreads, pillow shams, canopies, and dust ruffles. Prices for curtains start at around $8 a pair for tiers, $13 for long curtains. A quilted eyelet-ruffled coverlet, twin size, in natural or white costs $45; a tailored quilted "Colonial" print bedspread, $60. You'll find a guide to measuring windows as well as ideas for treatments for extra-wide windows. MO

III-8
CONSTANCE CAROL, INCORPORATED
P.O. Box 899
Plymouth, MA 02360

Constance Carol Collection of Curtain
Fabrics and Trims, $4, published seasonally,
42 pages, illustrated, color, with fabric and
trim swatches.

Constance Carol has some of the most attractive ready-made curtains we have seen. With a few exceptions, these are tab curtains of the traditional American type, with 3″ tabs that are hung on wood rods, available with or without tiebacks. The selection of fabrics is exceptionally good—gingham and calico, sprigged prints, prints by Waverly and Schumacher, whites, naturals, and solid colors. Some of the curtains have stenciled borders, others trim—eyelet lace, ruffles, and fringe. We were particularly taken with the Meissen stripe pattern, the patchwork, the curtains with hand-stenciled borders, and the delightful traditional prints. The collection con-

Hand-tied fishnet canopy, pine tree border Lover's Knot coverlet, Peacock Tail fringed petticoat, and reeded Honduras mahogany four-poster canopy bed are all from Laura Copenhaver, III-9.

Ready-made quilted polyester and cotton blend muslin bedspread and shams, with matching ruffled curtains, are machine wash/dry, no-iron, and inexpensive. Colonial Maid, III-7.

Muslin curtains, bleached or unbleached, with crochet edging, also available in permanent-press fabric, from Country Curtains, III-10.

tains over 120 swatches in a variety of colors, textures, and weights so you can try them against your furniture and walls. Prices are reasonable, starting at around $16 and varying according to length, width, and fabric. The most expensive are around $226 for a pair 102″ long x 160″ wide with lining. Wooden rods and brackets are also available. MO

III-9
LAURA COPENHAVER INDUSTRIES, INC.
P.O. Box 149
Marion, VA 24354

Rosemont, 50 cents, 32 pages, illustrated, black and white.

The Rosemont craftspeople are best known for beautiful handmade quilts, coverlets, and hand-tied fishnet canopies. The quilts can be made in any size or combination of colors in simple, traditional designs, such as the lovely Wild Rose pattern, usually made in three soft shades of rose with pale apple-green leaves, and the Virginia Beauty, a gay and primitive pattern in turkey red, yellow, and green. Both are $250 for twin and double sizes, $300 for queen and king. There are also pieced quilts in Goose Tracks and Flower Pot patterns. (As quilts are hand-sewn and quilted, orders may take up to twelve months for pieced quilts, twelve months or more for appli-

quéd quilts.) The coverlets, while not woven on hand looms, are made almost exactly like the old ones. Every detail of the original process is carefully followed and all hems and fringes are made by hand. Coverlets, in one color on white warp, are either all wool or a mixture of wool and cotton. There is the Honeycomb, which has a raised effect and looks antique; the intricate Morning Star; and the unusual Lover's Knot with pine-tree border, copied from an heirloom, in the summer and winter weave, the lighter side for summer, the darker for winter ($125 for double size in wool and cotton, $105 in cotton only). The fishnet canopies in four different designs are authentic copies of very old designs, for straight or curved frames, and cost from $140 to $245 according to pattern and size. Prices quoted here are from an old price list; they may have risen by now. Rosemont also has petticoat valances, coverlet material 90″ wide sold by the yard for matching upholstery or curtains, curtains of natural or white muslin, hand-tied fringes, and a muslin blanket cover with an insert of hand-tied lace. This engaging little catalogue carries the reassuring message that fine hand-craftsmanship is still with us. MO

III-10
COUNTRY CURTAINS
Stockbridge, MA 01262

Country Curtains, no charge, published semiannually, 64 pages, illustrated, black and white.

The emphasis here is on country charm with unbleached or white muslin shams, dust ruffles, canopy covers, and a patchwork quilt in the crisp, fresh tradition of colonial New England. The country curtains come with ball, tassel, short-knotted, old-fashioned, or bedspread fringes. Also available are crochet-type edging, pompom trim, or Irish lace ruffles. The curtains may be ordered in cotton muslin, permanent press, lawn, dotted swiss, organdy, and gingham, in tiers or tiebacks. Country Curtains also has wooden rods and brackets, unfinished or in a dark walnut or warm pine finish, in 31″, 36″ or 48″ lengths, from $6. The "city" curtains, inspired by the type of window treatments in houses on Boston's Beacon Hill, made up in a soft, pearly white fabric by Schumacher that looks like raw silk, edged with a tassel fringe, are priced from $20 to $46 a pair, according to length, plus $13 for a valance and $5 for a pair of tiebacks. Prices for the other curtains are lower. MO

Pure white or patterned vertical louver blinds with reflective vinyl to the outside deflect heat in summer, reflect in winter. LouverDrape, III-22.

III-11
CUMULOUS DESIGNS
42 Plympton Street
Boston, MA 02118

Comforter Kit, free brochure.

Cumulous Designs sells a Polarguard Comforter Kit (Polarguard is a light, warm, durable polyester fill used for sleeping bags and insulated jackets) that includes two layers of fill over 2″ thick, and complete instructions for making the comforter from machine-washable fabrics such as flannel, corduroy, or bed sheets. The kits come in twin, full, queen, and king sizes and are priced from $22.50 to $36. The company is planning to publish a catalogue listing their complete line of comforters, comforter covers, and kits, so request information if you are interested. MO

III-12
FEATHERED FRIENDS
2130 First Avenue
Seattle, WA 98121

Feathered Friends Down Comforters, free, published annually, 12 pages, illustrated, color.

Feathered Friends makes comforters filled with goose down and the superior Polish goose down in three styles—Old American, quilted in a traditional pattern of concentric squares; European, constructed with a system of small baffles or "fabric walls" inside the comforter that give an even layer of insulation; and the channeled Scandinavian model. The European is made of 100 percent tightly woven Egyptian cotton, the Scandinavian in Egyptian cotton or a non-slip cotton blend, and the American in the cotton blend. Color choices are off-white or light blue for the European, light blue or yellow for the others. The company also makes sheeting covers for comforters (you can send them two of your own flat sheets of the desired size or buy a kit for making the cover for $4.50), pillows, a baby quilt, and a quilted cocoon robe that zips and snaps around you. Prices for the comforters range from $133 to around $500. MO

III-13
GARNET HILL, INC.
Box 262 HDC
Franconia, NH 03580

Garnet Hill, 50 cents, refundable with purchase, published annually, 26 pages, illustrated, color.

In these energy-conscious times, keeping warm is a problem and Garnet Hill has a catalogue filled with good ideas for staying cozy in bed. They sell cotton flannel sheets in a variety of colors (samples are attached to the inside cover) and sizes, mostly flat; merino wool blankets; and goosedown comforters of the European duvet type. Flat sheets range in price from $14.75 for twin to $26.25 for king-size. There are also fitted flannel sheets and comforters for cribs; baby blankets, one made of pure Welsh wool in a thermal honeycomb weave; and the Feathernest, a down-filled garment you wear like a robe in the evening, zipped up, and then unzip to convert to a lightweight comforter ($85 in blue or tan). If you like the comforting touch of a hot water bottle, Garnet Hill has an elegant red velveteen covered version for $25, or one with a tartan flannel cover for $8.75. Then there are Welsh tapestry bedspreads in all wool or wool and cotton, both double-weave and reversible. In addition to bedding, Garnet Hill offers flannel nightgowns and robes as well as a range of pure wool and cotton underwear, both American and imported, to ward off the chill from outdoors. A great catalogue for those who love natural fibers and their insulating qualities. MO

III-14
GILL IMPORTS, INC.
P.O. Box 73
Ridgefield, CT 06877

Gill Imports, Inc. Hand-Embroidered Crewel Fabrics, 50 cents, 8 pages and price list, illustrated, color.

Gill imports crewel fabrics from Kashmir of 100 percent natural hand-loomed cotton with 100 percent wool embroidery. The amount of embroidery determines the price, which ranges from $13 to $30 a yard, and the fabric is between 52" and 54" wide. There is a 10 percent discount on bolts, which measure approximately 50 yards.

One swatch is enclosed to represent the fabric quality and larger swatches will be sent on request at $1 each. The patterns are mostly traditional and quite lovely. MO

III-15
VIRGINIA GOODWIN
Box 3603
Charlotte, NC 28203

Brochure of leaflets, 50 cents (refundable with purchase), illustrated, black and white.

Weavers since 1812, the Goodwin family continues the tradition of craftsmanship using antique patterns and handmade antique looms to create elaborate fishnet canopies, woven bedspreads, and a woven-in-the-round fringed tablecloth in the colonial Honeycomb pattern. The tablecloth is available in various colors; napkins, a runner, and place mats in this pattern can also be ordered. The Goodwins will be happy to send any further information or swatches on request. MO

III-16
HAGERTY COMPANY
38 Parker Avenue
Cohasset, MA 02025

Cohasset Colonials by Hagerty, $1, published semiannually, 40 pages, illustrated, color.

To tie in with their traditional furniture kits, Hagerty has a line of fabrics in the Colonial style, including documentaries from the Old Sturbridge Village collection, that range from checks and plaids to stencil designs. These are priced from $5.50 to $8 a yard. They will also make up curtains in these or in plain fabrics in two styles, tab or pleated, and supply wooden rods and brackets to fit your windows. For an accurate color match, send 25 cents for a sample of any one printed fabric or $5 for the decorator pack of over 25 color swatches. In addition to curtains, they offer traditional coverlets, spreads, dust ruffles, and a fishnet canopy for a four-poster bed that can be made to fit an arched or flat frame if you send a sketch and dimensions. MO

III-17
HOMESPUN FABRICS AND DRAPERIES
10115 Washington Boulevard, Box 352
Culver City, CA 90230

Seamless Beauty, brochure and fabric samples, free.

This company specializes in fabrics, custom draperies, bedspreads, and tablecloths of heavy 100 percent cotton in white or off-white loomed for a handwoven look. The fabrics come in five textures. Four are preshrunk and can be machine-washed and tumble-dried; Towcloth, an open weave, must be dry cleaned. One of the great advantages of these fabrics is their width, from 100″ to 120″. Prices range from around $8.50 to $12.80 a yard, according to width and whether the fabric is preshrunk and bleached. The 118″ and 120″ widths come raw from the loom and need to be shrunk in washing (120″ will shrink to 110″). Homespun will sell you fabric, pinch-pleat and fan-pleat headings if you wish to make your own draperies or will custom-make them to your order. Fringed bedspreads come in twin to king sizes at prices from about $37 to $73; fringed tablecloths, 90″ or 60″ in diameter with six napkins, from $28.95 to $37.95. MO

Cover big window areas with curtains of seamless 8'- or 10'-wide fabrics with custom-made or do-it-yourself pleats from Homespun House, III-17.

III-18
JENSEN–LEWIS COMPANY, INC.
156 Seventh Avenue
New York, NY 10014

Jensen-Lewis Canvas, $1, published annually, 16 pages, illustrated, black and white.

In addition to selling furniture with canvas coverings, this company offers canvas by the yard. Lightweight canvas in a choice of 12 colors, 31″ wide, is $3.95 a yard; heavyweight canvas in 28 colors, 35″ wide, is $4.95. The heavy canvas is perfect for upholstery, making screens, or tents; the lightweight for slipcovers, draperies, and bedspreads. For outdoor use, Jensen–Lewis has mildew-and-fadeproof Acrilan canvas, 31″ wide; however, this is sold only at their store, not through the mail. MO / RS

III-19
KENNEY MANUFACTURING COMPANY
1000 Jefferson Boulevard
Warwick, RI 02887

Creative Windows, Volume II, $1.95 plus 25 cents postage, 112 pages, illustrated, color.

This booklet illustrates dozens of window treatments using curtains and draperies, Roman shades, and roll-up blinds and the many styles of drapery hardware made by Kenney. While most of the window treatments are conventional, there is a very useful how-to section in the center of the booklet that gives detailed information on

measuring for curtains and draperies, selecting appropriate rods and hooks, and mounting rods and valances. MO

III-20
KIRSCH COMPANY
Dept. GU
Sturgis, MI 49091

Windows Beautiful, Volume VII, $2.50, published every two years, 140 pages, illustrated, color.

Kirsch is a leading manufacturer of drapery hardware and supplies and this complete window book is primarily devoted to various treatments in colorful room settings with an indication of the type of hardware used in each. There are also tips on the cleaning and care of draperies. A center how-to section tells you how to measure for rods and draperies and make your own curtains and window treatments. A selection of Kirsch rods is shown in the back of the book. RS

III-21
LEVOLOR LORENTZEN, INC.
720 Monroe Street
Hoboken, NJ 07030

Window Magic, $1, published annually, 42 pages, illustrated, color.

Levolor makes attractive thin-slat Venetian blinds and vertical blinds in more than 200 colors, metallics, and patterns, as well as woven shades called Levolor Weaves. Primarily a source of inspiration, this booklet is packed with imaginative window treatments and decorating ideas by well-known interior designers using Levolor products. With their most popular blind, the 1"-slat Riviera, you can combine different colors for a striped effect. By using stripes of color to carry through the lines of a wall graphic, the window can be made part of the design. You can paint a motif on a plain blind or cover it with fabric to match upholstery. Blinds need not be restricted to windows. Put them in a frame and they become a screen or a room divider; hang them from the ceiling as a roll-up partition between sleeping and seating areas in a one-room apartment or to disguise a laundry center or Pullman kitchen. A 16-page Designer's Workbook in the booklet shows you how to solve design problems with blinds and gives you all the necessary information about measuring windows, installing blinds and shades, cleaning, removing, and taking blinds apart, and covering slats with paint, fabric, plastic, or paper. RS / ID

III-22
LOUVERDRAPE, INC.
1100 Colorado Avenue, Dept. HD-2
Santa Monica, CA 90401

Vertical Imagination, $1, 36 pages, illustrated, color.

This handsomely illustrated booklet shows the vertical louvered blinds in a variety of settings. The flexibility and design of the blinds enables them to solve problems such as fitting the triangular shape of a gable-type window. An added advantage is that vertical blinds do not accumulate as much dust as the horizontal type and so require less frequent cleaning. LouverDrape offers 300 choices of color and texture in solid vinyl, designer fabrics, and metallics. One type of louver is perforated with tiny holes that give a clear view even when blinds are closed. RS / ID

III-23
NIZHONIE FABRICS, INC.
East Highway 160, P.O. Box 729
Cortez, CO 81331

Bahah-Zhonie. Indian Designed Fabrics, free brochure, illustrated, color.

This Indian-owned enterprise produces handprinted, silk-screened fabrics adapted from traditional American Indian designs by Navajo artist Bahah-Zhonie. The patterns are drawn from such varied inspirations as Navajo rugs and sand paintings, kachina dolls, the thunderbird, petroglyphs, and typical basket designs. Shown in the brochure are overall design prints, 45" wide, at $5.50 a yard, and border prints with designs from 11½" to 25½" high, also 45" wide, priced from $9.50 to $13.50. These unusual and beautiful textiles make stunning bedspreads, curtains, and tablecloths, or clothing. MO

III-24
PUCKIHUDDLE PRODUCTS LTD.
Dept. 2HDC
Oliverea, NY 12462

Puckihuddle, $1, published semiannually, 38 pages, illustrated, color.

Puckihuddle specializes in pretty, frilly, and flowered bedding, although they do show a few tailored ensembles. They have embroidered muslin pillowcases with a coordinating cotton flannel sheet, down comforters, an eyelet blanket cover, and charming crocheted bedspreads and pillow shams in white or ecru. There's just about everything you could imagine for the bedroom including patchwork quilts, pillows, cushion covers, topcloths for a skirted table, and lots of pillows, plus towels, tablecloths, placemats, and runners. If you like to make your own patchwork, you can buy a bundle of 30 assorted calico strips, a yard long and 3" wide, or 100 precut 6" calico squares, $8 for either one. A delightful little catalogue loaded with temptations. MO

III-25
ROCHE–BOBOIS
200 Madison Avenue
New York, NY 10016

Roche-Bobois, $5 (refundable with purchase), published every 18 months, 148 pages, illustrated, color, with illustrated price list.

Some extremely attractive ideas for window treatments are to be found in this company's catalogue. Curtains of natural and synthetic voiles with decorative designs of branches, Chinese pagodas, and Indian motifs can be hung in the traditional way or in Japanese screen fashion; this updating of the old-style "net" curtain imparts a poetic kind of lighting and a see-through quality that blends indoors and outdoors. There are also vertical-slat fabric blinds, a palm-tree-patterned automatic roller blind, and a Roman shade. Estimates on these are given to order. MO / RS

III-26
RUSSELL'S QUILT COMPANY
1173 West Central Avenue
Brea, CA 92621

Custom Made Comforters, *brochure with fabric samples, $1 (refundable with purchase), illustrated, black and white.*

This family business makes goose-down comforters in European (squares), Scandinavian (vertical channels), or Down (vertical/horizontal edges, central motif) quilting patterns. Prices vary according to the amount of goose-down fill used. Cold-climate twin size with two pounds of fill is $139; the same size for cold-to-mild climate uses 20 ounces of fill and costs $90. Dacron filling is also available for mild climates at $49 for twin size in any quilting pattern. Pillow prices for down or feathers range from $19 to $79 for king size (20" x 36"). Russell's also will recover comforters and pillows starting at $39 for twin comforter, $5 for standard pillow. Extra fill is $40 a pound for goose down, $7 a pound for feathers. MO

III-27
SUNSHINE LANE
P.O. Box 262
Millersburg, OH 44654

Handmade Quilt Collection, *50 cents, published semiannually, 12 pages, illustrated, black and white and color.*

Sunshine Lane's one-of-a-kind quilts are done entirely by hand on old-fashioned quilting frames, using patterns handed down from generation to generation, but they are made with modern wash-and-wear materials, and the batting is 100 percent Dacron. Each quilt is cut and stitched by hand, and the skill and loving attention of the individual worker makes them treasures, for no two are exactly alike. A few of the quilts are illustrated in color on the center pages, with sketches of the piece patterns in black and white. Among the patterns are the Double Nine Patch (various pastels or prints on white, a variety of pink patches on white, or the same variations in green, tangerine and dark brown); the Lone Star, Dresden Plate, and Boston Five, a combination of patches in series of five on a quilted center design on white. In addition to the full-size quilts, Sunshine Lane offers baby quilts, pieced pillows, and pillow shams. Prices range from around $170 to $385 for the full-size quilts, pillows are $36.50. If you want to see a

A city bedroom decorated with country cottons for ruffled bed hangings, ready-made tablecloths, cushion covers, sewing and trinket boxes, several bags and rolls, plus a patchwork quilt, all from the Laura Ashley Collection, III-1.

quilt in color, you can send $5 for a color photograph or $35 for the Decorator's Book, which has over 60 color photographs. The $5 is deducted from the price of any order, the $35 from the price provided the book is returned. MO

III-28
TOUCH OF CLASS
North Hampshire Common
North Conway, NH 03860

Touch of Class, *$1 (refundable with purchase), published semiannually, 20 pages, illustrated, color.*

Touch of Class has adopted the European idea of replacing the blanket and top sheet with a comforter in a sheet casing cover, which maximizes the insulating qualities of goose down, providing snuggly warmth without weight; Velcro tabs anchor comforter to casing. Their current catalogue shows 18 pattern and color combinations to match bed linens by Wamsutta, Utica, Springmaid, and Fieldcrest, with complementary sheets, pillow cases, and dust ruffles. They sell two types of goose-down comforter for mild and cold climates, covered with 100 percent cotton fabric in a tight weave, stitched in channels to

Comforter made from two full flat sheets and the Cumulous Designs Comforter Kit, III-11.

prevent the down shifting, with baffles that allow the down to expand. These come in twin, full, queen, and king sizes at prices ranging from $154 for a mild-climate twin size with 20 ounces of fill to $300 for a cold-climate king size with 48 ounces of fill. They also have goose-down pillows in various sizes and shapes. If you already own a comforter, you can order a sheet casing to fit and Velcro tabs at 35 cents each (a twin will use four tabs, a full/queen six, and a king eight). Casings range in price from $30 to $50. Touch of Class also monograms the casings and bed linens for an additional charge. To keep you warm until bedtime, there's a down snuggler with Velcro closures and a ¾-length zipper ($95). MO

III-29
TRIBLEND MILLS INC.
P.O. Box 548
Tarboro, NC 27866

How to Sew Draperies, free booklet, 16 pages, illustrated.

Triblend's mill-end store offers open-weave drapery fabrics at $2.99 a yard, batiste sheers at $1.99 a yard, a self-lined weave called Barrier-Lok that has insulating qualities and comes in a variety of patterns and colors at $2.99 a yard, and a pleater kit. The company sends out a flyer on the fabrics. With your order (which comes with a guaranteed refund provided the fabric has not been cut) you receive the booklet which contains basic information on making draperies, selecting hardware, measuring, and estimating yardage. MO

III-30
UNIROYAL, INC.
Attention: Lynn Russell
1230 Avenue of the Americas
New York, NY 10020

Naugahyde, the Finest in Decorative Vinyl Fabrics, $5 for folder of samples.

Naugahyde, the vinyl look-alike for leather, is shown in this folder in all its variety of colors, textures, and patterns, each keyed by color, number, and pattern name. These are actual samples, not just color matches. A chart on the back of the folder helps you figure yardage for upholstering. RS

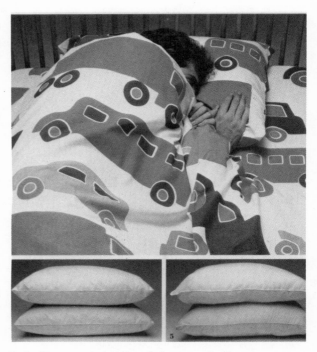

Bed pillows, auto-patterned sheets, and pillow covers from Conran's, I-26.

IV
Lamps and Lighting Fixtures

IV-1
ABITARE
212 East 57th Street
New York, NY 10021

*Abitare, $10, published annually, 234 pages
in ring binder, illustrated, black and white.*

This exceptionally beautiful catalogue of contemporary furnishings from around the world has some striking lamps and fixtures, most of them impossible to describe because their shapes are so avant-garde. There's the Topo table lamp with clamp, double-joint arm and swivel reflector designed by Joe Columbo; Tetto, an airy tent-shaped hanging lamp with a removable, dry-cleanable white linen shade and natural ash frame ($185); and Gigia, a cube-shaped table lamp with white or striped linen shade. The rest must be seen to be comprehended. MO / RS

IV-2
ETHAN ALLEN, INC.
Ethan Allen Drive
Danbury, CT 06810

*The Ethan Allen Treasury of American
Traditional Interiors, $7.95, published every
two years, 394 pages, illustrated, color.*

There are both traditional and contemporary lamps in this huge catalogue from a major home furnishings manufacturer—some with metal bases with a hand-burnished bronze finish, others of cut crystal, ceramic, handblown glass, and wood—as well as a selection of lanterns and chandeliers in traditional styles. RS

IV-3
ATELIER INTERNATIONAL LTD.
595 Madison Avenue
New York, NY 10022

*AI Cassett, $2, published annually, 90 pages,
illustrated, black and white.*

Some highly original lighting fixtures are included in this collection of contemporary furnishings. A floor lamp with a white marble base and a long, curving, adjustable stainless steel stem that can be poised over a desk or chair is as starkly beautiful as a piece of sculpture. A table or floor lamp designed by Castiglioni consists of a clear glass cylinder housing a glass diffuser and reflector that provides a selection of lighting effects. An unusual wall or ceiling lamp gives diffused light by means of fabric stretched over a bent tubular fiberglass frame. No prices are given. ID

IV-4
AUTHENTIC DESIGNS
330 East 75th Street
New York, NY 10021

*Catalogue of Early American Lighting
Fixtures, $2, 64 pages, illustrated, black and
white.*

This catalogue presents a collection of well-researched handcrafted reproductions and adaptations of eighteenth- and nineteenth-century chandeliers and sconces in solid, natural-finished brass and soft tobacco-brown hand-waxed maple. Chandeliers come with two feet of

IV

A. Classic French brass oil lamp, La Lampe-Pigeon; French Country Stores, IV-12. B. Moorish-style wrought iron wall lantern; Mexico House, IV-29. C. American Colonial round globe brass bracket lantern; Heritage, IV-15. D. Eighteenth-century candle-burning brass wall bracket with glass shade; Ball & Ball, IV-5.

brass suspension chain and a ceiling canopy. The designs lean to the rustic but are varied and quite beautiful in their simplicity. As the fixtures are made when ordered, any size adjustments may easily be accomodated. Special finishes, such as pewter-plated brass, add around 15 percent to the cost. The price for fixtures taking candles is 15 percent less than the price for electrified fixtures. Authentic Designs will also sell you the clear flame-tip imported bulbs for electrified chandeliers. Prices range from around $35 to $75 for wall sconces, from $120 to $400 for chandeliers. Any fixture may be returned for a full refund within five days of its receipt for any reason whatsoever. MO / RS

IV-5
BALL AND BALL
463 West Lincoln Highway
Exton, PA 19341

Fine Quality Hardware by Ball and Ball, $4, *108 pages, illustrated, black and white.*

In addition to their extensive line of fine brass reproduction hardware, Ball and Ball make reproduction lighting fixtures in Colonial styles. They have elegant eighteenth-century brass chandeliers, electrified or candle-burning, including a copy of the magnificent and enormous Independence Hall chandelier, hanging fixtures, wall sconces, candelabra, and hurricanes. An electrified three-arm chandelier with shades is around $585; the candle-burning model without shades, $385. There are also simple tin and pewter sconces, copper lanterns, and hand-forged iron candlestands and chandeliers. MO

IV-6
BLACKWELDER FURNITURE COMPANY
Highway 21 North
Statesville, NC 28634

Blackwelder's Fine Home Furnishings, $3, *published annually, 108 pages, illustrated, color.*

This comprehensive catalogue from a company that carries the lines of many of America's leading manufacturers of home furnishings (for details of their operation, see page 19) includes some good examples of contemporary floor and table lamps and lighting fixtures by Koch & Lowy and Laurel as well as traditional lamps by Stiffel, Wildwood, Knob Creek, and Milford Guild. They also carry mirrors by Friedman, LaBarge, and other companies. MO

IV-7
THE BURNING LOG
P.O. Box 438
Hanover Street
Lebanon, NH 03766

The Burning Log Woodburner's Catalog, 25 *cents, published annually, 32 pages, illustrated, black and white.*

Although primarily devoted to stoves and fireplace equipment, this catalogue also has some interesting lamps. Maple bobbin lamps with bases that were actually used in New England textile mills are $22.50 to $25.50. A candlestand lamp with hand-forged black wrought-iron stand, arm, and spindle and natural burlap shade, 52" high, costs $55.50. Reproductions of

Colonial lanterns, electrified for indoor or out-door use, range from $44 to $53 and a couple of most attractive stoneware oil lamps handcrafted by a Vermont potter, 13" high, are each $26. MO

IV-8
COLONIAL TIN CRAFT
7805 Railroad Avenue
Cincinnati, OH 45243

Colonial Tincraft Catalogue, $2, 40 pages, illustrated, black and white.

Extremely handsome handcrafted reproductions of early Colonial, eighteenth-century, and Williamsburg tin lighting fixtures, authentic in every detail, are the specialty of Christopher Nordloh, proprietor of Colonial Tin Craft. Many are made exactly as they were 200 years ago, with the same hand tools and forms used for the originals, and are works of art. Included in this extremely unusual, attractive catalogue are many chandeliers of plain and pierced tin, sometimes in combination with wood; pierced tin lanterns and lamps; tin candelabra; sconces; pierced tin hanging fixtures; and ceiling fixtures. There are also some antiqued solid copper lanterns with glass panels that can be hung, wall-mounted, or put on a post. Most of the fixtures can be bought electrified or fitted with candles; some chandeliers combine candle arms with an electric fitting in a center cone; the ceiling and hanging fixtures are only electrified. Prices are very reasonable for hand work, with many pieces under $100. A simple sconce costs around $17. The most expensive item is a 24-arm electrified wood and tin chandelier at $625. MO

IV-9
CONRAN'S MAIL ORDER
145 Huguenot Street
New Rochelle, NY 10805

Conran's, $2.50, published annually, 112 pages, illustrated, color.

Conran's has a fairly large selection of contemporary lamps, spots, track lighting, wall lights, and hanging fixtures, all reasonably priced. The designs are simple and functional, in keeping with their furniture. Especially attractive pieces are a hanging lamp with a graduated, curvy-ribbed acrylic shade in white, cream, or peach that can be raised or lowered ($65) and hanging lamps with natural cane shades in various shapes ($23 to $33). MO / RS

Paper lanterns, large and small, from Conran's, IV-9.

IV-10
EDMUND SCIENTIFIC COMPANY
7082 Edscorp Building
Barrington, NJ 08007

Edmund Scientific Catalogue, $1, published semiannually, 100 pages, illustrated, black and white and color.

This catalogue contains some unique lighting devices, many of which are used in nightclubs and light shows. Mirrored balls plus pinspot lamps and color filters enable you to give your family room a disco effect. There are strobe lights, color organs (electronic devices that control groups of colored lamps whose flashes are triggered by music), special dimmers, black-light fixtures and bulbs, and visual projection kits. *The Edmund Scientific Lighting Handbook*, a fully illustrated manual, explains how it all works ($9.95). MO

IV-11
FAIRE HARBOUR LTD.
44 Captain Pierce Road
Scituate, MA 02066

Faire Harbour Ltd., $1 (refundable with purchase), 12 pages, illustrated, color.

Aladdin kerosene mantel lamps, most of which have optional electric converters to combine turn-of-the-century charm with modern convenience, are Faire Harbour's specialty. There is a wide choice of shelf, table, wall, and hanging styles with brass- or chrome-finished bases and a selection of glass shades in the original designs, all at moderate prices. The company also has a complete list of replacement parts such as mantles, chimneys, wicks, shades, lamp bowls, and wall brackets. MO

**IV-12
FRENCH COUNTRY STORES, INC.**
P.O. Box 5287
New York, NY 10017

Leaflet on lamp, free, illustrated, black and white.

French Country Stores imports La Lampe-Pigeon, a fascinating oil- or kerosene-burning lamp that was created around 1840 for use in the wine caves of Bordeaux and the Loire Valley and then became popular in rural French homes. It is still being produced today in limited quantities, just as it was over a century ago, by the small company that owns the original patent. The simplicity of this all-brass, handcrafted lamp, 9½" high with bubble-shaped globe, would fit easily into a traditional or contemporary setting and, when the energy crunch arrives, could be a very useful addition to the house. It will burn ten hours before it needs refilling. The lamp is available direct from French Country Stores at around $42.50. MO

**IV-13
FURNITURECRAFT, INC.**
Box 285c
Stoneham, MA 02180

FurnitureCraft, Inc. Distinctive Early American Furnishings, 50 cents, published semiannually, 32 pages, illustrated, color.

Some charming and simple lamps are shown. One is a white ceramic ginger-jar shape with a Chinese pheasant and flower design, 20" high, for $66.50; others are of solid brass with antique bronze finish in Colonial styles. There are also working oil lamps in various shapes, including a London parlor lamp in brass, a pewter-and-brass French pump lamp, and a Lampe-Pigeon, as well as an Early American pewter nutmeg lamp and two brass wall sconces at prices ranging from $35 to $65. MO

**IV-14
HAGERTY COMPANY**
38 Parker Avenue
Cohasset, MA 02025

Cohasset Colonials by Hagerty, $1, published semiannually, 38 pages, illustrated, color.

Reproductions of Colonial lighting fixtures, all electrified, including chandeliers, sconces, an iron candlestand (converted to a floor lamp), and a selection of simple lamps with candlestick or whale-oil-lamp bases. Prices range from $29 for a sconce to $175 for a six-light Hanover chandelier with brass arms and maple post. MO

**IV-15
HERITAGE LANTERNS**
70A Main Street
Yarmouth, ME 04096

Heritage Lanterns, $2, published annually, 52 pages, illustrated, black and white.

Reproductions and adaptations of Colonial lights in copper, brass, pewter, and wood, handcrafted from designs used since the company's inception in the late 1800s. An enduring and pleasing blend of utility and simplicity, the fixtures include carriage, tavern, Salem, and globe lights; ship's lanterns; post lights; chandeliers; sconces; and table lights. All are available electrified; indoor chandeliers and sconces are available with the option of candles. The Mary Light and the Hamilton sconce can also be bought as oil lamps, for which Heritage has a bayberry-scented lamp oil. A special feature for electrified indoor fixtures is pure beeswax candles that take clear or flame-colored chandelier-base bulbs, carefully hand-dripped over the candle cup for a realistic effect. All the pieces have the charm of authenticity, but some, like the Beacon Hill (a six-sided light that originally came from the foyer of a Beacon Hill house) and a scalloped chandelier with a down light in the cone, are especially graceful. Prices for the fixtures range from around $35 to almost $700. Heritage recommends and sells an English wadding metal polish for cleaning brass; unlike liquid polish, it does not build up residue in the crevices. MO

**IV-16
HISTORIC CHARLESTON REPRODUCTIONS**
51 Meeting Street
Charleston, SC 29401

Historic Charleston Reproductions, $3.50 (refundable with $25 purchase), 56 pages, illustrated, black and white and color.

The reproduction lamps shown may not be the lighting of the period, but the bases are typical accessories that would have been found in Charleston homes—either China Trade porcelains or brass candlesticks in classic designs. One exceptionally handsome lamp has a blue-and-white Canton wig stand base and box-pleated pongee shade ($325); another has a Sacred Butterfly pattern fruit cooler as a base, adapted from an original in an old Charleston dinner service. MO/RS

IV-17
MARTHA M. HOUSE

1022 South Decatur Street
Montgomery, AL 36104

Southern Heirlooms from Martha M. House, *$1, published annually, 48 pages, illustrated, black and white.*

Among the Victorian reproduction furnishings sold by this company are some typical lamps. One is a banquet lamp with hand-painted pink roses on the shade, another has a hand-cut lead crystal globe and an elaborate gold-plated cherub base. MO

IV-18
HUBBARDTON FORGE AND
WOOD CORPORATION

P.O. Box SRX
Bomoseen, VT 05732

Hand-Wrought Iron from Hubbardton Forge, *$3 (refundable with purchase), published annually, 13 pages, illustrated, black and white.*

This company, which is reviving the almost lost art of ornamental blacksmithing, has a small but excellent collection of handwrought iron chandeliers, sconces, and candlesticks. A four-arm chandelier, 18″ high and 22″ in diameter, is around $56; an unusual socket candlestick in a swirling shape is $32. They also have accessories, including ceiling swag hooks, chain links, and a swing crane in two sizes that could be used to hold a chandelier over a wall table or to hang a plant. MO

IV-19
HURLEY PATENTEE LIGHTING

R.D. 7, Box 98a
Kingston, NY 12401

Hurley Patentee Manor—Handcrafted Lighting, *$2, published annually, 24 pages, illustrated, black and white.*

Hurley Patentee Manor is a Hudson Valley restoration that combines a 1696 Dutch cottage and a 1745 English country mansion, and is a national historic landmark. It is also the home of Hurley Patentee Lighting, which makes hand-crafted reproductions of seventeenth- and eigh-

Tiffany-type hanging shade assembled or as a kit from Rainbow Art Glass, IV-34.

Display your prettiest shells inside this melon glass lamp from Hilo Steiner, IV-36.

teenth-century chandeliers, sconces, candle-holders, lanterns, and Betty lamps, adapted from originals in museums and private collections. The materials used are tin, wood, iron, and brass; the tin and wood are finished to give the mellowed look of age. The fixtures are electrified or may be fitted with candles. Chandeliers are supplied with complete ceiling canopy and two feet of chain (longer chains may be requested) and come in a fascinating variety of styles including a rare design in hand-forged iron of a ring with three lights, a stately 13-arm meeting-house model, and an early multiple-lighted fixture with a tin extinguisher above each candle. The sconces are equally varied in design. Prices range from under $10 for a simple candleholder to around $300 for the multiple-light chandelier. A folder on the Manor, which is open for public viewing from June 30 to Labor Day, or by appointment at other times, comes with the catalogue. MO

IV-20
IRVIN'S CRAFT SHOP
R.D. 1
Mount Pleasant Mills, PA 17853

Early American Handcrafted Tin, Copper and Brass Reproductions, *$1 (refundable with purchase), published annually, 26 pages, illustrated, black and white.*

Chandeliers, lamps, lanterns, and sconces in antique copper, antique brass, and tin are the major offerings in this catalogue of Early-American-style handcrafts. The electrified table lamps have pierced tin shades in traditional motifs and bases in the shape of coffee pots, candle molds, and tavern lamps. There are also pierced tin shades for hanging fixtures, and chandeliers with pierced or plain tin cones that have a rustic charm. A pierced tin chandelier with six S-shaped arms for candles, 24" wide x 12" deep, is $42.50 (if completely electrified, $83.50); a matching chain and ceiling plate are included. Most of Irvin's lanterns and sconces are electrified, though some will take candles. Other Early American pieces include candleholders and chambersticks, tin or copper coffee pots, candle molds, ladles, a Betty lamp, cookie cutters, and the traditional Pennsylvania Dutch pierced round or heart-shaped molds for making egg cheese. A heart-shaped tin mold is $8.50. MO

IV-21
GEORGE KOVACS LIGHTING, INC.
831 Madison Avenue
New York, NY 10021

George Kovacs, *$1, published annually, 20 pages, illustrated, black and white.*

This catalogue shows a fairly large selection of the lamps and lighting fixtures imported or made by George Kovacs, a company with branches around the country. These contemporary designs range from simple white globes to the light fantastic—Hebi, the lightheaded snake, a sinuous stem shape that can be bent, curved, stretched, or swerved to put the light just where you need it. A wide variety—simple and classic swing-arm lamps, desk lamps, floor lamps, wall lamps, table lamps, pendant lamps, and spotlights, as well as the popular high-tech factory shade lamp—in polished aluminum or brass, or colors. The bamboo-and-rice-paper fans designed by Ingo Maurer and "Concentrics" by Wilhelm Vest, a nest of metal rings that collapses like a concertina for storage, are most intriguing. There is also a tripod lamp with grow bulb for your plants that adjusts to different heights from 24" to 52". Prices on request. MO/RS/ID

IV-22
LABARGE
P.O. Box 905A
875 Brooks Avenue
Holland, MI 49423

LaBarge Lamps, *free color brochure.*

The lamps shown have elegant and beautiful hand-decorated porcelain or ceramic bases, many in oriental shapes and designs. There is also a solid brass Oriental vase. Simple plain or pleated shades do not detract from the originality of the bases. RS

IV-23
LAUREL LAMP MANUFACTURING COMPANY, INC.
230 Fifth Avenue
New York, NY 10001

Laurel Lamp, *$1.50, updated semiannually, 36 pages, illustrated, color.*

This company has been designing and manufacturing modern lamps for over fifty years and their catalogue contains a remarkably comprehensive, well-styled selection—table, desk, floor, even clamp-on piano lamps. Many are

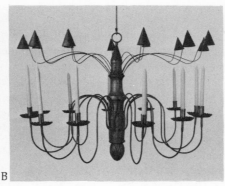

A. Satellite-like cluster chandeliers in opal or smoked glass; Lightolier, IV-24. B. Twelve-over-twelve iron and wood chandelier with a tin extinguisher above each candle; Hurley Patentee, IV-19. C. Tulip-shaped ribbed glass and brass turn-of-the-century-style fixture; Lightolier, IV-24.

sculptural in shape, others have travertine bases that look like pieces of sculpture. The materials are chiefly Swedish brass and polished chrome, with some bases in wood, travertine, opal case glass, clear acrylic, and porcelain. A "Light Shaft" floor lamp—70" tall, a cluster of three slender brass columns with reflective acrylic tips in clear or blue that look like space age candles—is very striking, as is a travertine table lamp shaped like a leaning column with a scooped-out center for the light source. Prices range from under $100 to over $400. Laurel Lamp has showrooms across the country in the main home furnishing centers and while their products are available only through stores and interior designers, the catalogue is well worth studying if you are looking for something different in modern lamps. RS/ID

IV-24
LIGHTOLIER, INC., Dept. LC
346 Claremont Avenue
Jersey City, NJ 07305

New Directions in Lighting, $2 *(comes with a $5-off certificate for chandelier purchase), 112 pages, illustrated, color.* **Guide to Track Lighting,** *25 cents, 36 pages, illustrated, black and white.*

Lightolier, probably the most innovative manufacturer of lighting, features an enormous selection of lights and lamps that are mostly contemporary. *New Directions in Lighting* contains an extraordinary and exciting collection of contemporary chandeliers. Some hang like sculptures in space, others are clusters of globes in chrome, clear, or smoky glass or luminous rectangles of translucent white acrylic. There are also more conventionally styled chandeliers in traditional shapes, and many pendant lamps including adaptations of old oil lamps, Tiffany-shaped shades of faceted crystal, smoky glass

globes, and drum and "stovepipe" shapes in brilliant colors. The ceiling fixtures are highly imaginative and beautiful, a far cry from the dreary center light of old; there are also wood-framed luminous panels with fluorescent tubes behind plain acrylic panels to give evenly diffused light over a wide area. In addition, you'll find mirror lighting for making up, outdoor lanterns in contemporary and traditional styles, recessed lighting, accent lighting, table and desk lamps, and a great variety of the track lighting for which Lightolier is famous. This is a very informative, detailed catalogue that fully de-

Golden oak and brass two-tier chandelier with opal globes from Lightolier, IV-24.

scribes each type of fixture, with dimensions and recommended bulbs; the pages are filled with ideas for using the various types of lighting for different areas and activities, plus advice on choosing the right scale of fixture and estimating the right mounting height for chandeliers.

Guide to Track Lighting is a concise and invaluable little book that gives you all the information you could need about Lightolier's track systems —where and how to use and how to install them. It covers such things as choosing the right position for the track according to whether you want accent lighting, general illumination for a whole wall, or highlighting for textures of draperies, brick, or stone wall surfaces; selecting a power feed-in for permanent or plug-in wiring; and judging the light intensity level for different ceiling heights. Eleven pages are devoted to the different shapes and styles of Lightolier lamps available for track lighting, including specialized types for accenting art or sculpture. You can learn a lot about lighting in general from these publications. RS/ID

IV-25
LUIGI CRYSTAL
7332 Frankford Avenue
Philadelphia, PA 19136

Unique Collection of Crystal Lamps, 25 cents, published annually, 48 pages, illustrated, black and white.

Luigi's catalogue shows chandeliers, candelabra, table lamps, wall sconces, and hurricanes of crystal, stained glass, and etched glass with gilded metal and marble, a look of shimmering opulence at amazingly modest prices. A pair of lamps with hand-cut crystal bases and prisms are in the $40 range; the five-light crystal chandelier is around the most expensive item at $170. The company also sells imported crystal prisms, bobèches, bulbs, and some lovely stemmed crystal bowls for centerpieces that can be made to match their hurricane or shower lamps. MO

IV-26
MAGNOLIA HALL
726 Andover
Atlanta, GA 30327

Yesteryear Furniture, $1, published semiannually, 80 pages, illustrated, black and white.

Magnolia Hall's Victorian furniture is complemented by electrified oil lamps and typical pe-

riod lighting fixtures. A lily pad lamp in bronze finish with frosted glass shade, inspired by a Tiffany design, is $25; a hurricane lamp with crystal pendants is around $40; the "Gone with the Wind" parlor lamp with hand-painted flowers on the bowl is around $90. You'll find here every kind of lamp to give an authentic Victorian look. MO

IV-27
MANHATTAN AD HOC HOUSEWARES
842 Lexington Avenue
New York, NY 10021

Ad Hoc/High-Tech Catalog, $1 (refundable with purchase), published annually, 16 pages, illustrated, black and white.

Although this store specializes in housewares of the no-frills, functional type associated with the high-tech movement, they also carry a few equally well-designed and straightforward lighting fixtures and lamps. One is a sleek work lamp from Sweden with an adjustable rubberized gooseneck in black matte finish, a choice of 8"-diameter table base, C-clamp, or magnetic base that will cling to metal shelving, and a halogen bulb that gives perfect light for precision work. It's not cheap—just under $100—but it looks as if it would last forever. Extra halogen bulbs are around $6. There are photographers' studio lights that swivel and can be mounted on a portable aluminum stand or fastened to a post or shelf with gaffer grips to provide portable lighting wherever it is needed. A tiny quartz light in unobtrusive black or white finish with C-clamp or other mounting devices floodlights paintings, walls, and work spaces. Hot spots (portable low-voltage fixtures available with a wide choice of spots or floods) and optional accessories such as louvers, beam spreaders, diffusers, and over fifty different colored filters are great for accent or mood lighting and cost between $75 and $82. MO

IV-28
EPHRAIM MARSH COMPANY, Dept. 753
P.O. Box 266
Concord, NC 28025

Ephraim Marsh—Distinctive Furniture, $1, published semiannually, 140 pages, illustrated, black and white and color.

Ephraim Marsh has some simple and attractive lamps to complement the eighteenth-century styling of their furniture. Included among them are a brass candlestick lamp, a twin-burner stu-

Living-dining-music room lit by track lighting only. Lightolier, IV-24.

dent lamp, a round caddy lamp, a lead-crystal lamp, and two Japanese Satsuma crackle porcelain lamps. Prices are in the $70 to $250 range. MO

IV-29
MEXICO HOUSE
P.O. Box 970
Del Mar, CA 92014

Mexico House, $1 (refundable with purchase), published annually, 42 pages, illustrated, black and white.

The hanging and wall-mounted lamps, chandeliers, wall sconces, candlesticks, and post lamps of hand-forged iron from Mexico are executed today as they were in the days of Cortez, in typical Moorish styles. Lamps come with flat black or hand-rubbed gilt finish (to give a soft antique effect) and Mexico House also offers white wrought iron. Some lamps combine iron and hand-chiseled wood. The standard glass color is amber but you can also order clear, blue, green, red, or a combination of colors for an additional $4. Most of the chandeliers and lamps come completely wired; some sconces are electrified, others take candles. Prices are reasonable—the most expensive is $115 for a 16-light chandelier in two

tiers of iron curlicues and leaves, 32" high x 32" wide. A single candle sconce is just $5.50. MO

IV-30
GATES MOORE
River Road
Silvermine
Norwalk, CT 06850

Early American Designs of Lighting Fixtures, $2 (refundable with purchase), 36 pages, illustrated, black and white.

Gates Moore started in the lighting-fixture business in 1950 after several years of repairing antiques. They follow the finishes, shapes, and construction methods of early American craftsmen. Although the metal and wood chandeliers, sconces, and lanterns are electrified, they have the authentic hand-crafted look. The fixtures are available in a choice of painted, pewter-coated, distressed tin, or oxydized copper finishes, and some of the painted chandeliers can be matched to your color sample. All hanging fixtures are supplied with a ceiling canopy painted to match the fixture, crossbar, hook, and handmade chain, ready to fasten to the electrical outlet. Prices range from $25 for a simple metal sconce to $750 for a multi-armed painted chandelier. MO

String shades and brass lamps from Hilo Steiner, IV-36.

IV-31
NESSEN LAMPS, INC.
3200 Jerome Avenue
Bronx, NY 10468

*Nessen Lamps, Catalogue #13, free,
published every three years, 54 pages,
illustrated, black and white.*

This company designs and manufactures simple, sleek contemporary lamps for residential and commercial use. Included in the catalogue are floor lamps with and without tables, as well as hanging, wall, table, and desk lamps. Nessen is perhaps best known for many kinds of swing-arm lamps—floor, wall-mounted, and desk types, all with a very functional look. Prices range from just under $80 to around $300. RS/ID

IV-32
PERIOD FURNITURE HARDWARE
COMPANY, INC.
123 Charles Street
Boston, MA 02114

*Authentic Reproductions of Furniture
Hardware and Lighting Fixtures, $2,
published every two years, 126 pages,
illustrated, black and white.*

About 30 pages of this catalogue are devoted to lighting, including Early American handcrafted sconces and chandeliers in antique or polished brass or antique pewter, lanterns in various metals, square or hexagonal ceiling light fixtures, and Victorian wall brackets and hanging fixtures. The Barbary Coast, a turn-of-the-century pool table light copied from a 1904 catalogue, with green cased-glass shades would be great fun in a family room. Prices on request. Fixtures can be made to your order if you send a picture or sketch. MO

IV-33
PROGRESS LIGHTING
P.O. Box 12701
Philadelphia, PA 19134

*Progress Lighting Ideas Book, $1, published
every two years, 160 pages, illustrated, color.*

No matter what type of lighting fixture you are looking for—chandelier, hanging lamp, wall bracket or sconce, ceiling fixture, outdoor lantern, makeup lighting strips, fluorescent, track, or recessed lighting, Progress has it. There are many styles, traditional and contemporary, including Victorian type fixtures, Tiffany-type shades, and the simplest of white cord- or rod-hung globes. Each fixture is fully described, with dimensions and finishes. An introductory section tells you how to select fixtures for function and decoration, and gives general lighting suggestions for different rooms. When writing, ask for the name of your nearest dealer. RS/ID

IV-34
RAINBOW ART GLASS, Dept. CHC2
49 Shark River Road
Neptune, NJ 07753

*Adventures with Color and Light, $1
(refundable with purchase), published
semiannually, 14 pages, illustrated, color.*

Rainbow Art Glass specializes in Tiffany-style hanging, table, and floor lamps of stained opalescent and cathedral glass constructed by the copper foil and solder method. The shades come in a wide variety of shapes and patterns and the hanging ceiling fixtures are also equipped with chain and wire, canopy, and canopy kit. While the complete lamps are not inexpensive, from $192 to over $1000 for hanging fixtures, the company also provides do-it-yourself kits for most of the styles and models. MO

IV-35
THE RENOVATOR'S SUPPLY
71 Northfield Road
Miller's Falls, MA 01349

The Renovator's Supply, $2 (refundable with purchase), 48 pages, illustrated, black and white.

This catalogue of supplies for those engaged in renovating or restoring an old house has a large lighting section. Fixtures include Victorian-style wall brackets and hanging parlor lamp; a table student lamp, either single ($165) or double ($268), and a hanging student lamp; various reproductions of old gaslight fixtures, electrified for modern use; tin sconces; an unusual pierced tin overhead light; chandeliers; lanterns and post lamps. Also included are heavy cast-brass shade holders; etched and pressed glass shades of different sizes, styles, and diameters; electric candles; replacement prisms for crystal chandeliers; and candlesticks of both solid brass and pewter. MO

IV-36
HILO STEINER
509 Broad Street
Shrewsbury, NJ 07701

Hilo Steiner, $2, published annually, 20 pages in folder, illustrated, black and white.

Hilo Steiner has good-looking simple and original designs in lamps, some with glass bases in

1929 Lenox China figure lamp called "Spring" lights from within and above. 21st Century Antiques, VI-38.

Modern classic Arco lamp designed by Castiglione, from Atelier International, I-7.

which you can put shells, one with a polished wood base on which you could display a large shell, piece of coral, or other small object. There's a swinger wall lamp in brass or chrome finish with a handmade string shade in a choice of 10 colors ($150); a slim swiveling floor lamp, 56" high, with a brass shell shade lined in white enamel ($85); a lamp with a celadon stoneware temple jar base from Thailand; a solid brass candlestick lamp; and a great little desk lamp with built-in magnifier. Prices include UPS delivery and purchases may be charged to major credit cards. There is also a toll-free number to call. MO

IV-37
TELL CITY CHAIR COMPANY
P.O. Box 329
Tell City, IN 47586

Tell City Primer of Early American Home Decorating, $4, published annually, 124 pages, illustrated, black and white and color.

Tell City has lamps in simple traditional styling to go with their Early American furniture. There are hanging chain lamps with bronze finish, table lamps with wood and metal bases, and table floor lamps of different designs. Also included are mirrored and plain sconces for candles. RS

V
General, Gift, and Museum Sources

V-1
AMERICAN HERITAGE PUBLISHING COMPANY, INC.
10 Rockefeller Plaza
New York, NY 10020

The American Heritage Collection, no charge, published annually, 32 pages, illustrated, color.

One of the more interesting specialized gift catalogues, *The American Heritage Collection* leans toward traditional Americana, from meticulously crafted reproductions of furniture to simple tole sconces. In a recent collection of reproduction furnishings from historic Deerfield in the Connecticut Valley, there was a superb eighteenth-century Mary Hoyt Williams chest with scalloped top, with the original brass pulls traced and reproduced exactly ($1,950). Other interesting items included painted tole sconces, copies of an original in the Hall Tavern; a pierced-brass sconce from an original now in the Van Cortlandt Manor ($95); a luncheon set of Pennsylvania "Gaudy Dutch" ware; a copy of a seventeenth-century brass candlestick with a footed triangular base; a fluted silver plate shell scoop with rosewood handle; and an amusing cast-iron black-cat silhouette, originally a boot-scraper, that would make a great doorstop ($29). Also included were Chinese antiques and *objets d'art*, a lovely tole chandelier, hand-colored collector's engravings of nineteenth-century streets, needlepoint kits, a sailing-ship pattern hooked rug kit, and a charming stencil-on-velvet kit of a bowl of fruit taken from a painting in Old Sturbridge Village ($85). There are always some out-of-the-ordinary things in this carefully chosen collection. MO

V-2
BEREA COLLEGE STUDENT INDUSTRIES
CPO 2347
Berea, KY 40404

Handcrafted Gifts from Berea College, free, published annually, 28 pages, illustrated, black and white.

In addition to handcrafted Colonial furniture, the students of this college make and sell a wide variety of handcrafts. There is an excellent selection of ceramics, woven hangings, pillows, throws, table mats, brooms, toys, and wooden board games. Wrought iron is another of their crafts, and you'll find here well-designed log holders and fireplace sets, a sea horse or horseshoe doorknocker, shelf brackets, towel bars, and rings. They will also give quotes on custom work for some items, among them andirons and hinges. Prices are reasonable for handcrafts—starting from around $2.50 and going up to $125 for a 34" x 72" woven wool and acrylic rug. MO

V-3
BRENTANO'S
545 Fifth Avenue
New York, NY 10017

Brentano's, free, published seasonally, illustrated, color.

The gift catalogues issued by this well-known chain of bookstores contain both books and a good selection of the other things they sell—reproductions of art and sculpture, handcrafts, decorative accessories, prints and posters, calendars, engagement books, and desk sets. In a recent issue we noticed simple, beautiful terra-

Marriage chest, reproduced from the Connecticut Valley original, in cherry and white pine. American Heritage, V-1.

cotta bowls and a ginger jar designed in Portugal; Korean temple rubbings on rice paper, signed and stamped by the artist, matted and framed for $85; and a unique sculpture by Carol Marks of movable, flexible jeweler's bronze figures that can be positioned in various ways on a rectangle of aluminum, polished to mirror brightness to reflect the forms ($250). A lovely leaded glass box with hand-etched iris design was $38, an Art Deco hand-blown rainbow glass bell signed by the artist was $60. Included in Brentano's sculpture collection were an endearing replica of a cat from the Benaki Museum in Athens and a replica of the sculpted head of Alexander the Great's horse, Bucephalus. For needlepointers, a design taken from a Pompeiian floor mosaic representing sea creatures is sold as a kit with 19"-square canvas, yarn, and instructions for $35. MO

V-4
THE CLIPPER TRADE, INC.
720 Beacon Street
Boston, MA 02215

The Clipper Trade, $1 *(refundable with purchase), published quarterly, 24 pages, illustrated, color.*

Clipper Trade specializes in extremely attractive imports from the Orient and reproductions of Oriental porcelains and art works, although there are some more general items of American extraction, including a Paul Revere pierced tin lantern and a schoolhouse clock with octagonal face. A reproduction of a nineteenth-century Korean jewel box lined with calligraphy parchment with brass fittings and goldfish lock is around $50; a most attractive rattan rocker with matching lamp stand and magazine rack costs $165 for the rocker, $55 for the lamp stand; a Quantong embroidered silk scroll, handmade in the People's Republic of China, with bird and flower scene, brocade frame, and scroll hanger costs $33; and a Japanese lamp with a silk shade and beautiful porcelain base in the iris pattern costs $150. Handmade cloisonné vases, a hand-painted Japanese screen with cherry-blossom design, and Chinese vases are other temptations. MO

V-5
EMERALD MAIL ORDER
Ballingeary
County Cork, Ireland

Emerald Catalog, free, published semiannually, 116 pages, illustrated, color.

The offerings in the Emerald catalogue include a wide variety of Irish products, such as Waterford crystal from Galway, Royal Tara china, Connemara marble desk accessories and clock, Newbridge flatware in the traditional King's pattern or the delicate Celtic pattern, Donegal table linens, and Foxford Connemara plaid throws. A lambskin rug, 36" x 25" (around $27) would be delightfully cozy at bedside; a snuggledown Continental quilt with pretty flowered covers designed by Mary Quant comes in feather and down or pure duck down at prices ranging, according to size and fill, from $66 for a 54" x 78" feather-and-down quilt to $222 for a 90" x 86" pure duck-down quilt. Covers are extra. We also liked the beautiful cut-crystal Waterford lamp bases (around $50 and $60), the hand-knitted cushion covers in natural wool, and a silver lotus bowl with three candle holders that would make a very attractive centerpiece ($42.90). Prices given in the catalogue are subject to change, and you are asked to confirm orders at revised prices before they are shipped. Payment can be made by check, money order, or charge cards. Shipping charges quoted are by surface mail, which takes about five to six weeks. Air mail is double or more. Duty, of course, is payable when the package is delivered. MO

V-6
GUMP'S
250 Post Street
San Francisco, CA 94108

Gump's Gift Book, $1, published seasonally, 82 pages, illustrated, color.

The catalogue of this famous and elegant San Francisco store is always packed with temptations, many of them one-of-a-kind antiques or pieces made especially for Gump's. Orientalia is their forte and in a recent catalogue there was an antique white jade carving of two herons holding a lotus blossom from the Tao-Kuang period, 3″ high including the rosewood stand, for $2,500; antique hand-carved gilt-wood panels from China; handmade jewel trees from the Orient; hand-cast bronzes from Japan; Oriental porcelains; and some beautiful lamps with bronze, brass, and porcelain bases. They also have the best of other worlds—Baccarat crystal, antique and modern silver, capiz shell bowls, boxes, and trays, and some delightful Italian earthenware. A set of six plates, each with a different hand-painted vegetable motif, made for Gump's, cost $36. Many of these offerings of outstanding quality would make unusual and charming accessories or table appointments. MO

V-7
HOFFRITZ FOR CUTLERY
515 West 24th Street
New York, NY 10011

Hoffritz for Cutlery, $2, published annually, 74 pages, illustrated, black and white.

Although fine cutlery is the name and fame of Hoffritz, they have many other interesting items —makeup and shaving mirrors, barometers and other weather instruments, a push-button telephone silencer, clock-radios, bar tools and ice buckets, and German porcelain trinket boxes. For the kitchen, Hoffritz has handsome counter-top knife blocks crafted in Denmark of lacquered pine, flatware holders of hardrock maple, and cheese and chopping boards. For the table, there are sets of six fruit knives, porcelain dessert plates in Meissen-style floral patterns, tea pots, and demitasse sets. Prices, which are subject to change, are given on an accompanying updated price list. The order form includes a gift certificate for $2 that can be applied to your first mail-order purchase. MO

V-8
THE HORCHOW COLLECTION
P.O. Box 34257
Dallas, TX 75234

TRIFLES
P.O. Box 44432
Dallas, TX 75234

The Horchow Collection, and Trifles, $2 for 12 monthly issues, illustrated, color.

These two leading gift catalogues have now merged their operations, although they each retain their own publication. Horchow's has traditionally been the Cartier of gift catalogues, with Trifles running a close second, and there is always a goodly amount of tableware and home furnishings in each. A recent Horchow Christmas catalogue had some lovely avocado-shaped glass bowls for serving that awkward fruit (set of four, $14), a quartz alarm clock in wood-grained case with brass touches, and one-of-a-kind antique blue-and-white Chinese bowls of the Ch'ing Dynasty period, 10″ to 12″ in diameter ($200). Trifles had a most ingenious tiny wall safe designed to look like an outlet ($15), a charming quilted white polyester satin comforter with brilliant butterfly embroidery, a dramatic Art Deco design black glass vase from Italy ($20), and a sleekly contemporary hurricane lamp with silver-plated base and round chimney. MO

V-9
MANHATTAN AD HOC HOUSEWARES
842 Lexington Avenue
New York, NY 10021

Ad Hoc/High-Tech Catalog, $1 (refundable with purchase), published annually, 16 pages, illustrated, black and white.

This nifty little catalogue comes from a store that specializes in housewares from professional restaurant and hotel equipment suppliers, but there's a great deal more than housewares in it. Most of the items are the kind of institutional and industrial equipment popularized by the high-tech style of functional decoration, when factory lights became sought-after lighting fixtures and laboratory flasks turned into flower vases or wine carafes. You'll find here the open wire Erecta shelving from Metropolitan Wire Corporation that comes knocked down to assemble with a rubber mallet, and is perfect for inexpensive bookshelves, or for storing linens, records, china, pots and pans, or home-office

Polished pewter English tankards, glass beer mugs, and stainless steel or aluminum wine or champagne coolers. Hoffritz, V-7.

supplies and is cheaper, lighter, and easier to move around than wood storage units. A freestanding shelf unit, 18″ x 42″ x 86½″ high with four shelves, is around $142. You can also get Erecta wall-mounted shelves, a dunnage rack to be used as a low coffee or end table, and a wire cart with chrome handles and three adjustable chromed-wire shelves that could be used as a serving cart, bar, or buffet. Other carts that can double as furniture are the Scotty cart, made for factories and classrooms, in red or black enamel finish with three shelves and a drawer, or a heavy-gauge stainless steel restaurant serving cart (this also comes knocked down and costs around $156).

Other things we noticed are nickel-plated egg baskets, 8″ and 12″ in diameter and 6½″ or 9″ high, that would make interesting holders for plants or magazines (you could spray-paint them if you wished); vinyl duckboard of the type used in factories, locker rooms, hotel kitchens, and gyms that could be used to cushion the cement floor of a garage or basement converted to a family room or be put down in a kitchen (it comes in red, black, green, or blue at $16 a foot, 10 percent off for a 33-foot roll); and the heavy quilted cotton movers' pads used to protect furniture and elevator walls that would make good bedspreads or upholstery material for plump, curvy seating

units. The pads come in three sizes—36″ x 76″ ($16), 72″ x 80″ ($30), and 76″ x 96″ ($35)—and each side is a contrasting color with matching border. The colors depend on factory stock but are usually available in reds, blues, purples, greens, browns, and neutrals (gray, beige, and cream). For bathrooms there are space-saving hotel towel racks; wall-mounted chrome rings in different sizes to hold washcloths, hand, and bath towels; a free-standing chromed steel towel rack with three hang-up rails and a shelf that would also be good in a guest room; and a sturdy stool with white enamel top and rubber-tipped, chrome-plated legs ($18.50). MO

V-10
THE METROPOLITAN MUSEUM OF ART
Dept. IPAO
Box 255, Gracie Station
New York, NY 10028

Museum shop catalogues, $1, published seasonally, illustrated, color.

Superb reproductions of fine china, silver, pewter, and brass objects, ancient sculptures, glassware, jewelry, and American folk art from the Museum's collections, produced either in the Museum's own studio or under their direct supervision. Descriptions, historical background,

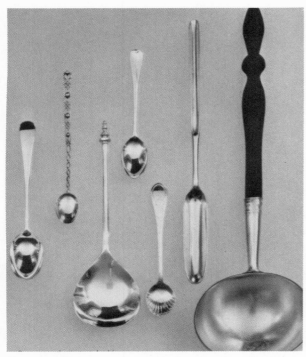

Silver and pewter spoons and ladle, reproductions from The Metropolitan Museum of Art, V-10.

and prices are given. This is an excellent source for really beautiful tableware, decorative accessories, and needlepoint kits, and the price range is wide. The Christmas edition of the catalogue also contains a big selection of Christmas cards with motifs taken from works of art, engagement and wall calendars, gift-wrapping paper, note paper, and many small inexpensive gifts. MO

V-11
MONTGOMERY WARD
393 Seventh Avenue
New York, NY 10001

General catalogues, published seasonally.

To get the Montgomery Ward catalogue and stay on the mailing list you must give the company three small orders or one order of at least $50 for each 6-month catalogue period, either by ordering from a borrowed catalogue or through the catalogue department of a Ward store. Everything you'd find in a department store and more can be found in this weighty mail-order catalogue, which can run as many as 1,400 pages. In addition to clothing, camping and exercise equipment, and a complete range of home furnishings, there are tools and materials for remodeling and do-it-yourself projects, kitchen and bathroom equipment, and energy-savers

such as insulating panels, rolls of fiberglass insulation, stoves, and built-in fireplaces (including a heat-convector built-in fireplace for mobile homes). You can shop by phone or by mail. There's a list of transportation and handling charges for mailable items and another for estimating delivery charges for non-mailable items. MO/RS

V-12
MUSEUM COLLECTIONS
140 Greenwich Avenue
Greenwich, CT 06830

Museum Collections, free catalogue, published seasonally, 28 pages, illustrated, color.

While this handsome catalogue originally offered sculptures and jewelry reproduced from works of art in major museums and collections, the scope has now been widened to include antiques, limited-edition graphics, handicrafts from around the world, contemporary designs inspired by and adapted from historical artifacts, Oriental objects, toys, needlepoint kits, glass paperweights, scarves, and other carefully chosen items in the general gift category.

In a recent issue we found many enticing things, including a four-panel hand-painted screen from Japan with a design of poppies on rice paper in a gold-leafed wood frame ($800), a floral cloisonné vase from Mainland China ($85), a signed original 19¼" x 15½" primitive on distressed wood showing a cat curled on a sofa ($95), an Art Nouveau-style bedside or desk lamp with a gracefully curved stem rising from a lily-pad base in antique brass finish with frosted glass globe, and a limited-edition bronze sculpture of a unicorn by Sterett-Gittings Kelsey ($295). There were Alvastone reproductions of some charming animal sculptures, bookends of the New York Public Library lions reduced in exact scale, and various prints taken from museum originals. *Museum Collections* always contains some unusual things for the home. MO

V-13
THE MUSEUM OF MODERN ART
11 West 53rd Street
New York, NY 10019

The Museum of Modern Art Gift Catalogue, $1, published annually, 28 pages, illustrated, color.

A recent gift catalogue featured three extraordinary pieces of modern furniture from the Museum's Design Collection, spanning the years from 1919 to 1929, authorized replicas of which were being offered in limited quantity. One was a sleek end table of shiny tubular steel with a thick smoked-glass top that can be raised or lowered, designed by Eileen Gray, who spent her entire career in France and produced some of the most original designs of the modernist movement. The table was designed between 1927 and 1929 for her house on the Riviera. A 90" long table by Le Corbusier combined a polished glass slab above a base of oval tubular black-enameled steel ($1440). A fascinating 1919 sideboard by Dutch architect Gerrit Rietveld, an abstract composition of lines and planes, could be custom built on special order. These will probably not appear in the current catalogue, but they give an idea of the quality of the Museum's offerings. Among other classic designs in the home field were a fluid, free-form crystal vase by Alvar Aalto, a beautifully crafted contemporary stainless steel espresso maker designed by Richard Sapper, and a marvelous portable AM/FM radio in a hinged double cube plastic case with pullout carrying handle ($150). If you're looking for the best in contemporary design, this is the place to find it. MO

Eileen Gray's 1927 table of tubular steel with smoked glass top, from the Museum of Modern Art, V-13.

V-14
THE MUSIC STAND
1457 Broadway
New York, NY 10036

The Music Stand, free, published semiannually, 16 pages, illustrated, black and white.

This catalogue's title is somewhat misleading, for while it includes many music-related items, from mugs decorated with heads of famous composers to jewelry with musical-instrument motifs, there's not a music stand to be seen. There are a canvas and wood cradle to hold records, also self-adjusting holders with a spring mechanism to hold anything from 1" to 18" of records, tapes, or books ($3.95), and laminated place mats with advertisements from turn-of-the-century music magazines (set of four, $5.95). MO

V-15
MYSTIC SEAPORT MUSEUM STORE
Mystic, CT 06355

Mystic Seaport Museum Store, $1 (refundable with purchase), published annually, 48 pages, illustrated, color.

This nifty little museum catalogue has many delightful things for the home—limited-edition marine prints, China Trade and Tobacco Leaf porcelains, whale sculptures, beautiful patchwork quilts, and numerous objects with a nautical flavor. We especially liked the dolphin andirons and fireplace tools of hand-cast brass (andirons, 15" high with log supports, are $195 a pair, the tools and stand, 32" high, $285 the set), the needlepoint kit of a whale designed to cover a brick doorstop ($17.50), the unusual ship's surgeon candleholder of bronze or brass with deep sides to catch wax drippings, reproduced from one salvaged from a sunken British warship ($42), and a copy of the old-fashioned ocean-liner deck chair in teak with brass fittings that just invites lounging ($295). The furniture line includes quite a few unusual pieces, such as a portable table, 21½" in diameter and 21" high, in glass and brass that would make a good deck end table, a chart cocktail table, hatch-cover table, ship's grating end and coffee tables, and a cocktail table with a slate top etched with the plan of a ship. There are also clocks, lamps, runners handwoven by the Mystic Seaport weavers, hurricane chimneys with brass candlesticks, brass shell bookends, and all kinds of things for the table—at home or on the water. A good source for gift shoppers. MO/RS

V-16
THE NATURE COMPANY
P.O. Box 7137
Berkeley, CA 94707

The Nature Company, free catalogue, published semiannually, 40 pages, illustrated, color.

An out-of-the-ordinary gift catalogue that uses nature as its theme. There are various Alvastone sculptures of animals, a delightful print of a watercolor of wildflowers of the California mother lode ($8), unusual and well-designed bird feeders, some elegant sundials and weathervanes, and a host of weather instruments. We liked the combination sculpture/mobile and prism, a hand-cast optical instrument that transforms light into rainbow colors when placed in a sunny location (around $20), a whale mobile, an amusing solid brass wall hook with a duck's head ($11), a dramatic bell sculpture by Paolo Soleri, and the enchantingly different glass oil lamps designed by Jon Wolfard—clear glass cylinders 6", 9" or 12" tall with interior clear globe-shaped flasks to hold the oil and wick. MO

V-17
PHILLIPS SON & NEALE, AUCTIONEERS
867 Madison Avenue
New York, NY 10021

Auction catalogue list, free.

The Phillips catalogue subscription list covers a wide variety of objects such as Oriental rugs and carpets, European ceramics, English and Continental furniture, clocks, decorations, and decorative paintings, collector's china, and Art Nouveau and Art Deco posters, all to be sold at auction in New York, Toronto, and Montreal. You can send for a single catalogue at prices ranging from $10 to $60, or subscribe to all the yearly categories. Each catalogue includes estimated prices and an order bid form and with it you get *The Auctioneer*, a quarterly publication about the offerings, and a calendar of auctions. MO

V-18
PRESERVATION SHOPS, NATIONAL TRUST FOR HISTORIC PRESERVATION
1600 H Street, NW
Washington, DC 20006

Gift Collection, 50 cents, published annually, 24 pages, illustrated, color.

Among the usual selection of gifts there are always some attractive reproductions and original pieces for the home. In a recent catalogue we found a classic pewter coffee service from the collection of Old Sturbridge Village (adapted from an original by R. Yates, late eighteenth century), two vases created for the National Trust in amber or cobalt blue glass with silver feathering, signed, numbered, and registered ($120 for the cobalt, $100 for the amber), and a simple pottery candlestick with the light buff-and-green Bennington glaze, a reproduction from an original in The Bennington Museum. There were attractive hand-cast reproductions of French jardinières in terra-cotta and gray, crewel and needlepoint kits, patchwork pillows ($28 each), a copy of a traditional New Hampshire blanket in blue and white plaid and a double-woven blue and white coverlet with Lover's Knot design and pine-tree border, 108" x 90", for $162.50. Rag rugs are usually rather dreary in design, but one with a beige arrowhead design run vertically on a brown background, a traditional motif probably taken from Indian weavings, was striking and different, with a very contemporary look. MO

V-19
S. T. PRESTON & SON, INC.
116-A Main Street Wharf
Greenport, NY 11944

Of Ships and Sea, 25 cents, published semiannually, 114 pages, illustrated, black and white and color.

Preston's catalogue hews to the nautical theme of its title and while some of the items are pretty gimmicky, many are honest and handsome, such as an oil-burning admiral's lamp of solid brass, 14½" high ($49.95), a solid cast-bronze armillary sundial, and a ship's bell striking clock and barometer set in brass by Schatz, makers of fine precision instruments. There's something here for every taste and budget—anchor doorknockers, a brass porthole mirror ($45), marine prints and reproductions of paintings on canvas, a large selection of table lamps, a ship's wheel cocktail table, and kits for building ship models. MO

V-20
SHIP 'N OUT
937 Harmony Road
Pawling, NY 12564

Ship 'n Out, $1 (refundable with purchase), published semiannually, 12 pages, illustrated, color, plus brochures.

This company specializes in brass, copper, and wood items, mostly with a nautical flavor or motifs. In addition to such things as diver's helmets and ship's wheels, there is a large assortment of brass doorknockers, door plates and hooks, brass shelf brackets, and racks. The Australian train or ferry baggage rack would make a nifty bookshelf or wine rack ($79.95). Ship 'n Out also has brass fire screens, fireplace sets, lanterns and candleholders, and a few pieces of wood furniture. A copy of the classic ocean-liner deck chair in teak is $198, a coffee table with a top made from an original hatch cover is $225.

One of the brochures we received with the catalogue showed solid copper weathervanes in classic rooster, eagle, horse, and whale shapes, the other showed a solid brass bar foot rail. MO

V-21
SHIP'S WHEEL, INC.
Nottingham Square Road
Epping, NH 03042

Romance of the Sea, 50 cents, published six times a year, 48 pages, illustrated, black and white.

Although this catalogue has a nautical name and theme, it offers a wide range of other gifts from clothing to "amusing" shower curtains lettered with sayings like "Paint and Body Shop" and "Water Works." For the garden there's a well-designed slatted wood bench, 5' long ($75), a park bench, patio furniture, sundials, and pool floats. For indoors you'll find trapunto pillows with sailing ship designs (around $25), brass hooks shaped like a whale, limited-edition marine prints, an authentic hatch-cover table ($375), and a glass-topped table with a 3"-deep base where you can display a collection. MO

V-22
SHOPPING INTERNATIONAL, Dept. 225
Norwich, VT 05055

Shopping International, $1, published semiannually, 48 pages, illustrated, color.

Since we first saw this gift catalogue it has in-creased the scope of its offerings enormously, while still concentrating on imports—clothing, jewelry, glassware, china, and decorative accessories—that reflect the cultures and crafts of different countries. We noted a copper candelabra from Santa Clara del Cobre, Mexico, hand-hammered so no two are exactly alike, 8½" tall with holders for seven candles ($75), and a pierced black pottery lantern from Coyotopec which comes with a 15" chain, wired or unwired. From Germany there were wine glasses with green stems and bases and multi-colored grapevine pattern ($49 for a set of six), a crystal stein etched with a design of hops, and pressed flowers encased in glass and framed in wood to hang as a picture. There are also patterned bedspreads from India; an onyx vase from Pakistan; a "Cracow Wedding" wall hanging by Polish weaver Maria Domanska, a traditional design interpreted in a contemporary style ($170); a millefiori glass paperweight from Italy; a beautiful Kwantun silk embroidery panel from China; an alpaca fur rug from Peru; and crystal candlesticks, vases, and sculptures from Sweden. The products of 30 countries, from Africa to Turkey, are represented. MO

V-23
SMITHSONIAN INSTITUTION
P.O. Box 2456
Washington, DC 20013

The Smithsonian Catalogue, free, published semiannually, 36 pages, illustrated, color.

The pieces shown reflect the wide spectrum of

"Han Flying Horse" cast iron replica sculpture, from Shopping International, V-22.

the Smithsonian's collections. Many are authorized reproductions, others have motifs taken from objects in the collections. Recently there were some charming kits for needlepoint, cross-stitch samplers, and crewel and bargello pillows. One delicate white-on-white needlepoint pillow was based on the pattern of an eighteenth-century English stoneware plate ($18 for the kit). Reproduction glassware included some magnificent pressed glass candlesticks, as well as a tall "spooner" that could be used for flowers or celery and a centerpiece or serving bowl, 8" in diameter, in the "Broken Column" pattern. A most unusual mirror had a wood frame stenciled with designs taken from a late nineteenth-century Bible quilt. Other items were an amusing pig wall hanging of weathered sheet metal inspired by an old weathervane, a handsome solid brass carriage clock ($360), and various art reproductions including a replica of a late Han Dynasty dragon tomb figure in Alvastone. Selections, naturally, change with each edition of the catalogue. MO

V-24
SOTHEBY PARKE BERNET/
PB EIGHTY-FOUR
　　Subscription Department
　　980 Madison Avenue
　　New York, NY 10021

List of annual subscription rates for catalogues and price lists, no charge.

If you are too far away or too busy to attend the fascinating auction sales at Sotheby Parke Bernet and its offshoot, PB Eighty-Four (171 East 84th Street), it is still possible to participate in their auctions. You can subscribe to a year of catalogues, ask for an estimate of what the item you are interested in will bring, then place a bid by mail or phone. Price lists sent after each sale give you a good idea of how prices are running. This New York combination of the famed London and New York auction houses has tremendous sales of Americana, art, furniture, rugs, porcelains, silver, and lots more. PB Eighty-Four has more moderately priced selections than the Madison Avenue branch. MO

V-25
SPIEGEL, INCORPORATED
　　P.O. Box 6340
　　Chicago, IL 60680

Spiegel Catalogue, $2 (refundable with purchase), 604 pages, illustrated, color.

Contemporary living room charmingly furnished with purchases from Sotheby Parke-Bernet/PB Eighty-Four auction sales. V-24.

This giant, all-inclusive mail-order catalogue has a great many inexpensive home furnishings, from bed ensembles of matching linens, comforter, dust ruffle, and curtains to complete stereo systems. You'll find here brass beds, furniture of all kinds, decorative accessories, fireplace accessories, lamps and lighting fixtures, carpeting and rugs, plus a wide variety of ready-made curtains and slipcovers, blinds, shades, and shutters. A 4-panel shutter set, unfinished, 20" x 29", is around $20, with many other widths and lengths available. Recently they showed some extremely attractive rattan and wicker furniture and accessories. A rattan headboard was priced at $45 for twin size, a latticework 3-panel screen was $199, and an armchair with lattice back and cane seat was $159. Spiegel also has tableware, appliances, cookware, and energy-saving wood-burning heaters, including one with a built-in cooktop (around $250). Everything you'd find in a big department store is here. Orders may be placed by calling a toll-free number and charging your purchases to major credit cards. You can also open an account with Spiegel over the phone at the time you make your purchase. MO

V-26
STURBRIDGE YANKEE WORKSHOP
　　Brimfield Turnpike
　　Sturbridge, MA 01566

Sturbridge Yankee Workshop, 50 cents, published three times a year, 48 pages, illustrated, color.

While Sturbridge Yankee Workshop specializes in Americana—reproductions, adaptations, and current pieces—there's a great deal more in this gift catalogue, a grab-bag of items ranging from the souvenir type to well-designed furniture and accessories. So many things are packed into each page that you have to use a selective eye. Picking at random, we noticed French Quimperware, hand-painted pottery with a traditional rustic design, at $82.50 for a 5-piece place setting, a simple wrought-iron ratchet chandelier, tulip-shaped hurricane candleholders of old-fashioned wavy glass ($26.50 a pair), and a graceful Prosper Windsor chair and settee with delicately shaped back flowing down into thin arm rests. A hand-blown cranberry glass footed hurricane and flared bowl in the Paul Revere shape would be lovely on a table. There are also a large assortment of brass lanterns and many different types of lamps. MO

Miniature enamel boxes reproduced in England for the Horchow Collection, V-8.

V-27
LILLIAN VERNON CORPORATION
Box LV, Dept. ESS
510 South Fulton Avenue
Mount Vernon, NY 10551

Lillian Vernon, free catalogue, published five times a year, 108 pages, illustrated, color.

This well-known mail-order gift catalogue covers a wide range of items from jewelry to a draftsman's kit and includes many good ideas for the home. We noticed in a recent catalogue capiz shell candleholders in a graceful water lily shape, $14.98 the pair, and a matching hexagonal box; strawberry-pattern earthenware by Old Foley of Staffordshire; German hand-crafted crystal candleholders and serving pieces by Goebel; and a striking contemporary quartz wall clock, a circle of brilliant red plastic with a single numeral (12) and white hour, minute, and second hands, for $21.98. There were also some simple and well-designed heavy clear Lucite bathroom accessories, such as shower caddy, shelf-towel rack and double hooks, and Italian-made storage shelves and racks of steel with a white vinyl coating. One exceptionally useful piece was the wall grid, 26" x 17", with S-hooks for hanging tools and utensils ($7.98 with four hooks, extra hooks $1 for a set of four). MO

Eclectic bedroom inexpensively furnished from the Spiegel catalogue. V-25.

Antique silver tankard and tea caddy from England. Gump's, V-6.

VI
Decorative Accessories

VI-1
ABITARE
212 East 57th Street
New York, NY 10022

Abitare, $10, published annually, 234 pages in ring binder, illustrated, black and white.

The accessories featured in this high-style catalogue of the best in international design are limited but excellent. There is a wall mirror with a flat, sleek stainless steel frame, marble and travertine ashtrays, bowls, boxes, and platter, and a really good-looking umbrella stand, a simple cylinder of white or black perforated steel ($88) with a matching wastebasket ($73)—hardly inexpensive but worth the price. MO/RS

VI-2
ETHAN ALLEN, INC.
Ethan Allen Drive
Danbury, CT 06810

The Ethan Allen Treasury of American Traditional Interiors, $7.95, published every two years, 394 pages, illustrated, color.

Part of the vast Ethan Allen home furnishings collection shown in this catalogue consists of traditional wall and floor clocks in a range of styles and woods. There are also over a dozen mirrors in different shapes, sizes, and styles, including a Chinese Chippendale mirror, an upright mirror with decorated side panels, and a Queen Anne mirror with hand-carved gilded wood frame. Among the more interesting decorative accessories are lacquered and polished brass imports—lanterns, boxes, a temple jar, garden seat, and samovar—from the Far East, glass sculptures from Murano, and ceramic figures. Framed pictures of traditional subjects (still lifes, landscapes, portraits, birds, and flowers) and throw pillows to coordinate with Ethan Allen upholstery, drapes, and bedspread fabrics are also included in this section. RS

VI-3
BHS INDUSTRIES LTD.
P.O. Box 59
Yalesville, CT 06492

Brochures, 50 cents (refundable with purchase), published annually, illustrated, black and white.

Unusual wall clocks of hand-cast solid pewter or pewter and pine are the specialty of BHS Industries. Seventeen different models, four with pendulum movement, are shown in the clock brochure. Circular clocks are 10″ in diameter, others are 11″ to 11½″ high. The designs are simple and restrained, our favorites being the Taft and the Hourglass, which resemble pewter plates in shape. The second brochure features the solid pewter belt buckles made by BHS. Prices on request. MO

VI-4
THE BIGGS COMPANY
Mail Order Department
Attention: Mrs. Frances W. Street
105 East Grace Street
Richmond, VA 23219

Biggs Reproduction Furniture, $5 (refundable with purchase), published annually, 90 pages, illustrated, black and white.

In addition to a wide range of furniture, Biggs has many attractive reproduction mirrors in their collection, such as Chippendale mirrors, a Queen Anne lacquered mirror, an oval-top wheat mirror, an Empire mirror, a delightful oval Adam mirror, and two Old Sturbridge Village mirrors, one with a circular carved wood gilt frame topped by an eagle. Prices range from around $150 up. The catalogue also has a few decorative accent pieces, including a mahogany étagère and a muffin stand. MO/RS

A collection of wicker, straw, reed, and grass baskets, trays, and mats from Conran's, I-26.

VI-5
BINSWANGER MIRROR PRODUCTS
P.O. Box 17127
Memphis, TN 38117

Book of Mirrors, $2, *published annually, 56 pages, illustrated, color.*

Binswanger makes a comprehensive collection, from wall mirrors to pier, console, and cheval mirrors to sliding and bi-fold mirror doors and unframed door mirrors. While the emphasis is on traditional designs with metal frames and gold or bronze finish, there are also mirrors with wood frames, hand-painted frames, inlays of cork and cane, white frames in lattice and bamboo designs, as well as some unusual contemporary mirrors framed in suede cloth. Virtually every size, shape, and type of mirror is available, and the prices are reasonable, ranging from $40 to $400. RS

VI-6
THE BOMBAY COMPANY
P.O. Box 53323
920 Valmont Street
New Orleans, LA 70153

The Bombay Company Catalogue, $2, *published annually, 40 pages, illustrated, color.*

While furniture comprises the major part of the catalogue, there are also some unusual and well-crafted accessories. One is the Bond Street Post Office Bar, modeled on the British scarlet mail box and fitted as a bar ($150). Also included are decorated map and chart boxes, a tavern clock with painted dial and temperature gauge, a nest of three mahogany and brass serving trays, and a very handsome cribbage board of solid rosewood inlaid by hand with solid brass, 10¼" long x 3¼" wide for just $19. MO/RS

VI-7
THE BRASS BUTTERFLY
P.O. Box 261
Bomoseen, VT 05732

Plant Rooters, free leaflet, illustrated, black and white.

The delicate airy plant "rooters" sold by The Brass Butterfly consist of copper-coated steel hangers in simple decorative shapes that hook onto a pole or rod and clear glass rooting pots suspended from wooden rings through which the plant is trained upward. There are single pots, clusters, and heart, round, or teardrop metal shapes. The prices are very reasonable for hand-crafted work, from $3.50 to $7 for a 4-pot hanger. MO

VI-8
COLONIAL TIN CRAFT
7805 Railroad Avenue
Cincinnati, OH 45243

Colonial Tin Craft Catalogue, $2, 40 pages, illustrated, black and white.

While the specialty of Colonial Tin Craft is reproduction lighting fixtures, they also have some unusual and interesting accessories. There are pierced-tin planters that hold standard 4″, 6″ and 8″ clay pots, with jute rope or chain for hanging, priced from $9.75 to $19.25, and charming wall decorations of pierced tin in traditional pie-safe motifs (star, sunflower, tulip cluster, eagle), framed in barnwood or maple, $37.50. MO

VI-9
DESPARD DESIGNS LIMITED
1150 Fifth Avenue
New York, NY 10028

Time Design Clocks, $1 (refundable with purchase), one illustrated color page and information sheets.

Despard's Giro Time Design wall clocks are unique and rather hard to describe, although easy to read when you see them. Instead of having the conventional moving hands, each clock is a moving picture, continually changing as the hour and minute discs revolve, and is operated by a transistorized movement (guaranteed for a year) and a standard 'C' battery. The designs are fascinating. The most conventional, "Turning Numbers," is a digital clock with red hour markings, dark blue 5-minute markings, a white read-out wedge for the time and a red sweep-second hand. On "Stars and Stripes," red and blue stars on a white background tell the time. "Yin-Yan Whales," which would be great fun in a child's room, has red and blue dots for quarter-hours and minutes and the dorsal fins of interlocking whales of different colors indicate the time. Most sophisticated is "Moonstar," with gold moons and silver stars on a black background. The clocks are made of high-quality plastic, measure 9″ in diameter and 2⅝″ in depth, weigh 15

ounces and come with a wall hanger. They are around $30 each. MO/RS

VI-10
DEUTSCH, INC.
196 Lexington Avenue
New York, NY 10016

Catalogues, $2, published annually, 48 pages, illustrated, black and white and 26 pages, illustrated, color.

This firm of wicker and rattan importers has a great variety of attractive accessories, such as mirrors with wicker and bamboo frames, three-panel screens, planters, wastebaskets, wine racks, display ladders, a hanging lamp shade, wall shelves, and towel stands. There's also a good selection of trunks (including campaign-style) and cubes in cane camphorwood, brown rattan, and burnt rattan. Prices are reasonable. MO/RS/ID

VI-11
EDISON INSTITUTE
20900 Oakwood Boulevard
Dearborn, MI 48124

Reproductions from the Collections of Greenfield Village and the Henry Ford Museum, $2.50, 46 pages, illustrated, black and white and color.

Among the authentic reproductions commissioned by the Edison Institute are case and wall clocks by Colonial of Zeeland. There are two handsome grandfather clocks, the Thomas Jackson tall-case clock in curly maple and the Aaron Willard tall-case clock in mahogany, the Aaron Willard banjo clock with reverse glass painting on the tablet depicting a naval scene, a steeple

Natural red clay bean pot reproduction from Edison Institute, VI-11.

clock, regulator wall clock (available only in kit form), and a school clock. There are also two mirrors by LaBarge, one a Federal girandole from an original made in Philadelphia between 1810 and 1830 in pine finished in black with burnished gold metal leaf, the other a Philadelphia Chippendale mirror in burled elm with carved gilt trim and a carved phoenix atop the pediment. MO

VI-12
THE FENTON ART GLASS COMPANY
Caroline Avenue
Williamstown, WV 26187

Fenton 1979–80, $3, published every two years with seasonal updates, 78 pages, illustrated, color.

Beautiful illustrations of the art glass lamps, baskets, serving dishes, vases, and miscellaneous pieces that are sold only through Fenton representatives listed in the back of the catalogue. No prices. RS

VI-13
FURNITURECRAFT, INC.
Box 285c
Stoneham, MA 02180

FurnitureCraft, Inc. Distinctive Early American Furnishings, 50 cents, published semiannually, 32 pages, illustrated, color.

Some of the decorative accessories offered by FurnitureCraft include a handsome Thai brass noodlestand (used by street vendors to sell hot noodle soup) that could be used as a portable bar, an end table, or a planter (around $150), as well as an amusing cast-iron green-eyed black cat doorstop, 10" long x 5½" high (around $14).

Pewter reproduction tavern tankards from Great Americana, VI-16.

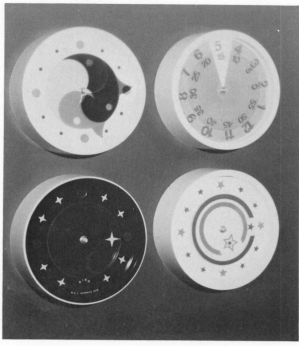

Giro Time Design wall clocks are transistor operated and tell time in moving pictures. Despard Designs, VI-9.

There are various clocks, such as the elegant Montreal clock in walnut with glass panels and brass trim that runs on a flashlight battery and the chiming Canterbury mantel clock, also battery operated. Worthy of note are the reproductions of the blue-and-white "cracqule ware" produced by the Dedham Pottery Company during the late nineteenth and early twentieth centuries and again today, which has a delightful border design of floppy-eared rabbits. A 6"-square tile with a circle of rabbits is $16, a 3" x 6" half tile is $8.75, and the Dedham rabbit figure itself, originally used as a knife holder, is $30. MO

VI-14
GLASSMASTERS, INC.
27 West 23rd Street
New York, NY 10010

Window Art: The Glassmasters Collection, $1, 5 loose pages, illustrated, color.

Stained glass hanging plaques in many beautiful designs—flowers, birds, sun and moon faces, mythical beasts, animals, and fruit—some with solid brass frames, would turn a plain window into a picture. Sizes range from miniatures, just over 4", up to an 11¼" x 9½" harbor scene in the

American Heritage series. These are some of the loveliest examples of stained glass art we have seen. Prices on request. MO/RS

VI-15
GOLD MEDAL, INC.
1700 Packard Avenue
Racine, WI 53403

Casual Furniture Collection, $1, *published annually, 32 pages, illustrated, color.*

This company that makes simple, well-designed casual furniture has a couple of very attractive screens with frames that take panels of fabric. An interesting hardwood frame Planterack, 66" high, with slatted top and bottom designed to hold and hang potted plants, comes knocked down with an unfinished frame and can be assembled easily to make an unusual indoor garden center. RS

VI-16
GREAT AMERICANA STORE
P.O. Box 98
Great Neck, NY 11021

The Great Americana Store, brochure, 25 cents, published quarterly, illustrated, black and white.

This is the familiar Americana of the recent past —metal candy, cookie, and coffee boxes and serving trays bearing nostalgic names like Rudd's Sunshine Candies, Pabst, Pepsi, and Dr. Pepper; woodenware such as a 5-foot-tall cigar-store Indian, a barber pole, and a figurehead; plus reproductions of pewter mugs, napkin rings, a porringer, candlesticks, and a Jefferson cup in statesmetal with pewter finish. Prices range from around $5 to around $23 for a solid brass Victorian doorknocker. MO

VI-17
GREEN BOUGHS
2021 Valentine Drive, N.E.
Grand Rapids, MI 49505

Fire Screens, brochure, 50 cents, illustrated, color.

Needlepoint fire screens handcrafted by Green Boughs cabinetmakers come in solid cherry in dark, medium, or light color, or with antique or distressed finish in Chippendale, Hepplewhite, Sheraton, and Queen Anne styles, as well as one contemporary model. They will send a full-color catalogue of their tapestries (the brochure shows only a few designs) for a $5 deposit, postage paid both ways, which will be refunded on return of the catalogue. Prices range from around $95 for the contemporary fire screen to $300 for the hand-carved Chippendale reproduction, 50½" high. They will also make frames to fit your own needlepoint at no extra charge. MO

VI-18
P. E. GUERIN, INC.
23 Jane Street
New York, NY 10014

Catalogue of Artistic Hardware, $4, 64 pages, illustrated, black and white and color.

An 8-page color section at the back of this fabulous hardware catalogue shows some superb eighteenth- and nineteenth-century reproductions of glass, steel, and bronze doré tables, bouillotte lamps, a Louis XVI dressing-table mirror, and obelisks and candlesticks of rock crystal and malachite. These elegant pieces are available only on special order. There are also more contemporary designs, including a Parsons table in onyx and a leaf table by Robsjohn–Gibbings (around $1575). MO/ID

VI-19
GUILD OF SHAKER CRAFTS, INC.
401 W. Savidge Street
Spring Lake, MI 49456

Shaker Furniture Reproductions, $2.50 (refundable with purchase), published seasonally, 28 pages, illustrated, black and white and color.

Among the Guild's interesting offerings are five sizes of lidded oval storage boxes from 4½" x 3" x 2" up to 11½" x 8" x 5¼", $26.50 to $40, as well as many sizes and types of serving and storage trays, and candlesticks based on early Shaker designs. MO

VI-20
HABERSHAM PLANTATION CORPORATION
P.O. Box 1209
Toccoa, GA 30577

The Habersham Plantation Workbook, $8.50 (refundable with purchase through dealer), published semiannually, 56 pages, illustrated, color.

Habersham Plantation's catalogue of American Colonial country furniture reproductions in-

Beveled mirror with hand-decorated border over gold leaf with gold aluminum frame, from LaBarge, VI-23.

Hobnail milk glass, handcrafted, from Fenton Art Glass, VI-12.

cludes a "Primitive Arts" collection of prints and accessories. There are colorful hand-painted boards and wooden wall plaques, inn and tradesmen's signs, a running-horse weathervane suitable for the wall of a family room, and copies of original English and American seventeenth- and eighteenth-century prints and paintings. RS

VI-21
HISTORIC CHARLESTON REPRODUCTIONS
51 Meeting Street
Charleston, SC 29401

Historic Charleston Reproductions, $3.50 (refundable with $25 purchase), 56 pages, illustrated, black and white and color.

In this catalogue of reproduction home furnishings from one of America's most famous historic cities are some superb mirrors, handcrafted with century-old frame-making techniques and ornamented with a special molded composition perfected in the eighteenth century. Middleton, with ribbed moldings and unusual offset corners with fluted carvings, is a copy of an eighteenth-century original from a Charleston house ($630). There's a Queen Anne mirror in black lacquer over wood with raised chinoiserie decoration, a girandole, a Chippendale rectangular mirror, and a simplified adaptation of a Hepplewhite

mirror with frame finished in antique metal leaf with light red rub, the center beveled plate set forward, and the sides angled to give an interesting reflective effect ($650). MO/RS

VI-22
MARTHA M. HOUSE
1022 South Decatur Street
Montgomery, AL 36104

Southern Heirlooms from Martha M. House, $1, published annually, 48 pages, illustrated, black and white and color.

There are some period accent pieces in this catalogue of Victorian furniture reproductions, among them a cheval mirror with gold-leafed wood frame, a solid mahogany grandfather clock, upholstered footstools (including a gout stool), and a marble-topped plant stand. MO

VI-23
LABARGE
P.O. Box 905A
875 Brooks Avenue
Holland, MI 49423

LaBarge Mirrors and Tables, free color brochure.

Shown in the brochure are many beautiful mirrors, most with hand-carved frames, some imported from Spain and Italy. The variety of styles, shapes, and finishes includes antiqued gold leaf, pickled pine, walnut burl veneer with gold metal leaf trim, and rattan. Some have matching consoles. One especially handsome mirror is hand-decorated on gold metal leaf and signed by the artist. In addition to mirrors, La-Barge has screens—coromandel, a four-panel mirrored version, a bamboo from China with hand-painted panels—and an assortment of tea tables, cocktail tables, and serving carts in glass and metal as well as various decorative accessories. RS

VI-24
MAGNOLIA HALL
726 Andover
Atlanta, GA 30327

Yesteryear Furniture, $1, published semiannually, 80 pages, illustrated, black and white.

In this company's catalogue of Victoriana, a magnificent mirror with an elaborately carved frame with a gold finish is around $100, a "triple wedding band" of three interlocking oval mirrors is around $200. These are but two of the many types of mirrors shown, which embrace everything from an oak hall tree with mirror to a head-to-toe "bedroom primping mirror" that tilts in its frame. Other accessories include reproduction wall and mantel clocks and a fascinating tiered curio stand in walnut ($80). MO

VI-25
EPHRAIM MARSH COMPANY, Dept. 753
P.O. Box 266
Concord, NC 28025

Ephraim Marsh—Distinctive Furniture, $1, published semiannually, 140 pages, illustrated, black and white and color.

Ephraim Marsh has four clocks that harmonize with their traditional furniture. There are three wall clocks, including one regulator clock, and a bracket clock with Westminster chimes. The cases are of cherry, ash, and mahogany, with solid brass hardware. Prices run from around $230 to $532. MO

VI-26
MEXICO HOUSE
P.O. Box 970
Del Mar, CA 92014

Mexico House, $1 (refundable with purchase), published annually, 42 pages, illustrated, black and white.

Some attractive decorative items of hand-wrought iron are featured in the Mexico House catalogue—fanciful birdcages, wall baskets for greenery, wine racks, a baker's rack, a corner rack, a hanging magazine rack, and a table base with hand-carved wood top, 24" in diameter (around $50). An unusual wall decoration from Cuernavaca is an Aztec calendar made of *piedra malaquita* with velvet backing, which comes with historical explanation sheet in English and Spanish. This is available in 7½", 11¾" or 14" diameter ($15, $20, or $25). MO

VI-27
HOWARD MILLER CLOCK COMPANY
860 Main Street
Zeeland, MI 49464

Howard Miller Brochure of Antique Adaptations and Grandfather Clocks, no charge, 4 pages, illustrated, color.

Howard Miller clocks come in many traditional styles. The handsome grandfather clocks include the John Goddard, reproduced from the original by the famous Colonial cabinetmaker, with individually carved shell motif and pediment rosettes, a triple chime movement that plays three different cathedral chimes, and a moon phase dial. Shelf clocks include an Eli Terry mantel clock, the elegant Montreal, of brass and walnut with beveled and etched glass panels with mirrored back panel, and The Princess, a French carriage alarm in brass finished case, with luminous hand and hour markers. There are also various wall models, such as a railroad regulator clock, one shaped like a pocket watch, a calendar clock, and a world time clock that automatically indicates the time in 70 locations on a map of the world, an unusual conversation piece. No prices are given in the brochure. RS

VI-28
MILL HOUSE
Scotts Corners
Pound Ridge, NY 10576

Free color catalogue, 6 pages with price lists, illustrated.

Mill House imports handmade faience, blown glassware, tiles, linens, and desk accessories from Europe. Among their most lovely items are the Portuguese faience accessories, some of which are copies of eighteenth-century pieces from museum collections and all of which evidence the quaint charm and originality of design one has come to expect from the Portuguese. There are enchanting rabbit and bird candlesticks ($22.50 a pair), dog bookends, various boxes, and attractive pottery hurricane candlesticks with a raised back and handle. A delightful rivière flower holder of five small joined vases would make a good low centerpiece on a small table. This is around $25 in color, $21 in white. MO

VI-29
NUTONE DIVISION, SCOVILL
Madison & Red Bank Roads
Cincinnati, OH 45227

NuTone—Making Homes Better, $2,
published annually, 164 pages, illustrated,
color.

While the NuTone catalogue is primarily concerned with bathroom equipment and other products for the home, they also show a variety of attractively framed mirrors in different shapes and sizes, some decorative wall lights with globes and hurricanes, and valance lights for bath and powder room, both incandescent and fluorescent. RS

VI-30
PALMETTO WAREHOUSES
& COLLECTABLES
Route 1, Highway 321
Norway, SC 29113

Palmetto Warehouses—Nostalgia
Unlimited, $2 (refundable with purchase),
published annually, 100 pages, illustrated,
black and white.

The nostalgia consists of advertising Americana from our recent past, such as reproductions of the Coca-Cola 1922 "Autumn Girl" tray ($5.95) or glass ashtray and tin signs from the good old days of the 10-cent Napoleon cigar and the Murphy harmonica. Coca-Cola seems to dominate this catalogue. There's even an original Coca-Cola metal chest (circa 1890–1915) that was used at ball games or on railroads and horse-drawn wagons for transporting bottles of the precious stuff. Only two of these old chests are shown— one is embossed "Augusta, Georgia," the other "Danville, Virginia"—and each is priced at $250. MO

Willard Shepard carving a 6' eagle in the Mystic Seaport Shipcarver's Workshop. VI-33.

VI-31
RAINBOW ART GLASS, Dept. CHC2
49 Shark River Road
Neptune, NJ 07753

Adventures with Color and Light, $1
(refundable with purchase), published
semiannually, 14 pages, illustrated, color.

In addition to its large selection of Tiffany-style lamps, this company has unusual stained-glass clocks in a variety of designs. Some are battery-operated, others have clock movements and are electrified and softly illuminated. Prices range from around $92 for the 11"-square battery-operated clocks to $192 for the 13"-square electrified models. There are also wall mirrors in free-form shapes with opalescent stained-glass trim, stained-glass ceiling panels leaded into a brass frame and reinforced with a brass strip, and terrariums of clear and stained glass to hang or stand. A 16" x 24" barn-shaped terrarium with red hinged door, hinged roof section, and end panels in a flowered design is $231. All of these are sold either assembled or, at a lower price, in kit form. MO

VI-32
RIDGEWAY CLOCKS
GRAVELY FURNITURE COMPANY, INC.
Dept. HDC
Ridgeway, VA 24148

Ridgeway Clocks, The Heartbeat of Your Home, free 8-page booklet and small brochure, published annually, illustrated, color.

The booklet and brochure show the many different styles of case, wall, and shelf clocks made by Ridgeway, with ideas for using them in different rooms. The clocks are available in various wood finishes and decorator colors. One of the most unusual is the Madame Sushi case clock with black lacquer finish and chinoiserie decoration in gold, 79" high x 15¾" wide x 9¼" deep. Prices range from $139 to $359 for mantel and wall clocks, and from $699 to almost $1,500 for case clocks. RS

VI-33
SHEP'S SHIP SHOP
Jordan Cove
Waterford, CT 06385

Shep's Ship Shop, no charge.

One of the best woodcarvers in the country, Willard Shephard can and will carve practically anything from simple name boards to a cigar-store Indian (the latter is by special order only). He conducts his mail order business from his home in Waterford and will send you the illustrated price list of his standard works and confer on special orders. MO

VI-34
SKYWORD INTERNATIONAL, INC.
400 West Palatine Road
Arlington Heights, IL 60004

Free color brochure, illustrated.

Skyword has an attractive line of indoor planters that combine natural wood with denim, cane, burlap, and polyester. MO

VI-35
SYROCO
P.O. Box 4875
Syracuse, NY 13221

Syroco Decorative Accessories Catalogue, free, published annually, 42 pages, illustrated, color.

A comprehensive collection of decorative accessories in many styles. There are mirrors, wall plaques, and prints with frames of wicker, bamboo, rattan, wood, brass, or metal with antique gold finish, and matching clocks and sconces in almost every style and material. Syroco showrooms in many cities are listed, or you may request the name of a retail source in your locality. Syroco also maintains clock service stations throughout the country. RS

VI-36
TELL CITY CHAIR COMPANY
P.O. Box 329
Tell City, IN 47586

Tell City Primer of Early American Home Decorating, $4, published annually, 124 pages, illustrated, black and white and color.

The mirrors shown are basically simple in design, with maple frames that blend with Tell City's furniture. There are oval wall mirrors, an octagon mirror, a shaving mirror, a hall mirror with a small shelf and pegs for hanging up hats and coats, a square mirror with a black plywood liner that gives a sculptural effect, and a skinny rectangular mirror that can be used above a shelf. Other accessories in the Early American mood include wall shelves and brackets, plant stands adapted from antique candlestands, and a quilt rack. RS

VI-37
TOUCH OF CLASS
North Hampshire Common
North Conway, NH 03860

Touch of Class, $1 (refundable with purchase), published semiannually, 20 pages, illustrated, color.

While this catalogue is heavy on bed and bath linens and accessories, there are quite a few attractive decorative accessories. An unusual blown glass lamp with a delicate feathered design in the opalescent shade and base, numbered, signed, and dated by the artist, is $155; appliquéd suede pillows with pine tree, geometric, or cattail designs are around $40, and an Imari petit point box with 1600 stitches per a mirror with cane frame accented with bamboo trim ($29), a bamboo cabinet with shelves above that would make a good bedroom storage piece, a wastebasket, and three-tier floor stand. There are also some nice ideas for children's rooms, including a hand-painted porcelain lamp with figurine base of a little girl in a nightshirt and hand-painted music boxes with Beatrix Potter figures of Jeremy Fisher Frog and Benjamin Bunny on top ($25). MO

VI-38
21ST CENTURY ANTIQUES
Hadley, MA 01035

21st Century Antiques—Second Collection,
$3.40 (includes postage), published annually,
32 pages, illustrated, black and white.

A fascinating collection of what owner Peter Rakelbusch describes as "the applied art of an epoch recently called the Modern Movement—the Arts and Crafts/Mission, Art Nouveau and Art Deco periods." His catalogue has over 500 objects (offered subject to prior sale) including Art Deco and Art Nouveau desk lamps and vases, assorted pieces of furniture such as a Mission oak standing shelf and chair, and a marvelous tubular brass bedstead in a rolling geometric design ($280). You'll also find mirrors, light globes, chunky Bakelite radios, bookends, flatware, dinner services, cocktail shakers and glasses, and loads of female figures, dressed and undressed, in arch poses. It's handsomely illustrated, amusingly written, highly entertaining, and full of goodies from our not-so-distant past at prices that are eminently reasonable, from $5 up. Not the least of the merits of this well designed and conceived catalogue is the order form, a marvel of clarity and personal attention. You can phone to find out if the item you want is still available and it will be held for four post office days to allow time for your written order to arrive. If you order furniture you will be told the shipping charges before you send in the order. For other articles the packing, shipping, and insurance charge is given after the price.

Mr. Rakelbusch also has a series of what he calls "minilogs," smaller and more frequently published catalogues at $1 each, and intends to carry books about Art Deco and Art Nouveau. He will also work with any customer who has a specific interest or special request, and will purchase on commission or sell on consignment. MO

VI-39
WEST RINDGE BASKETS, INC.
Rindge, NH 03461

Hand-Woven New England Baskets,
brochure, no charge, published annually,
illustrated, black and white.

The Taylors of Rindge have operated a family business for three generations, making simple, functional hand-woven baskets of ash strips with oak hoops. Here are all the old-fashioned baskets so hard to find these days—baskets for gardening and for shopping, covered lunch and picnic baskets, covered pie and cake baskets (including an open pie basket), a fruit basket, a knitting basket, a tall basket for bottles, and small and large wastebaskets. All are sturdy, scrupulously handcrafted, and made to last. Prices on request. MO

VI-40
YIELD HOUSE, INC.
Route 16
North Conway, NH 03860

Yield House, free, published quarterly, 74
pages, illustrated, color.

This extensive catalogue, although mainly devoted to pine furniture, has many accessories, among them mirrors, clocks, lamps, brassware, pillows, and figurines. MO

Colorful giraffe and elephant plaques for children of all ages from Syroco, VI-35.

VII
Art and Collections

VII-1
ALADDIN HOUSE, LTD.
654 Ninth Avenue
New York, NY 10036

Orientalia Collection—799, $1.50, 16 pages, illustrated, black and white.

A catalogue of Oriental antiquities from the fourteenth to the nineteenth centuries and reproductions, usually in limited editions, from earlier periods. Among the originals are nineteenth-century hand-carved Chinese wood panels, lacquered red with gold leaf, 19" x 2½", $49.50 with floral motif, $59.50 with floral and bird motif; a Japanese Imari covered bowl, c. 1830, for $145; Indian peacock motif brass temple lamps; Hindu shrine brass altar pieces of Shiva on his horse and with his wife, Parvati; fourteenth-century Sawankaloke Siamese pottery and celadon wine cups and some rare Tibetan rugs up to 75 years old. The rugs are priced from $435 to $475 (color Polaroid shots are available on request for $1.50 each). Among the reproductions are a standing Bodhisattva, from an eighteenth-century bronze in the Springfield Museum of Fine Arts, and a Chinese lion, 6½" high, from the bronze original in the Peabody Museum, $34. Aladdin House sells originals and replicas from ancient Egyptian, Persian, pre-Columbian, Roman, Greek, and Oriental cultures. Catalogues and brochures are only produced as material becomes available and a $3 annual subscription to their mailing list covers all their publications. MO

VII-2
W. GRAHAM ARADER III
1000 Boxwood Court
King of Prussia, PA 19406

W. Graham Arader III, Rare Maps, Books and Prints, $24 for six catalogues a year, single issues $5 (refundable with purchase), 42 pages, illustrated, black and white.

Americana is one of Mr. Arader's specialties and a recent catalogue contained a representative selection from his stock of maps, prints, rare books, and reference books. It included Karl Bodmer prints of the American West, four original woodblocks by Thomas Nast, a chromolithograph edition of Audubon's *Birds of America*, printed by Julius Bien, and many old maps of North and South America and various states and cities. Mr. Arader also does book repairs and hand binding and has a restoration service for all works on paper, such as prints, maps, and globes (see details on page 175). MO

VII-3
RICHARD B. ARKWAY, INC.
114 East 61st Street
New York, NY 10021

Catalogue of rare books and maps, free, published quarterly, 58 pages, illustrated, black and white.

For the map collector, Arkway offers rare and interesting books with maps, including sixteenth-century first editions. You'll find a few non-American maps, and a large selection of American maps, starting in a recent catalogue with a 1552 map of the New World by Sebastian Muenster. MO

VII-4
ART POSTER COMPANY
22255 Greenfield Road
Southfield, MI 48075

Catalogue, $2 (refundable with purchase), published semiannually, 8 pages, illustrated, color, with discount price list.

Over a hundred posters are listed, some silk-screened, some in limited editions, in sizes averaging 30" x 24". Contemporary art posters of shows by artists such as Helen Frankenthaler, Frank Stella, Georgia O'Keeffe, and Alexander Calder make up the major part of the catalogue, but there are also posters of botanical subjects, pop art, photography, and earlier artists like Renoir, Miró, Monet, and Picasso. Prices start as low as $10 and go up to around $25, with silk-screened prints rather more expensive at $30 to $40. Custom framing in gold, silver, or bronze metal with plexiglass adds $30 or more to the price. MO

VII-5
BENJANE ARTS
320 Hempstead Avenue
West Hempstead, NY 11552

Seashells and Natural Sea Life Specimens, $3, published annually, 32 pages, illustrated.

This lavish, beautifully illustrated color catalogue will fascinate anyone who collects shells and other forms of sea life, such as coral, sea urchins, sea horses, starfish, shark's teeth, and turtle shells. There's a wide range of prices, from 20 cents for common shells to $80 for a rare *Cypraea tessellata.* An extra-large piece of brush coral is $25. Benjane also sells display stands of Lucite, brass, or a combination of the two. A small Lucite ring stand is 50 cents, an extra-large Lucite and brass tripod holder is $7.50. MO

An 1854 signed Rembrandt Peale oil on wood rural scene. Frank S. Schwarz & Son, VII-35.

VII-6
BERNARDO
2400 Westheimer Road, Suite 108W
Houston, TX 77098

Pre-Columbian Temple Ruins of Mexico, a Collection of Rubbings and Serigraphs by Patric, $2 (refundable with purchase), 24 pages, illustrated, black and white and color.

Bernardo imports rubbings and serigraphs (the latter are silk-screen multicolor prints) by the woman artist, Patric, who lives and works in Yucatán. The serigraphs are offered in limited editions, hand-numbered and signed. Her motifs are based on scaled-down bas-reliefs taken from Mexican temple ruins, particularly those in ancient Mayan cities, and each work is accompanied by a printed explanation of the figure, its legend, and date and place of origin. The hand-crafted rubbings are offered in various colors and multicolors, achieved by the careful blending of many different tones, layer upon layer, until the nuances of the desired color are achieved. These decorative and unusual works of art on textured cloth-paper composition range in price from $3.75 to $75, quite a bargain. The catalogue gives a clear depiction of the works and provides information on their origin and history. MO

An oil painting by Burt Procter of a Navajo Indian youth. Trailside Galleries, VII-39.

VII-7
BUCK HILL ASSOCIATES
Garnet Lake Road
Johnsburg, NY 12843

Posters and Handbills of America's Past, 25
*cents, published annually, 20 pages,
illustrated, black and white.*

This offbeat catalogue lists over 1,000 posters,
handbills, broadsides, prints, and advertisements, authentic reproductions that trace the po-
litical and social history of America from earliest
times. Most are printed in black ink on white
paper, like the originals, but some posters are
printed in full color or on colored paper. Among
the offerings are the original 1706 New England
Thanksgiving proclamation, a Civil War recruit-
ing poster, a Butch Cassidy reward poster, an
1884 cartoon of Belva Lockwood, the first female
presidential candidate, and posters and handbills of such movie greats as Chaplin, Harold
Lloyd, Rudolph Valentino, and Humphrey Bo-
gart. Categories are American Colonies, Revolutionary War, George Washington, Slavery, Civil
War, Lincoln, Later 1800s, Wild West, Guns,
Turn of the Century, Medicine-Dentistry, Circus, Automobiles, Movies, and Miscellaneous.
Prices range from 35 cents to $4.95 for Western
color prints, and there is a $3.95 minimum order
plus 50 cents postage and handling. Buck Hill
also has reprints and facsimiles of old books on
cookery, housekeeping, and eighteenth- and
nineteenth-century schoolbooks such as Mc-
Guffey's *Pictorial Eclectic Primer* (facsimile reprint, $2.50). MO

VII-8
BURGUES PORCELAINS
P.O. Box B
183 Spruce Street
Lakewood, NJ 08701

Burgues—Porcelains of Limited Editions,
$5, *illustrated, color.*

A folder containing an impressive collection of
fifty full-color photographs of both present limited editions and past closed editions of Burgues
porcelains. The main body of the artist's work
consists of animals, birds, and flowers, beautifully and intricately portrayed in their natural
settings. They are from 4½" to 18" in height,
priced from just under $100 to around $3,300.
The editions vary from 75 to 950. A number of
the porcelains shown are in museum collections.
MO/RS

*"Lollipop Louie" porcelain clown from an edition of 250
by Burgues, VII-8.*

VII-9
CHARRETTE
31 Olympia Avenue
Woburn, MA 01888

Charrette Catalog, $2.50, *published
semiannually, 260 pages, illustrated, black
and white.*

Charrette's catalogue of office, architectural, and
art equipment has the widest selection of frames
we have seen—plexiglass; white or black plastic
frames with glass insert; the Eubank metal framing system that holds prints equidistant from the
wall on all four sides so that the print appears to
float in space (adjustable from 16" x 16" to 40" x
40", $7); the various Kulicke frames of wood,
welded aluminum, and polished aluminum; the
crystal-clear acrylic box frame; and the WK frame
that stands vertically or horizontally, originally
designed as a way of displaying two-sided
graphics. Also included are the metal section
frames, a system based on modern classic museum frames, in chrome or gold-finished aluminum in lengths from 8" to 40", a framing kit,
Swiss framing clips, gallery clips, and precut

mats. If you are looking for picture lamps, you'll find three here. The Futurist, a slim cylindrical chrome lamp with spun-metal end pieces, 9″ long, is around $29. MO/RS

VII-10
COMMEMORATIVE IMPORTS, INC.
Box D
Bayport, MN 55003

Commemorative Imports Limited Edition Review, free, published quarterly, 12 pages, illustrated, black and white.

This company specializes in collector's plates, in first and later editions, and they send out this periodic review of some of the plates they have in stock. They also have porcelain figurines, Christmas bells and ornaments, and steins. MO

VII-11
DOVER SCIENTIFIC COMPANY
P.O. Box 6011
Long Island City, NY 11106

Shells, Fossils, Minerals and Display Stands, $2, published annually, 44 pages, illustrated, black and white, with separate color folder.

Not only an invaluable source for collectors of shells, fossils, minerals, and gem stones but also for anyone looking for beautiful and original decorative pieces: a violet spider shell from Mauritius; a polished lapis lazuli ashtray ($250); polished mineral eggs; an Australian fossil fern on a cream-colored matrix slab, over 185 million years old; Indian artifacts and art from the Pacific, such as carved wooden face masks, figures, bowls, and shields. Dover has a nice selection of brass-and-glass display cases and brass display stands for treasured shells, ranging in price from

Pueblo Indian pottery pieces, flint ceremonial spear point, blades, stunners, and two red clay Indian pipe bowls from Dover Scientific, VII-11.

Serigraph of prehistoric cave painting of prancing horses. Gallery of Prehistoric Paintings, VII-17.

$5 to $47.50, and also offers books on nature, anthropology, archaeology, geology, and the arts and crafts of different peoples. MO

VII-12
ELIZABETH F. DUNLAP
6063 Westminster Place
St. Louis, MO 63112

Maps of North American Interest, free list (stamps appreciated).

Quality maps at low cost, as well as some original and valuable maps for the serious collector, are offered by the Dunlap collection, which covers North America, the United States, states and cities, Canada and provinces, Mexico, Central America, and the West Indies. The collection is extensive, the descriptions are clear and concise, and the prices seem moderate, with many maps available for as little as $10. The most expensive are around $250. Elizabeth Dunlap also has a list of books of general Americana. MO

VII-13
EDITIONS LIMITED GALLERY, INC.
919 East Westfield Boulevard
Indianapolis, IN 46220

Brochure, $2, published quarterly, 12 pages, illustrated, color.

This gallery sells posters and prints by such contemporary artists as Calder, LeRoy Neiman, Jurgen Peters, and Will Barnet at prices ranging from $30 to $1,200. MO

VII-14
FIESTA ARTS, INC.
Greenvale, NY 11548

Belle Epoque, Ricordi Art Poster Collection, $2 (refundable with purchase), published annually, 6 pages, illustrated, color.

Fiesta Arts has a special arrangement with the

Ricordi Company of Milan, and among their offerings are opera posters, 19½" x 27½", printed on heavy stock from archive stone matrices, originally prepared for La Scala in the first decades of the century. *Turandot, Tosca, Manon Lescaut,* and *Parsifal,* done in the Art Nouveau style, are $7.95 each. Another series of Ricordi posters of the same era, $7 each, has marvelous bold designs advertising liqueurs and aperitifs, motorcars like the Isotta Fraschini and Mercedes, and even Michelin tires. The company also sells reproduction Victorian footstools with removable tops that may be covered with your needlepoint or crewel ($27.95). MO

VII-15
THE FLYING COLORS COLLECTION
225 Park Avenue South, Suite 816
New York, NY 10003

Mailers, free, illustrated, color.

The mailers show a series of ten lithographs created by Alexander Calder, including one originally executed for a Braniff jet plane. These are sold in signed and numbered editions, and cost from $950 to $2,000. There are also six plate-signed lithographs from *Flying Colors* (a mural painted on a Braniff jet), measuring 20" x 26", delivered framed for $75 each plus shipping charges. MO

VII-16
FRAME HOUSE GALLERY
110 East Market Street
Louisville, KY 40202

The Art of Print Collecting, $2.50 (refundable with print purchase), published annually, 80 pages, illustrated, color.

Wildlife, nature, and the American West are the themes in this catalogue, which includes the prints and biographies of over 30 artists for a wide variety of styles—from realistic to the abstract patterns of planes and simple geometric shapes of Charles Harper to the delicate Oriental subtleties of Diana Kan and Manabu Saito. A collector's price guide to published prints gives the name of each print, the year, size of edition, issue price and, where applicable, estimated collector price. As the majority of the editions are large, the original prices of the prints are reasonable, mostly well under $100. In addition, the catalogue offers signed and numbered art books and portfolios, and a handy glossary of terms used in connection with prints. MO

VII-17
GALLERY OF PREHISTORIC PAINTINGS
20 East 12th Street
New York, NY 10003

Prehistoric Paintings: Collector Editions, $3 (refundable with purchase), 16 pages, illustrated, color.

An unusual collection of over 50 limited-edition serigraphs representing the earliest known works of man, hand screen-printed by Douglas Mazonowicz, founder and owner of the gallery. Mr. Mazonowicz spent sixteen years of research in the caves and rock shelters of France, Spain, Italy, Central Sahara, and early American Indian sites, making tracings and color scale photographic studies to ensure that the serigraphs are faithful to the originals. Included in the collection are a standing bison from the Altamira cave in Spain, horses from the Lascaux cave in France, figures and animals from the Tassili Plateau of the Central Sahara, Etruscan tomb art, and rock art of American Indians. Most of the serigraphs are in limited editions of 75, signed and numbered, and range in price from $75 to $4,500. The color illustrations in the catalogue are exceptionally good. MO

VII-18
GIUST GALLERY
261 Newbury Street
Boston, MA 02116

The Giust Collection, $1 (refundable with purchase), 42 pages, illustrated, black and white.

The specialty of the Giust Gallery is fine hand-crafted reproductions of sculptures, friezes, and reliefs from masterpieces in the great museums. Lino Giust follows the tradition of Florentine master craftsman Piero Caproni, who made his molds directly in the museums and constructed the Caproni Gallery Building in Boston at the turn of the century to cast and house his reproductions. Mr. Giust personally casts and finishes every piece shown in the collection, each of which bears the Giust-Caproni hallmark. Among the pieces shown are a head of Zeus from the Louvre, busts of Sophocles, Socrates, and Julius Caesar from the British Museum, a gargoyle from Notre Dame Cathedral, a Gothic sconce, Egyptian and Assyrian friezes, and a Moorish rosette from the Alhambra. Materials are black and green bronze, stone, sandstone, terra-cotta, and black iron. The price range is from $30 to $525

Trompe l'oeil "Still Life With Pipe," 1879, oil by William Harnett. Kennedy Galleries, VII-23.

with the exception of Michelangelo's head of David, original size, from the colossal statue in the Accademia, Florence, priced at $1850. MO

VII-19
GUILD OF SHAKER CRAFTS, INC.
401 W. Savidge Street
Spring Lake, MI 49456

Shaker Furniture Reproductions, *$2.50 (refundable with purchase), published seasonally, 28 pages, illustrated, black and white and color.*

Among the items in the Guild's catalogue are Shaker inspirational or "spirit" drawings in silk-screen reproductions, including the Mother Ann spirit drawing, *Old Chatham 1848,* 14" high x 20" wide with blue mat; the Mother Lucy spirit drawing; a wreath of flowers; the tree of light and tree of love. Prints range in price from $4.50 to $22.50, with smaller spirit drawings at $1. Frames are extra. MO

VII-20
HOTCHKISS HOUSE
18 Hearthstone Road
Pittsford, NY 14534

Catalogue of Books on Antiques & Collectibles, *free, with seasonal supplements, 12 pages, black and white.*

The catalogue lists over 1,400 selected titles of books in stock, divided and indexed into sixty categories of antiques, arts, hobbies, and collecting. Each book is listed by title and author with a brief résumé of the contents. Of interest to lovers of antiques are such recent additions to the list as the second edition of the *Pictorial Price Guide to American Antiques,* which shows over 5,000 items in group photos, each keyed to a dealer or auction price ($8.95), and *The Antique Restorer's Handbook* ($8.95). Also listed are books on Oriental rugs, nineteenth-century glass, antique tin and toleware, prints, antique wicker furniture, pottery and porcelains, silver and silver plate, American Indian and Eskimo art and crafts. A useful source for reference books. MO

VII-21
ICART VENDOR
8111 Melrose Avenue
Los Angeles, CA 90046

Louis Icart—Art Deco Artist, $1, 14 pages,
illustrated, black and white and color.

Reproductions of the work of Louis Icart are the
specialty of this company, and the catalogue
shows about two dozen prints at $7 each (there's
a minimum order of 5 prints). They also have
French turn-of-the-century posters by Toulouse-
Lautrec, Cappiello, Mucha, and Cheret. MO

VII-22
**INTERNATIONAL CENTER
OF PHOTOGRAPHY**
1130 Fifth Avenue
New York, NY 10028

Books, Catalogs and Posters, $1, published
*annually, 24 pages, illustrated, black and
white.*

Apart from books on photography and photographers a recent catalogue from ICP had posters
by great photographers such as Diane Arbus,
Edward Weston, Eugene Atget, and Brassai at
$12.50 each. Four portfolios of the work of An-
dreas Feininger (*New York, Forms of Nature,
Shells,* and *Trees*), each series with twelve original prints signed and numbered by the photographer in a limited edition of 100, were $1750 a
portfolio. There was also a Jerusalem portfolio—
a collection of twelve prints (six color-dye transfer and six black and white photographs) in a red
velvet box published in a limited edition of 100
for the benefit of the Israel Museum. There are
always some very offbeat limited-edition prints
in this catalogue. MO

VII-23
KENNEDY GALLERIES, INC.
40 West 57th Street
New York, NY 10019

Selected American Masterworks, $10,
*special exhibition catalogue, 66 pages,
illustrated, color.*

This is a top New York gallery primarily devoted
to figurative art by American artists of the eighteenth, nineteenth, and twentieth centuries.
This special exhibition catalogue shows the work
of, among others, John Singleton Copley,
Thomas Cole, Fitz Hugh Lane, John F. Peto, John
Singer Sargent, Edward Hopper, John Marin,
Ben Shahn, Andrew Wyeth, and Thomas Hart
Benton. As catalogues are issued periodically, it
is best to write requesting current offerings. The
Kennedy Gallery also has a graphics collection
catalogue of signed limited editions by distin-
guished artists. MO/RS

VII-24
LOVELIA ENTERPRISES, INC.
P.O. Box 1845, Grand Central Station
New York, NY 10017

Tapestries, $2, published annually, 20 pages,
illustrated, color.

Gobelin and Aubusson tapestries from France,
Belgium, and Italy, woven of 100 percent cotton
or wool on old looms from original jacquards, are
shown in this catalogue. Some are copies of masterpieces hanging in museums all over the
world. There is also a page of do-it-yourself ideas
for decorating with tapestries—upholstery,
headboards, valances, pillows, and so on. Sizes
are available from 10" x 10" to 10' x 20' in a variety
of period motifs. Prices are low to moderate. MO

VII-25
MILLVILLE ART GLASS
P.O. Box 344
Millville, NJ 08332

Free brochures.

Millville Art Glass, previously known as Holly
City Bottle, is engaged in making handcrafted
commemorative bottles and paperweights. Recent brochures had paperweights and bottles
commemorating the 1980 Winter Olympics at
Lake Placid, the visit of Pope John Paul II, the
tenth anniversary of the Apollo XI moon landing,
and the demise of Skylab in Australia. Prices for
the colored glass bottles range from $10 to $30,
the paperweights are mostly $6. There are also
some handcrafted pitchers and vases made from
turn-of-the-century molds in cobalt blue or ame-
thyst by the Wheaton Village Craftsmen. The
pitchers are $15 each, the vases $12.50. MO

VII-26
MODERN ART EDITIONS, INC.
80 Fifth Avenue
New York, NY 10011

The Poster Collector, $2 (refundable with
*purchase), published annually, 20 pages,
illustrated, black and white and color.*

If you are looking for inexpensive art, there are some great buys in this handsomely produced catalogue of art and museum exhibition posters, Art Nouveau posters, pop art, and photo posters by many famous names. The posters are sold unframed, or with a Framekit of metal moldings in silver or gold finish cut to the size of the poster, all the necessary hardware for easy assembly and hanging included, or framed under Plexiglas. Prices for unframed posters run from $12 to $42. MO

VII-27
MODERN MASTER TAPESTRIES, INC.
11 East 57th Street
New York, NY 10022

Tapestry—The Useful Art, free brochure, published annually, 24 pages, illustrated, color.

A fabulous collection of contemporary tapestries with designs by great twentieth-century artists —including Picasso, Klee, Miró, Léger, Arp, Calder, Frank Stella, Robert Motherwell, Theodoros Stamos—handwoven in India and France. The tapestries come in all shapes and sizes from 4' x 6' to 10' x 10' and larger, in a variety of contemporary art styles, weaving techniques, and materials, in limited editions from six to twenty. You can also have tapestries custom designed. While the prices are high, from $2,200 to $16,000, the tapestries are really limited-edition works of art by artists whose paintings command much higher figures. RS/ID

VII-28
NEW CHINA ARTS CORPORATION
225 Park Avenue South, Suite 816
New York, NY 10003

Free brochures, illustrated, color.

The brochures offer a fascinating glimpse of contemporary art from the People's Republic of China in a variety of styles and techniques. From Kwangtung Province come wheatstraw collages —brightly dyed straw trimmed and glued in designs of birds, flowers, animals, and landscapes. Tientsin watercolors on silk, executed in the traditional style, depict birds and flowering branches. Watercolors on rice paper are done in a bold, free-form style with vigorous brush strokes and slashes of color. A series of water-

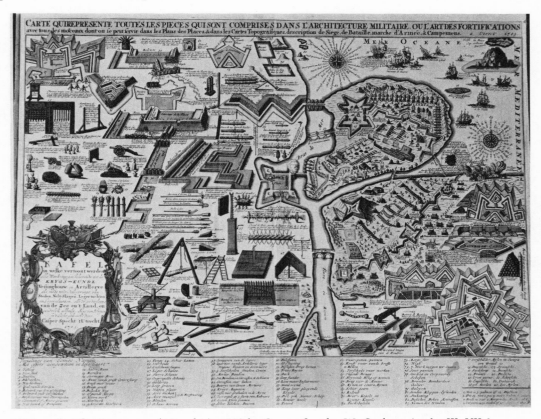

Military fortifications map of Utrecht in 1703 by Casper Specht. W. Graham Arader III, VII-2.

color landscapes by artist Shui-Yi show the fantastic limestone hills and caves of Kweilin. Among various woodblock prints, the most charming are the primitives of village life by untrained peasants of Huhsien County. Prices range from $30 for a wheatstraw collage to $250 for a Huhsien woodblock print. MO

VII-29
OESTREICHER PRINTS, INC.
43 West 46th Street
New York, NY 10036

Oestreicher's Reference Book of Fine Art Reproductions, $5, 160 pages, illustrated, color.

This company may well have, as the catalogue states, "the most complete, comprehensive cataloguing of available full-color reproductions ever published by any print dealer." The catalogue contains 1,100 miniature color illustrations from Oestreicher's collection of over 500,000 prints, which embrace the entire spectrum of art from old masters to contemporary artists, and the list of prints is truly impressive. Prints are listed alphabetically by the artist's name, with title, size, and price (moderate), and a page-reference number beside any print shown in color. Inquiries about artists and prints other than those listed are welcomed, provided you enclose a stamped, self-addressed envelope for a reply. Prints may be "permanized," which means they are laminated to masonite and given a permanent matte finish of clear lacquer that eliminates the need for glass. Oestreicher also has frames of every type and a framing service and will suggest appropriate styles and moldings for the print and your room scheme. MO

VII-30
ORIGINAL PRINT COLLECTORS GROUP, LTD.
120 East 56th Street
New York, NY 10022

Catalogues and newsletters, free to members, published bimonthly, 16 pages, illustrated, color.

An excellent mail-order source for original graphics by contemporary artists (and, from time to time, fine old master prints as they become available) and well worth the annual membership fee of $25. Actually, if you are a serious buyer, membership costs you nothing, as the fee is applied to your first order within one year of joining. If you are interested in receiving literature describing the membership plan, an application form, sample catalogues and newsletter, just write to the Original Print Collectors Group, or OPCG for short. Who are the OPCG? According to their direct-mail letter, they are "a relatively small group of art lovers who have banded together to take advantage of our collective buying power so that, with professional expert advice, we can acquire the finest modern graphics by both known and yet-to-be-recognized artists at the most advantageous prices . . . because of our contacts in the art world, and because we purchase graphics directly from the source, we can offer our members truly great works of art before the general public even knows of their existence." Their expertise provides a valuable service for those not in touch with the art market and the selections are reasonably priced, especially when you consider that the prints are sold attractively framed and the price includes framing and insured delivery to any address in the continental United States. Some of the prints are under $100, others under $200. Prices, naturally, vary according to the artist and the size of the edition. In a recent issue, Victor Vasarely's *Nebulus,* an original serigraph in a signed edition of 250, was $650 framed, a Miró lithograph in a signed edition of 150 was $1,695, while a charming lithograph by Jean-Pierre Cassigneul in a signed edition of 75 was just $295. An extra service of benefit to members is a listing in the newsletter of prints sold out in previous offerings that members wish to buy, in some cases at double or more the original price. MO

VII-31
DONALD T. PITCHER
P.O. Box 64
North Haven, CT 06473

Catalogues of antique prints, free.

Donald Pitcher specializes in early Americana. He publishes about a dozen different print catalogues a year on various regions and subjects such as original wood engravings by Winslow Homer removed from old magazines (similar listings are available for the work of other artists of the 1800s, Thomas Nast and Frederic Remington among them), canals, the Western states and Mexico, New York City, and nineteenth-century prints showing the Shakers at work and at worship. Prices are reasonable. MO

*Left, "Mame" original poster from Triton Gallery,
VII-42. Right, Casa Ricordi poster of Puccini's "Madama
Butterfly," Fiesta Arts, VII-14.*

VII-32
POSTER ORIGINALS LIMITED
924 Madison Avenue
New York, NY 10021

Poster Originals Limited, $5, published
seasonally, 124 pages, illustrated, color.

An exceptionally handsome and well produced
catalogue of poster art. In addition to the comprehensive and excellent selection of American
and European art posters, there are Polish circus
and zoo posters by leading artists, original
comic-strip pop posters, botanical posters, 1972
Olympic posters, a special collection of art im-
ages published in France, and a group of posters
by Milton Glaser and Seymour Chwast. Trans-
world Art Posters is a collection of lithographic
and silk-screen posters, including many by Dali.
Folon Posters are by prominent French artist
Jean-Michel Folon. One very interesting group,
Amnesty International Posters, consists of works
by contemporary artists who volunteered their
services. Poster Originals has books on poster
art, a custom-framing service with a wide choice
of frames, and an inexpensive Framekit, aluminum sections in gold or silver finish custom cut
to the size of each poster, with hardware for assembly and hanging ($20 to $45, according to
size). Prices for the posters are mostly in the $15
to $40 range. A useful and informative section in
the beginning of the catalogue includes a glossary of print terms and advice on framing and
preserving works of art on paper. MO

VII-33
PRINT WORLD
P.O. Box 6601
Philadelphia, PA 19149

Print World, free.

The catalogue lists steel engravings, wood engravings, photogravures, and typogravures of
the mid- to late nineteenth century, mostly on
popular historical, fictional, and artistic themes.
Information about each print includes the size,
name of the artist, and the engraver as well as, in
some cases, the name of the publisher and the
copyright date of the print. A current catalogue
featured steel engravings of Shakespearean
scenes by various artists at $21, steel engravings
of paintings by Landseer at $17, photogravures
of official portraits of U.S. presidents at $25, and
steel engravings of scenes from early American
history taken from paintings by Alonzo Chappel,
dated 1857–1859, for $17. Prints are priced ac-
cording to their artistry, topic, and rarity. MO

VII-34
ROYAL COPENHAGEN PORCELAIN
575 Madison Avenue
New York, NY 10022

Royal Copenhagen Porcelain, 34 pages,
illustrated, color, and **Come Dine with
Kings,** folder of 28 leaflets and sheets,
illustrated, color, $1 for both.

The Royal Copenhagen Porcelain catalogue is devoted mainly to their figurines of people, birds,
animals, fairy-tale characters such as Hans

*Bacchic Dance plaque, originally from Herculaneum,
in sandstone or terra-cotta. Giust Gallery, VII-18.*

Christian Andersen's "Little Mermaid," hand-decorated vases, boxes, plates and ashtrays, and bas-relief plates. The folder also shows some figures and one leaflet features the Royal Copenhagen Christmas plates, but the emphasis is on the various porcelain and faience patterns. Price lists are included. RS

VII-35
FRANK S. SCHWARZ AND SON
1806 Chestnut Street
Philadelphia, PA 19103

Philadelphia Collection, $3, published semiannually, illustrated, color.

Schwarz specializes in fine paintings, antique furniture, and silver and periodically sends out catalogues of his current offerings. When writing, specify subjects you are interested in. MO

VII-36
THE SCULPTURE STUDIO, INC.
441 Lafayette Street
New York, NY 10003

Metal Sculpture, 50 cents, 8 pages, illustrated, color.

Artist William Bowie specializes in metal sculptures, both for the wall and on stands for table display. Some are abstractions, others stylized studies of birds, flowers, trees, and sailboats. The sculptures have both delicacy and a great sense of movement, from the arrow-straight lines of a bunch of cattails to the airiness of a flock of birds. There's a fascinating abstract city skyline, a glittering starburst, and a multiple sunburst. In most cases the works are gold-leafed steel with silver-leaf accents and brazed bronze joints. Prices vary, according to size and subject, from $60 to $1,200, and special sizes and different finishes of almost all works can be made to order. MO

VII-37
L. H. SELMAN, LTD., Dept. HDC
761 Chestnut Street
Santa Cruz, CA 95060

Price Guide and Catalogue of Collector's Paperweights, $5, published annually, 120 pages, illustrated, color.

If you have never considered collecting or buying paperweights, one look at this glorious catalogue would hook you—for these are no mere decorative objects, but exquisite works of art.

Antique paperweights from L.H. Selman, VII-37.

There are pages and pages of contemporary and antique paperweights, each illustrated in color, described, identified, and priced. Some are so breathtakingly beautiful you yearn to own them. Each time Selman puts out a catalogue there is an even greater selection. This time the first part of the catalogue, on modern paperweights, has been considerably expanded. In addition to modern Baccarat, D'Albret, St. Louis, and Perthshire weights there are intriguing designs by Lundberg Studios and Orient & Flume in California, and by individual craftsmen-artists like Ray and Bob Banford, Charles and David Lotton, Paul Stankard, Paul Ysart, and Francis Whittemore. The variety and individuality of patterns and styles is amazing, and many are in limited editions. Prices range from around $30 for a simple millefiori Perthshire paperweight to $1,000 for a one-of-a-kind weight, with most in the $100 to $500 range. Some of the antique Baccarat, Clichy, St. Louis, English, and American paperweights are surprisingly reasonable, but most are fairly expensive. The costliest are a large, beautiful and rare antique American weight with a variegated Mount Washington rose, at $14,000, and a couple of the Baccarat and St. Louis at over $3,000.

Selman will look for specific types of paperweights, buy fine paperweights, and do insurance appraisals and cataloguing. All offerings in the catalogue are subject to prior sale. MO

VII-38
STEUBEN GLASS
715 Fifth Avenue
New York, NY 10022

Steuben Glass, $4, published annually, 224 pages, illustrated, black and white and color.

Steuben is famous for lead crystal of the finest

Solid crystal apple from Steuben Glass, VII-38.

design and workmanship, and their yearly catalogue consists of superb photographs of the pieces on fine-quality paper with a detailed description and, where applicable, the name of the designer. One of the most dramatic sections of the current catalogue we received showed the prismatics—abstract sculptures in crystal that owe their form to the cold techniques of cutting, grinding, and polishing. These optical illusions resulting from prisms and lenses are incredibly beautiful. Of course there are vases and bowls, animals, jewelry, handsome pieces for entertaining from glasses and decanters to candlesticks to canapé plates, as well as sections for the collector and the executive featuring pieces that are truly works of art, plus major engraved works, complex creations in which the form of the engraving and the crystal are one. Prices for these crystal masterpieces range from $90 for a small paperweight to over $15,500 for one of the magnificent engraved pieces, a pyramid in a limited edition of 30. A number of publications about Steuben crystal are available. MO/RS

VII-39
TRAILSIDE GALLERIES
Box 1149
105 North Center Street
Jackson, WY 83001

Trailside Galleries, $8.50 (refundable with purchase), published annually, 96 pages, illustrated, black and white.

Trailside is a major gallery of Western Americana: paintings, sculpture, exciting and original American Indian jewelry, wood carvings, and prehistoric ceramics of the Mesa Verde region. This handsomely illustrated catalogue shows

works of art by some seventy-six artists and craftsmen represented by Trailside, with dimensions, prices, and some background on the artists. Trailside has two galleries, in Jackson and Scottsdale, Arizona, and also sells limited-edition prints, at prices from around $110 up. As the catalogue price is refundable with purchase, presumably they will accept mail orders and send you current catalogues if you express an interest in the work of any of their artists. MO

VII-40
TREASURE–HOUSE OF WORLDLY WARES
1414 Lincoln Avenue
Calistoga, CA 94515

A Mini-Trip Around the Globe, free with stamped, self-addressed business-size envelope.

Mrs. Stevie Whitefeather, who runs a small personal business in folk art from all over the world, will send her current list of items on hand. Although these change all the time, they usually include American Indian pueblo pottery, masks from many countries, Navajo tapestries, San Blas molas, woven hangings from South America, Navajo rugs and sand paintings, Peruvian alpaca rugs, and American Indian baskets that rank as collector's pieces. MO

VII-41
ELIZABETH CAPACCIO TRENT
5221 N.E. 15th Avenue
Fort Lauderdale, FL 33334

Dance in Sculpture, brochure, $1 (refundable with purchase), illustrated, black and white.

Out of the artist's ballet background grew sculptures of dancers that are modeled in wax, cast in a compound stronger than marble, and hand-finished in antique bronze. Most of the graceful figures, a *pas de deux* from *Romeo and Juliet* and a Nureyev *corsaire arabesque* among them, have an

Gold- and silver-leafed sculptured steel eagle by William Bowie for Sculpture Studio, VII-36.

Italian marble base and measure from 10″ to 18½″ high. There are also sculptures *en l'air,* leaping figures designed for hanging. Prices range from $35 to $95, postage is extra. MO

VII-42
TRITON GALLERY
323 West 45th Street
New York, NY 10036

Brochure and inventory list, 50 cents.

Triton is a great source for posters from the theater, ballet, film, opera, and related arts, all of fairly recent vintage. Some of their selections are shown in color and black and white in the brochure, the current inventory is printed on a four-page list. Recent offerings included the marvelous stylized poster for *Equus,* one for the Rolling Stones' 1972 American tour, and a signed and numbered poster for *A Midsummer Night's Dream*

at Stratford-upon-Avon ($40). Prices range from $2 to $60, with many under $10. MO

VII-43
VIGNARI ART ENTERPRISES
P.O. Box 335
Main Street
Ogunquit, ME 03907

Sea, Men and Ships, $2, *published annually, 36 pages, illustrated, black and white.*

Compiled by marine artist John T. Vignari, this catalogue encompasses over 300 years of marine art by artists from Canaletto through English painters and French Impressionists to American painters like Hopper, Homer, and Wyeth. There are 140 black and white reproductions of the color prints, which range in price from around $8 to $22. Prints are mailed in tubes, insured. MO

"Gathering the Grapes," an Aubusson tapestry faithfully reproduced from Cluny Museum original by Lovelia, VII-24.

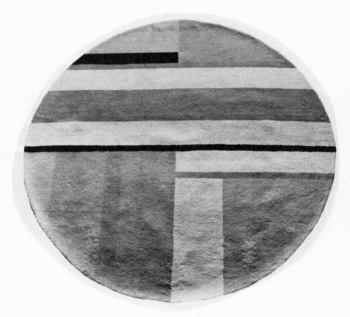

"Yellow Fondo," 7'-diameter handwoven wall tapestry, by Ilya Balotowsky for Modern Master Tapestries, VII-26.

VIII

Tableware and Accessories

VIII-1
BAILEY/HUEBNER
10 West 57th Street
New York, NY 10019

Bailey/Huebner at Henri Bendel, free
brochures, published seasonally, illustrated,
black and white.

Everything in these little brochures from the Bailey/Huebner section of the Henri Bendel store has a look of carefully chosen simplicity and timeless contemporary design. Some of the pieces recently shown were an ovenproof glazed white ceramic tray with brushed steel server that could be used for desserts or for cheese; a slatted pine box and serrated knife for slicing and serving French bread at the table (crumbs fall neatly into the box); classic bottle-bottomed bar glasses; an 8-quart stoneware salad or soup serving bowl, also white and ovenproof; and super 12-inch buffet plates of cream-white china, only $6 apiece. Handsome flatware combining stainless steel with ivory-colored handles was $15 for a 5-piece place setting. There were also charming fruit- and vegetable-shaped ceramic containers, oven and freezer proof, that could be used for *sorbets* or individual servings of soup—one had a matching pumpkin-shaped tureen. The offerings change constantly and include a wonderful selection for stylish entertaining indoors and out. MO/RS

VIII-2
COLONIAL CASTING COMPANY
443 South Colony Street
Meriden, CT 06450

Hand Crafted Pewter, 30 cents, published
annually, 12 pages, illustrated, black and
white.

Handsome reproduction and original pieces in simple, graceful Early American designs—either a Colonial or scalloped edge—handcrafted in solid, lead-free pewter safe for table use are offered by Colonial Casting. Among their eighteenth-century reproductions are goblets, tumblers, mugs, vases, plates and chargers, a sugar and creamer, bowls and serving trays, napkin rings, ladles, and spoons. A lovely Queen Anne compote with scalloped base and a matching oblong serving plate costs around $19 for the compote, $30 for the plate. The company also produces candelabra, candlesticks, and sconces. Prices range from $4 for a gravy ladle to $90 for a scalloped five-light candelabra. MO

VIII-3
CONRAN'S MAIL ORDER DEPARTMENT
145 Huguenot Street
New Rochelle, NY 10805

Conran's, $2.50, published annually, 112
pages, illustrated, color.

Clean-lined, inexpensive contemporary tableware and accessories are part of Conran's extensive home furnishings catalogue: a wide variety of glassware in classic shapes—tumblers, wine glasses, tankards, carafes, and pitchers; earthenware services in plain white, white banded with maroon or bordered with a delicate blue design, and white with a blue or red grid pattern; two more conventional patterns, Blue Denmark and Scenic, the latter a Victorian rural print in pink on white; Mora, shiny, handmade glazed rustic earthenware from Spain, would look good in a country home. A 20-piece service of the Grid pattern, with four place settings, is around $50. Stainless steel flatware with handles of steel, wood, or colored plastic is also reasonably priced, and informal in mood. There are quite a few accessory pieces in plain white, such as bowls, sauceboats, and butter dishes, plus crisply patterned tablecloths and napkins. MO/RS

Rangetoppers plain white cookware from Corning Glass Works, VIII-4.

Stoneware pottery table appointments from Denby, VIII-5.

Towne Garden pattern porcelain china, King Charles sterling flatware and crystal stemware, by Gorham. Historic Charleston Reproductions, VIII-9.

VIII-4
CORNING GLASS WORKS
Houghton Park
Corning, NY 14830

Corning Housewares Products, *free, published semiannually, 30 pages, illustrated, color.*

The catalogue shows the current lines of Corning Pyrex ware, Corning Ware cookware, and Corelle livingware or dinnerware, which comes in plain white or with border or center designs and can be used in microwave or conventional ovens. Some of the patterns, such as Meadow and Wildflower, are simple and attractive, with a country charm. In the familiar oven-to-table cookware, available in white or with a small floral design, there is an interesting variation—French White cookware with ridged sides, like the French soufflé dishes. The covered or open casseroles and pie or quiche plate would coordinate nicely with the dinnerware. There is a complete list of all the items in the Corning line at the back of the catalogue, plus order forms by means of which customers can order replacement parts direct from Corning at the listed catalogue price—a great service if you break a couple of pieces and can't find them at your local store. RS

VIII-5
DENBY, LTD., INC.
130 Campus Plaza
Edison, NJ 08817

The Dauntless Stoneware of Denby, *free, published semiannually, 16 pages, illustrated, color.*

Since 1909 the Denby pottery has been making handcrafted and hand-decorated stoneware. It is fired like fine china but the sturdier body and thicker glaze make it durable enough to use in a regular or microwave oven or in the freezer. The designs of the tableware and ovenware are simple and rustic, the colors are natural, brown, and blue, and some patterns are plain, others decorated. To accompany the pottery they offer good-looking stainless steel flatware with handles of colored stoneware as well as hand-blown goblets and tumblers in clear crystal or subtle pastels. Prices for a 5-piece stoneware place setting range from $41 to $70, the flatware is $65 and $70. RS

Contemporary hand-blown stemware and red and white Bistro pottery from Roche–Bobois, VIII-16.

VIII-6
EDISON INSTITUTE
20900 Oakwood Boulevard
Dearborn, MI 48124

Reproductions from the Collections of Greenfield Village and the Henry Ford Museum, *$2.50, 46 pages, illustrated, black and white and color.*

The reproductions in the catalogue are classic pieces of Revolutionary pewterware by Woodbury Pewterers, including a Rufus Dunham hops pitcher, a Benjamin Day tankard, a charger with coffee service, covered serving dishes, candlesticks, and a delightful pear-shaped teapot. There are also glass goblets, tumblers, dessert bowl, and plate in the Argus pattern, made by Fostoria, in colors approved by the Museum, a pair of Sandwich candlesticks, and a few pottery pieces, such as puzzle jugs and slipware plates and platters made by the Village craftsmen. MO

VIII-7
FURNITURECRAFT, INC.
Box 285c
Stoneham, MA 02180

FurnitureCraft, Inc. Distinctive Early American Furnishings, *50 cents, published semiannually, 32 pages, illustrated, color.*

This catalogue of Americana has reproductions from the Henry Ford Museum of eighteenth- and nineteenth-century pewter in traditional shapes such as a porringer, covered serving dish, pear-shaped teapot with sugar and creamer, tankards, a footed bowl, and a charming set of four miniature porringers and spoons, from originals by Paul Revere and Richard Lee, that could hold salt or condiments (the 8-piece boxed set is around $20). Made of tin, antimony, and copper, these lead-free pieces duplicate the originals in minute detail, down to some of the original casting flaws. MO

VIII-8
HAVILAND & COMPANY
11 East 26th Street
New York, NY 10010

Brochure, 50 cents, illustrated, color.

The brochure shows the 26 Haviland china patterns, from the very simple to the elaborate and beautiful Lotus and Kien Long designs, in the style of antique Chinese porcelains. Prices are given for three-piece and five-piece place settings, serving pieces, and special pieces such as chop plates and salad bowls. A 42-piece set of china ranges in price from $456 to over $7,000, according to the pattern. There is also a leaflet on their much less expensive informal line, which includes oven-to-table pieces such as soufflé and baking dishes. RS

VIII-9
HISTORIC CHARLESTON REPRODUCTIONS
51 Meeting Street
Charleston, SC 29401

Historic Charleston Reproductions, *$3.50 (refundable with $25 purchase), 56 pages, illustrated, black and white and color.*

Tableware and accessories are part of the fine

reproductions in this handsome catalogue. As Charleston was a major seaport in the eighteenth century, it received many shipments of China Trade porcelains. Gorham's Towne Garden china pattern, taken from a plate found in a 1799 private house, is one of the reproductions; a 5-piece place setting is $63. Other china services, by Vista Alegre for Mottahedeh, are the Sacred Butterfly and Ch'ing Dynasty Rose patterns and a superb Blue Canton service with matching serving dishes and accessories. To go with the china, there are Gorham's King Charles pattern in sterling flatware and crystal stemware. In addition, the catalogue has some fine silverplate serving pieces including a traditional Charleston rice spoon, candlesticks of brass or pewter, tea kettle, and trivet. The candlesticks are especially attractive; one is a reproduction of a Georgian stick with baluster turnings, another a copy of a seventeenth-century Flemish candlestick, 19¼" tall, that would make a good lamp base; two have slides to elevate the candle as it burns down. Among the accessories we particularly liked was a copy of an eighteenth-century Chelsea lattice basket ($150). MO/RS

VIII-10
JOSEPH H. KILIAN
39 Glen Byron Avenue
South Nyack, NY 10960

Antique Silver & Old Sheffield Plate, $2 for a 2-year subscription, 20-page descriptive price list.

An impressive listing of silver tableware and objects that makes fascinating reading. The lists, naturally, vary as things are sold, but there are always such items as teapots and tea trays, serving plates, spoons and forks, marrow scoops, sugar tongs, ladles, asparagus tongs, candlesticks, snuff boxes, and inkwells. The price of good antique silver increases every year, so it can always be regarded as a wise investment. Mr. Kilian mentions that asparagus tongs are now retailing in London for $500 and up, whereas those he lists range from $275 to $450. In addition to very expensive pieces like the Paul Storr silver, some of which commands $25,000 or $30,000 at current rates based on auction prices, Mr. Kilian has an 1880 silver salt shovel for as little as $25 and many pieces are under or just over $100. Each item on the list is fully described, with measurements and identifying markings. MO

Swedish crystal, hand-blown, from Kosta Boda, VIII-11.

VIII-11
KOSTA BODA USA LTD.
225 Fifth Avenue
New York, NY 10010

Portfolio of Pattern Brochures, 25 cents, published seasonally, illustrated, color.

The booklets enclosed in the brochure are quite varied, since this company which makes superb Swedish crystal also distributes for others. There are brochures on English Hornsea vitrified oven-to-table ware and Portmeiron pottery dinnerware, Swedish Gense stainless steel flatware, the Rörstrand dinnerware, and Liljeholmens dripless candles. The Kosta Boda line includes candleholders, glasses, plates, bowls, vases, compotes, and ornaments in clear crystal and colors. The Artist Collection of beautifully shaded colored glass flasks and bowls is exceptionally attractive. RS

VIII-12
LENOX CHINA, INC.
Old Princeton Pike
Lawrenceville, NJ 08648

Lenox China/Crystal, Oxford Bone China Created by Lenox, and Temper-ware, free brochures.

These three pattern brochures show the different lines of Lenox china and Temper-ware, a durable ware stronger than ironstone, stoneware, or earthenware that can go from freezer to oven. There are dozens of attractive china patterns from traditional to contemporary, banded in 24-karat gold or in platinum. Lenox china comes in six classic shapes, Oxford bone china in one. The China/Crystal brochure also shows the Lenox

Cuisine line of cooking and serving china, including soufflé dishes, casseroles, ramekins, a platter, a quiche dish, and a baking dish, and Lenox sparkling cut, etched, or colored crystal stemware, bar glasses, and decanters. The Temper-ware patterns, casual, colorful, and mostly floral, would suit a country setting. There are also cook-and-serve and accessory pieces in this line. A 16-piece starter set is $84 or $97, according to pattern. Price lists are included with the brochures, but the patterns are sold only through retail stores. RS

VIII-13
THE LION MARK
25 Maryland Avenue
Annapolis, MD 21401

The Lion Mark. English Sterling Silver, *$3 for postage and handling, published semiannually, 100 pages, illustrated, black and white.*

The Lion Mark specializes in British sterling silver pieces of the highest quality—late Victorian, Edwardian, or later, plus fine reproductions of eighteenth- and nineteenth-century designs. Each piece or set of pieces is described in detail and illustrated with black and white photographs. All antique pieces are properly hallmarked and in excellent condition. The range of antique sterling is wide. In flatware there are complete services; sets of forks; dessert spoons and forks; teaspoons; skewers; marrow scoops;

Designs by seventeenth- and eighteenth-century American silversmiths reproduced by The Metropolitan Museum of Art, V-10.

Lenox china Lace Point pattern, in open stock, is dishwasher-proof. VIII-12.

serving, dressing, and other special spoons; soup, gravy, and sauce ladles; butter knives; asparagus tongs; grape shears; and many more items. The wide variety of serving pieces includes coffee services; sugar baskets and cream jugs; platters; sauce boats; serving dishes; salvers; bowls; and cake baskets. You'll find here just about everything made in sterling. MO

VIII-14
MANHATTAN AD HOC HOUSEWARES
842 Lexington Avenue
New York, NY 10021

Ad Hoc/High-Tech Catalog, *$1 (refundable with purchase), published annually, 16 pages, illustrated, black and white.*

If you are in the market for tableware that is inexpensive, durable, functional, and simple in design, Manhattan Ad Hoc offers a very good selection of the kind of professional equipment used in hotels and restaurants. They sell the plain creamy-white Hall restaurant china and Buffalo china, white or banded in green (the two look well together if you like to mix and match). A Buffalo china dinner plate is around $4, coffee cup and saucer, $4, soup or cereal bowl, $2.60, and an oval platter, 13⅝" long, just $9. There is also silver-plated restaurant flatware, sleek and clean-lined, around $14 for a 5-piece place setting, stainless steel dinner or serving plates, round stainless steel serving trays, and the footed, covered stainless steel compote serving dishes used in Chinese restaurants ($15). The stainless steel instrument trays used by surgeons

Chemists' boiling flasks can be used as bud vases or wine carafes. Manhattan Ad Hoc, VIII-14.

come in three sizes and would make excellent bar or serving trays ($13 to $21.50). In sturdy Duralex French bistro tempered glassware you can get soup bowls, plates, cups and saucers, tumblers, and the non-stemmed bistro 9-ounce wine glasses (4 for $6.50). For classic design at a reasonable price, nothing could beat the Swedish stainless steel gravy boat ($17.50) with matching ladle ($2.25). The wide variety of laboratory glassware, flasks, and dishes makes perfect flower vases, wine or coffee carafes, soufflé dishes, and serving bowls—as the catalogue copy points out, the uses of laboratory glass are limited only by your imagination. MO

VIII-15
MILL HOUSE
Scotts Corners
Pound Ridge, NY 10576

Free catalogue, 6 pages with price lists, illustrated, color.

Mill House imports beautiful handmade Portuguese and French faience in traditional Moustiers, Montpellier, and Nevers (Revolution) patterns as well as hand-blown bubbly colored glass from Biot, a tiny factory, which they suggest as a perfect complement to the faience. The tableware includes place settings and individual pieces in any of 14 designs copied from old Nev-

ers faience, in green and polychrome Moustiers, and in yellow Montpellier. Prices run around $68 for a five-piece place setting of Moustiers and Montpellier, $85 for Nevers. The Biot line of glassware includes wine and water goblets, a water pitcher, decanter, salad bowl, fruit bowl, and hurricane lamps and is relatively inexpensive—$7.95 for a 5" fruit bowl, around $25 for a 7"-high hurricane. Mill House has a very clearly and knowledgeably written introduction describing the faience centers, techniques, and styles. MO

VIII-16
ROCHE–BOBOIS
200 Madison Avenue
New York, NY 10016

Roche–Bobois, $5 (refundable with purchase), published every 18 months, 148 pages, illustrated, color.

The voluminous and fascinating Roche–Bobois furniture catalogue also has some very stylish contemporary tableware, in some cases with tablecloths and fabrics to match the pottery. We noted the line of Bistro pottery in white with red edging and glasses with sturdy bases to team with it; glazed sandstone with a Scandinavian look; delightful flower-patterned Limoges porcelain designed by Marc Held; stainless steel flatware; a good selection of modern hand-blown tumblers and stemmed glasses; and a most unusual octagonal glazed china table set in various colors. We also liked the good-looking glassware for the table including plates, bowls, dishes, glasses, and a decanter, with relief designs for the seasons—grapes for summer, fish for winter, leaves for fall and spring—that would be lovely alone or to mix and match. While the tableware is not inexpensive, it is good value. MO/RS

Portuguese faience, handmade since 1741. Mill House, VIII-15.

Blue Fluted pattern with Half-lace border. Royal Copenhagen Porcelain, VIII-17.

Swedish Gense stainless steel flatware from Kosta Boda, VIII-11.

VIII-17
ROYAL COPENHAGEN PORCELAIN
575 Madison Avenue
New York, NY 10022

Come Dine with Kings, *$1, folder of 28 leaflets and pattern sheets, illustrated, color.*

Royal Copenhagen and Georg Jensen silver have merged, so within the folder you will find not only 16 patterns of porcelain and faience tableware, with retail prices for each piece given on the back of the sheet, but also some of Jensen's distinctive silver. Another leaflet features a line of place mats and napkins embroidered with the Royal Copenhagen hallmark, each one pictured with a china pattern and Jensen flatware. Place mats and napkins come in sets of four for $30. In addition, the folder contains a catalogue of Royal Copenhagen porcelain figurines and decorative pieces, described in more detail on page 111. RS

VIII-18
THE SILO
Upland Road
New Milford, CT 06771

Silo Kitchen Catalogue, *free, published three times a year, 24 pages, illustrated, color.*

While the main emphasis is on kitchen and cooking equipment, this catalogue also contains some attractive oven-to-table pieces, among them Lauffer's covered casserole, soufflé dish, and ramekins in brown stoneware, snail plates with tongs and forks ($25 for a set of 4), and brown-glazed earthenware onion soup bowls. A solid red-oak board with dual troughs for crackers and a flat center area for cheese is $10, a cheese knife and plane to go with it are $10 the set. MO

VIII-19
WOODBURY PEWTERERS, INC.
860 Main Street South
Woodbury, CT 06798

Woodbury Pewter, *no charge, 6 pages, illustrated, color.*

Woodbury Pewterers are famous for their careful workmanship and excellence of design and their accurate reproductions of early American pewter by Austin, Bassett, Day, Danforth, Revere, and other craftsmen, and for pieces from the Henry Ford Museum collection. The catalogue shows tea and coffee services, bowls, plates, tankards, goblets, candlesticks, and two electrified lamps, one a reproduction of an early whale oil lamp and the other a candlestick lamp. Prices are reasonable—a large Revere pitcher, 2-quart capacity, is around $58, a small plate for a syrup jug, $5, and the syrup jug, $25. RS

Hall restaurant china, oven- and freezer-proof, with harder-than-steel white glaze, resists scratches and chips. Manhattan Ad Hoc, VIII-14.

IX
Equipment and Hardware

IX-1
ADVENT CORPORATION
195 Albany Street
Cambridge, MA 02139

Advent VideoBeam® Large Screen Television, free brochure, illustrated, color.

Advent's VideoBeam® TV brings an exciting new experience to viewers. It operates like a regular color set but has two parts—a projector console and a 72"-diagonal screen onto which the picture is projected. After aligning projector and screen you tune in to the desired program. Sound is provided by a wide-range speaker/amplifier system built into the projector. Two models are available: model 710 is 26½" high x 16½" wide x 25⅝" deep; Model 761 is 17½" high x 32" wide x 23½" deep and has the added convenience of random access remote control. RS

IX-2
ARABESQUE
2322 Myrtle Avenue
El Paso, TX 79901

Arabesque Handcrafted Doors, and Mantels by Arabesque, each brochure $1, illustrated, black and white and color.

The handcrafted doors and mantels designed and executed by Mexican-American craftsmen under the direction of Arabesque's president, Carlos Morales, vary from typical Spanish designs to French Provincial, are shipped unfinished, and cost from $508 to $1,164. You can choose a door carved on one or on both sides. The company will make special sizes to order for an additional price. The mantels, of Honduras mahogany or ash, are also sold unfinished, and prices range from $770 to $850. Information on other materials and sizes, with prices, is avail-

able on request. Arabesque will also make a mantel to your specific design. MO

IX-3
BALDWIN HARDWARE MANUFACTURING CORPORATION
P.O. Box 82
841 Wyomissing Boulevard
Reading, PA 19603

Narrow Backset Mortise Locks, Quality Mortise Locks & Latches, and 18th-Century Colonial Lock Makers, 50 cents each, 8 pages, illustrated, color.

The special narrow backset locks are generally installed on exterior and interior residential doors. They have been designed to accommodate doors having a narrow side rail, or stile, that necessitates the use of lever handles. All lock cylinders have a full five-pin tumbler operation. There are chrome, brass, bronze, nickel, and silver-plated models, plus some truly striking Limoges porcelain handles and trim.

If the door has wider side rails, or a knob is desired, the quality mortise locks are made with the standard 2¾" backset, and feature an armored plate that resists tampering as well as an optional jimmy-proof deadbolt. Traditional and modern trim, knobs, latches, handles, and drop rings, come in steel, bronze, chromium, and brass, and there is a special line of plastic, crystal, or Limoges porcelain knobs.

The eighteenth-century colonial locks are authentic reproductions of knobs, locks, and pulls found in historical homes and museums, and have been adapted to include modern security functions. All working parts are forged of solid brass. Standard and dutch elbow rim locks, sectional handle locks, keyhole door latches, thumb latches, square plate latches, knobs, and lock

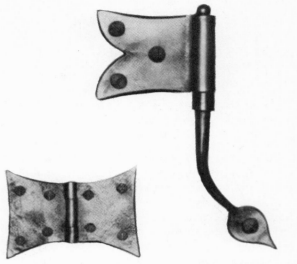

trim are available. When writing for the catalogues, request the name of your nearest Baldwin hardware dealer. RS

IX-4
BALL AND BALL
463 West Lincoln Highway
Exton, PA 19341

Fine Quality Hardware by Ball and Ball,
$4, 108 pages, illustrated, black and white.

Ball and Ball's latest catalogue is an impressive collection of more than 900 items in over 1200 sizes, with the emphasis on antique brass furniture and house hardware. The catalogue also contains a great deal of useful information about the manufacture of reproductions. You'll find brass hardware for furniture and cabinets in William and Mary, Queen Anne, Hepplewhite, and Chippendale styles; Sheraton and Chippendale knobs and drops; all kinds of hinges and catches; casters and feet; escutcheons; clock finials and fittings; cabinet locks and keys; doorknockers; and lamp finials. Also included are brass picture hooks and fireplace accessories, house hardware in brass and iron, and Victorian hardware for those who are restoring old houses. A special section covers Ball and Ball's reproductions of eighteenth-century lighting fixtures. A current price list and order form are enclosed with the catalogue. MO

Hand-forged butterfly and rattail hinges from Ball & Ball, IX-4.

IX-5
THE BAYBERRY
718 Montauk Highway
Amagansett, NY 11930

Handmade Weathervanes, $1, published
annually, 22 pages, illustrated, black and
white.

All the traditional weathervane figures are shown in hand-hammered copper, solid-bodied or in silhouette. Prices are quoted for complete vanes or for figures alone in natural copper, verdigris patina, or gold-leaf finishes. There are also handmade copper lanterns, and a most attractive pierced copper chandelier. Prices for the lanterns range from $32.50 to $166 for a Philadelphia street light. The 15"-diameter electrified chandelier is $80, the 18"-diameter, $110. Prices for weathervanes range from $78 for a complete arrow vane to $1,900 for a 96" complete eagle and arrow. MO

IX-6
BENDIX MOULDINGS, INC.
235 Pegasus Avenue
Northvale, NJ 07647

Mouldings/Carvings, free brochure and price
list, 11 pages, illustrated, two-color, plus 1
page on instant picture frames.

The brochure shows an extensive selection of the Bendix moldings—carved wood, embossed pine, hardwood, scalloped plywood—and decorative wood carvings in various shapes, sizes, and styles. On the back of each sheet is the catalogue number, size, and number of pieces per package. Prices for moldings range from $1.30 to $8.80 per piece, according to length and type, or from $17.50 to $65 for a standard order, depending on how many pieces are in the package. Bendix also makes do-it-yourself wood picture frames that simply snap together—no glue, screws, or tools are needed. Each frame is pre-stapled to hold in the picture and the glass. Frames come finished in black with gold trim line, bronze with embossed gold, walnut, or unfinished, ready to stain or paint. The company will, on request, supply the names of retail outlets in your vicinity. RS

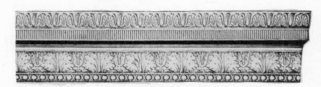

Ceiling cornice of ornamental wood from Driwood Moulding, IX-15.

IX-7
BILLARD'S OLD TELEPHONES
21710 Regnart Road
Cupertino, CA 95014

*Old Telephones & Parts Catalog, $1
(refundable with purchase), 8 pages,
illustrated, black and white.*

If you have an old telephone that isn't in working
condition, this company will probably be able to
supply the part or parts you need, from cords to
cranks to receivers. There's an identification
chart with sketches of many kinds of phones.
You supply the number of the phone that most
resembles yours and the make, if possible, and
Billard's can help you get the parts. They also
offer for sale a few vintage models, such as an
Art Deco pay phone in chrome case, rewired for
use ($59), and a remake of a 1901 style in a solid
oak cabinet ($139). MO

IX-8
BOULTON STEREO
380 Madison Avenue
New York, NY 10017

*Boulton Stereo Catalogue, free, published
semiannually, 11 pages, illustrated, black and
white.*

Unlike component stereo systems that can only
play in one or two rooms, a Boulton can put
music into every room, and you can even play
different selections in different rooms simultaneously. There are systems for everything from
tiny apartments to 20- or 30-room houses, and
over 100 accessories to tailor the system to your
home. Four basic setups are featured in the catalogue, and the absolutely top-notch components are described in detail. The technical
specifications (very important when selecting
equipment of this kind) are provided. The company will install and balance all the equipment

Control box for Boulton's component stereo system. IX-8.

for you; they also provide an extensive questionnaire so they can send prospective customers
more details on the appropriate components. RS

IX-9
THE BURNING LOG
P.O. Box 438
Hanover Street
Lebanon, NH 03766

*The Burning Log Woodburner's Catalog, 25
cents, published annually, 32 pages,
illustrated, black and white.*

This little catalogue has over forty items for the
fireplace, such as cloth or leather log carriers, bellows, andirons of polished brass, brass and iron,
or hammered steel (from $50 to $150), complete
firesets, firestarters including a handy Cape Cod
lighter in black cast iron (it works by means of a
porous clay ball that absorbs kerosene and is
placed under the firewood), and fire screens. In
fact, there's almost nothing you can think of for
your fireplace and chimney that isn't here, from
a sign that indicates the damper is open to a
Norwegian chimney brush to a fuel-miser grate
that keeps logs centrally located for more efficient burning ($24). You'll also find a good many
wood-burning stoves. An exact reproduction of
the original De Dietrich Alsace-Lorraine wood
stove with decorative sculptured castings is both
an efficient heater and a cooking stove ($635).
The De Dietrich combination coal/wood heater,
cast-iron with a sleek two-tone porcelain jacket,
is $550, a Franklin fireplace around $345. The
Burning Log also handles the Norwegian Jøtul
stoves, both the classic box types and the contemporary combifires with doors that open so
you can view the fire. MO

IX-10
C&D DISTRIBUTORS, INCORPORATED
P.O. Box 766
Old Saybrook, CT 06475

*Jiffy Makes Wood Burning Easier and Safer,
free brochure, illustrated, black and white.*

A log lifter which hooks, lifts, and clamps logs
into position for sawing, a woodsplitter for logs
and kindling, and a chimney-cleaning device
with 30' of chain, adjustable to any lined chimney flue from 7" to 12", are the three C&D products listed in the brochure. RS

IX-11
CAPE COD CUPOLA CO., INC.
78 State Road
North Dartmouth, MA 02747

Catalogue, $1 (refundable with $10 purchase), published annually, 48 pages, illustrated, black and white.

The company claims to offer the largest assortment of cupolas and weathervanes in the U.S. The weathervanes are made of cast aluminum, solid aluminum, copper, and with gold leaf. Full-bodied weathervanes are handmade from rare molds over 100 years old and include such traditional shapes as a pig, ram, goose, grasshopper, horse, whale, eagle, and running deer. Accessory items such as flagpole ornaments, chimney letters, script lettering, post signs, and antique cast-aluminum scroll brackets are also available. You'll find wall decorations and plaques for indoor or outdoor use showing eagles, seagulls, horses, and so on, as well as some attractive aluminum sundials and bird feeders. Prices for weathervanes range from around $19 for a small aluminum model suitable for a garden tool shed, small garage, or a 16″ to 18″ cupola to around $700 for some of the full-bodied 23-karat gold-leafed vanes. MO

IX-12
ALBERT CONSTANTINE AND SON, INC.
2050 Eastchester Road
New York, NY 10461

Constantine's Woodworker's Catalogue, *50 cents (or $1 with 20 wood samples), published annually, 100 pages, illustrated, black and white and color.*

Constantine's Woodworker's Catalogue contains a large selection of hardware for furniture, including brass hinges and drawer pulls, escutcheons, handles, backplates, and knobs, all at reasonable prices. Also here are locks for doors and drawers, catches for cabinets, and sliding hardware for record players, drawers, and sliding doors, plus such hard-to-find items as a spring for a platform rocker ($4.95). MO

IX-13
DA-LITE SCREEN COMPANY, INC.
P.O. Box 137
Warsaw, IN 46580

Slide and Movie Projection Screens, *free brochure.*

This company makes projection screens for home use, 40″ to 70″ square, as well as screens for auditoriums and electrically operated screens on rollers which come in various sizes. Most screens are available in either glass-beaded or non-gloss matte white fiberglass surface. Accessories include multiple-control systems for electric screens and replacement surfaces. All screens are described with dimensions and illustrations. RS

IX-14
DECORATORS SUPPLY CORPORATION
3610 South Morgan Street, Rear
Chicago, IL 60609

Wood Fibre Carving, *$1, 24 pages, and* ***Capitals and Brackets,*** *$2, 44 pages, and* ***Plaster Ornaments,*** *$2, 56 pages, all illustrated, black and white.*

For those who want to restore or add period architectural detail, this company is an invaluable source. In *Wood Fibre Carvings* there is an impressive assortment of decorative carvings for mantels, cabinets, and architectural trim, reproductions of motifs from Wedgwood urns to rococo shells to chinoiserie that can be either nailed (carvings have brad holes) or glued to the woodwork. Sizes and prices are given for each. *Capitals and Brackets* covers the major styles—Ionic, Doric, Corinthian, and Gothic—and style periods from Greek and Roman to Renaissance and Louis XVI. A separate price list is included with this catalogue and with *Plaster Ornaments*, which shows some of the many patterns in cast ornamental plaster, including cornices, moldings, pediment ornaments, grilles (with or without background), as well as examples of complete ornamentation for Empire, Colonial, Louis XV, Louis XVI, Old English, and Italian coffered ceilings. All patterns in this booklet can be made of exterior composition for use on the outside of buildings. There is a minimum order of $15 and

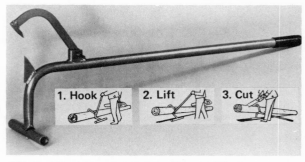

Jiffy log lifter from C & D Distributors, IX-10.

while the prices are not inexpensive, they would be nowhere near the cost of hand craftsmanship —if you could find it. Decorator's Supply also has other catalogues, including a 350-page art book of composition carvings in the various art periods ($13). MO/RS

IX-15
DRIWOOD MOULDING COMPANY
P.O. Box 1729
Florence, SC 29503

Driwood Period Mouldings, $3 (refundable with purchase), published seasonally, 32 pages, illustrated, black and white and color.

Driwood makes ornamented period wood moldings for cornices, wall and ceiling panels, pilasters, chair rails, door and window casings, and picture moldings, all authentic in design and architecturally correct. They are supplied in lengths from 6' to 16', with prices listed per lineal foot, and are stocked in poplar suitable for use in white or color work or made to order in maple, walnut, oak, or mahogany. The great variety of moldings are shown sketched and in profile, with dimensions, and also installed in room settings, illustrating their versatility. Special designs can be made to order. MO

IX-16
FURNITURECRAFT, INC.
Box 285c
Stoneham, MA 02180

FurnitureCraft, Inc. Distinctive Early American Furnishings, 50 cents, published semiannually, 32 pages, illustrated, color.

Fireplace tools and accessories are included in this jam-packed little catalogue of Americana. There's a brass coal scuttle, 8½" high (around $15); a pine and leather bellows; reproduction andirons with a forged loop head, 18" high and 18" deep (around $50); an old-fashioned iron poker and log roller, each 3' or 4' long; and a Cape Cod firelighter which holds kerosene to soak a ceramic torch that will burn for fifteen minutes, a boon to the unhandy (around $23). A hand-forged wrought iron tool set, in black or white Swedish finish, would be a handsome addition to any fireplace. Each piece is unique and bears the marks of the smithy's hammer and fire. If you like to hide your fireplace in summer, we noted a lacy fireplace fan of solid brass, 37" across the base and 24½" high at the center, for around $100. MO

IX-17
GRILLION CORPORATION
189–193 First Street
Brooklyn, NY 11215

Plygrilles, $2 (refundable with purchase), 12 pages, illustrated, black and white and color.

Decorative plywood grilles of all types and in many different patterns, including lattice, honeycomb, Moorish, diamonds, Greek square, and link circle. Prices for unpainted, unframed grilles start at $6.50 for a 15½" x 23½" grille, ⅛" thick. Grilles set in sturdy frames to use for screens, wall and window coverings, room dividers, headboards, and dropped ceilings can be bought with frosted white translucent fiberglass laminated between. The company also makes Japanese-style rectangle box shoji with fiberglass panels for sliding walls or to cover a window wall, and folding screens, assembled and unpainted or in a do-it-yourself kit. The brochure illustrates a number of ways to decorate with grillework. Grillion will also give quotes on custom work. MO

IX-18
P. E. GUERIN, INC.
23 Jane Street
New York, NY 10014

Catalogue of Artistic Hardware, $4, 64 pages, illustrated, black and white and color.

Beautiful builder's and furniture hardware, bathroom fittings, and accessories. If you can't find what you are looking for here (which is unlikely, as Guerin has never willfully discarded a model since 1857 and has over 50,000 registered and available on special order), the company can reproduce antique pieces from your sample and create new designs to your drawing. The hardware comes in many finishes—brushed or polished brass, antique silver, brushed or polished bronze, pewter, and gold plate among them— and is priced accordingly. For instance, a bamboo-motif door pull, 6" long, is $27.50 in polished brass, $36.75 in gold plate. The bathroom fittings and accessories are exceptionally handsome, with some basin sets in onyx, others sporting swan or dolphin handles. The furniture hardware section covers such style periods as Louis XV, Empire, Louis XVI, and Provincial designs in French steel or solid brass, and shows the items in stock, including pulls and escutcheons, wrought-brass moldings, galleries, and rosettes. There are also decorative tie-backs in the various finishes. The price list provides dimensions and finishes and recommendations for finish maintenance. MO/ID

IX-19
HORTON BRASS COMPANY
P.O. Box 95X
Nooks Hill Road
Cromwell, CT 06416

Furniture Hardware Catalogue, $1.50, 36 pages, illustrated, black and white.

The company makes authentic reproductions of period cabinet hardware in brass with antique or highly polished finish, and also in black iron. They can supply hardware for periods from 1680 to the 1920s and if they don't have a stock brass to match your sample, they will hand-make a copy for an additional charge. The stock brasses include a good selection of Queen Anne, Sheraton, Hepplewhite, Chippendale, and Victorian styles, all reasonably priced. Horton also sells bolts, irons, and clamps for beds, clock parts, and such miscellaneous items as mirror holders, molding hooks, cast-brass doorstops in animal shapes, and machine-made nails that look like the handmade originals ($3 a pound). They have a small but good collection of books on houses, furniture, and clocks, including a republication of Russell Hawkes Kettell's 1929 work, *The Pine Furniture of Early New England.* There's a minimum order of $10 for hardware and a discount for bulk orders. MO

IX-20
**HUBBARDTON FORGE
AND WOOD CORPORATION**
P.O. Box SRX
Bomoseen, VT 05732

Hand-Wrought Iron from Hubbardton Forge, $3 (refundable with purchase), published annually, 13 pages, illustrated, black and white.

Hubbardton Forge is pioneering the revival of the almost vanished art of ornamental blacksmithing, and their pieces have a sturdy, simple beauty that would be equally suitable to colonial settings or contemporary rooms. The selection is not large but includes some unusual bathroom and kitchen accessories and wrought iron tiebacks in addition to chandeliers, sconces, candlesticks, and fireplace tools. There are two handsome professional kitchen pan hangers, one a hoop of heavy-gauge iron, feathered and riv-

Honeycomb pattern room divider screen panels from Grillon, IX-17.

eted, with hand-forged hooks and chain links for suspending it from the ceiling ($42). MO

IX-21
JAMES B. LANSING SOUND, INC.
8500 Balboa Boulevard
Northridge, CA 90401

JBL Loudspeaker Systems, free 6-page color brochure, illustrated.

This company has some sleekly handsome bookshelf, floor-standing, and console designs in loudspeaker systems, mostly with cabinets finished in hand-rubbed walnut veneers and grilles in dark or neutral finishes. One console system, the Paragon, is sculptural in shape and a classic of acoustic and visual design. Each half of the complete stereo loudspeaker system contains massive component drivers and the center convex panel refracts the output of the middle-range horns to give an almost panoramic stereo effect. It is a piece of furniture that would be an asset to any room. JBL's technical credentials are impeccable, as the table of specifications on the back of the brochure attests. No prices are given. Write for the name of your nearest dealer. RS

IX-22
LEMEE'S FIREPLACE EQUIPMENT
815 Bedford Street
Bridgewater, MA 02324

Lemee's Fireplace Equipment, $1 (refundable with purchase), published every two years, 38 pages, illustrated, black and white.

This catalogue is considerably more eclectic than its name. In addition to the comprehensive selection of fireplace accessories, many of them seventeenth- and eighteenth-century Colonial designs in copper, brass, and iron, that make up the bulk of the catalogue, there are weathervanes, bookends in brass or black iron, a warming pan, colonial hardware, a doorstop, wall mirrors and hooks, trivets, sundials, mailbox signs, and even cast-iron, white-enameled garden furniture in a grapevine pattern. The fireplace equipment includes fire screens (folding and curtain), tools, handsome andirons, wood boxes and baskets, reproductions of Early American firemarks and firebacks, grates and grilles, and bellows. Everything is clearly depicted and described, with dimensions and shipping weight. A price list and order form are included. Prices are reasonable, mostly under $100, the most expensive item being the heavy solid brass Hampton andirons with lacquered finish at around $253. MO

IX-23
MEXICO HOUSE
P.O. Box 970
Del Mar, CA 92014

Mexico House, $1 (refundable with purchase), published annually, 42 pages, illustrated, black and white.

Mexico House has some very attractive and inexpensive hand-wrought iron hardware, including a scroll-shaped door pull, a wall bracket, and just $4.95 for a ceiling canopy with hook. In fireplace accessories, there are both hanging and standing firesets, a curlicued Spanish log basket, and a handsome screen at around $90 (this can also be handmade to your specifications). The company specializes in custom design work and will have their artisans in Mexico duplicate designs provided in the form of photographs, drawings, or specifications, so you can have grilles, railings, or a gazebo made to order if you wish. MO

IX-24
NU*TREND MANUFACTURING COMPANY, LTD.
Suite 1711, Two Penn Center Plaza
Philadelphia, PA 19102

*United Metal Catalogue, 20 pages, illustrated, color, and Nu*trend Idea Book, 4 pages, illustrated, color, $1 for both.*

Inspired by the high-tech decorating style, industrial products are now being brought into the home to provide functional and uncomplicated design. The United Metal catalogue shows a wide range of waste receptacles, wastebaskets, and utility barrels that can be used indoors and outdoors, among them a space-saving wall-mounted steel cabinet (also available in white or beige) that could be used as a laundry hamper in a bathroom, fireproof steel wastebaskets, and the familiar metal mesh or redwood-slat trash baskets seen on city streets, with flat base or a metal spike that can be driven into the ground. The Idea Book shows ways in which industrial products can be used in the home—a stainless steel cigarette sand urn as a plant stand, a large plastic barrel as an ice-filled beverage cooler. You could make a fascinating game out of devising new ways to use these sturdy products. RS

IX-25
PERIOD FURNITURE HARDWARE COMPANY, INC.
123 Charles Street
Boston, MA 02114

Authentic Reproductions of Furniture Hardware and Lighting Fixtures, $2, published every two years, 126 pages, illustrated, black and white.

This company has a considerable selection of brass cabinet hardware in period styles, with antique (dark) or bright finish, as well as porcelain knobs, carved wood legs, knobs, drops, and ornaments for furniture. While hardware constitutes about half the catalogue, that's only the beginning. There are reverse paintings on glass for mirrors and clocks; brass trivets and trays; solid brass doorknockers, name plates, and house numbers; door handles, knobs, and reproduction rim locks; fireplace accessories in brass and iron; fire screens; weathervanes; plus a large selection of Early American metal sconces, chandeliers, and lanterns and Victorian lighting fixtures. Prices are reasonable. MO

IX-26
PORTLAND WILLAMETTE COMPANY
6510 NE Columbia Boulevard
Portland, OR 97218

Complete Fireplace Furnishings, *$1, 36 pages, illustrated, color.*

This catalogue from a leading manufacturer of fire screens and fireplace accessories covers a great deal more than just the products. It contains sections on the history of the fireplace, on planning your fireplace (type, location, and size), on building a fire and the burning qualities of various firewoods, and on fireplace maintenance. A guide to fireplace styles shows different models, from the standard wall fireplace to corner and triple-face types (the latter is open on three sides). Fire screens include the Glassfyre models, which have folding tempered glass doors set in a metal frame with top and bottom damper controls, standing or portable fire screens with metal frames and sliding mesh curtains or wire cloth spark guards, and folding screens with hinged wire cloth panels. There are various ensembles of screens with matching andirons, firesets and woodholders, accessories such as top bars, canopies, and hoodscreens for attached firescreens, matching fenders, coal hods, bellows, hearth brooms, and bar grates. The fire screens come in many finishes, about eighteen in all, including satin or polished brass, smooth or hammered antique brass and copper, hammered Swedish steel, and satin black. The catalogue comes with an order form for fireplace screens and accessories that may be completed and returned to the company; they will refer it to your nearest Portland Willamette dealer who supplies the information on the product price and order time. RS

IX-27
RED BARON ANTIQUES
234 Hildebrand Avenue
Sandy Springs, GA 30328

Catalogue, free, published seasonally, 8 pages, illustrated, color.

We received the second annual gift catalogue put out by Red Baron's Antiques, featuring some of the stained and beveled glass which is their specialty. There are Art Deco and Art Nouveau patterns, beveled door panels, transoms, and sidelights, a 14½" x 25½" Victorian window ($585), a 4' x 6' jeweled landing window ($1850),

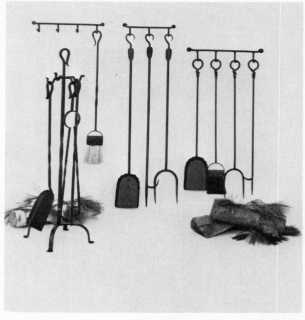

Wrought iron fireplace tools to hang on the wall or stand on the floor. Lemee's, IX-22.

and lots of other interesting pieces. As well as stained glass, the catalogue shows or lists all kinds of memorabilia from the not-so-distant past that would be fun to use around the house, such as corbels, a parlor stove in perfect condition, an old four-legged bathtub, marble mantels, gilt pier mirror frames, and small oak swinging doors. They have hundreds of stained and beveled windows in stock and obviously their catalogue changes according to what else they have picked up for sale. MO

IX-28
RITTER & SON HARDWARE
Gualala, CA 95445

Catalogue, $1, 16 pages, illustrated, sepia.

Ritter's selection of solid brass hardware includes bail sets, all kinds of ornamental pulls, keyholes, knobs and knob backplates, washstand brackets, hat hooks, a doorknocker, hardware for a French door, and a rolltop desk lock. The styles are decorative rather than classic. The company also offers a brass antiquing solution, embossed leather chair seat replacements, and hardware and nameplates for an old-fashioned three-door oak icebox, for which they also sell full-size professionally drawn plans. Prices are reasonable and you can place your order by calling a toll-free number. MO

High-tech round-top stainless steel waste receptacles from Nu*Trend, IX-24.

IX-29
THE JOHN P. SMITH COMPANY
P.O. Box 551
Branford, CT 06405

Free leaflet.

The leaflet shows four styles of custom-built fireplace screens in black-lacquered wire cloth with brass handles, and a wrought iron log holder available in two sizes that folds for easy storage. Although the leaflet is also an order form, no prices are given, so be sure to request them when writing. MO

IX-30
VINTAGE WOODWORKS
PO Drawer R 100
Quinlan, TX 75474

Victorian Gingerbread, $1, 4 pages, illustrated.

Summer houses, gazebos, walkways, stables, barns, and interiors are transformed by this decorative pinewood scrollwork, available in precut patterns or custom-designed to your specification. Prices are reasonable. A screen-door corner ¾" x 6" x 5" is $2.99, a Gothic circle ¾" x 8½" is $8.99. They also have various kinds of running trim. MO

IX-31
WOOD MOULDING & MILLWORK PRODUCERS
P.O. Box 25278
Portland, OR 97225

Wood Moulding & Millwork, $1.50, illustrated, color.

The wood moldings in standard patterns, including crowns, coves, quarter and half rounds, base caps, panel and picture moldings, chair rails, and casings of various types, are illustrated in diagrams and, in use, in photographs. These are generally available throughout the United States. RS

Victorian gingerbread wood trim designs revived by Vintage Woodworks, IX-30.

X

Energy Savers

X-1
APPROPRIATE TECHNOLOGY CORPORATION
P.O. Box 975
111 Green Street
Brattleboro, VT 05301

Window Quilt Information Package, $2, illustrated, color.

The package, a folder containing a sample of and illustrated information about the Window Quilt, gives a clear idea of how this multi-layered thermal shade helps to stop heat leakage through windows and so cut heating bills. The quilted roller blinds, which seal at the top, sides, and along the sill, are made of a five-layer sandwich of polyester fiberfill, aluminized plastic film, and an off-white polyester covering. Other brochures and information sheets include a rundown on percentages of energy-saving achievable, and instructions for measuring and installation. The price for a standard 2½' x 4' window, including all hardware, is $40. Write for the name of your nearest dealer. RS

X-2
ATLANTA STOVE WORKS
P.O. Box 5254
Atlanta, GA 30307

Winter Warmth, free brochures, 14 pages, illustrated, color.

This old, well-established company has a good selection of wood- and coal-burning stoves, more homely than sophisticated but made of infinitely durable cast iron and designed for ease of operation. They also make cast iron coal- or wood-burning ranges with heavy cooking surfaces and ovens that provide steady, even heat —the kind generations of Americans cooked on in the past, and are turning to again—and a Franklin model that can be used open or closed, free-standing or in the fireplace. The Franklin model also burns coal or wood. All stoves, properly stoked, should burn throughout the night. RS

X-3
BROOKSTONE COMPANY
Vose Farm Road
Peterborough, NH 03458

Hard-to-Find Tools and Other Fine Things, free, 68 pages, illustrated, black and white.

The Brookstone catalogue has a few good ideas for saving energy. One is a pressure-sensitive door sealer kit, a curved flexible brass surface that presses against opposite wood surfaces to block gaps ($14.95). A fuel-saver thermostat automatically drops heat at night or increases heat at a selected time. Adhesive insulating tape reduces heat loss on hot-water pipes. MO

X-4
THE BURNING LOG
P.O. Box 438
Hanover Street
Lebanon, NH 03766

The Burning Log Woodburner's Catalog, 25 cents, published annually, 32 pages, illustrated, black and white.

Two energy-savers from this company are a fan inside a grating that can be installed between ceiling joists or in walls to move heated air from around the stove to other rooms ($70) and a cast iron floor register that opens to let heat rise to upper rooms. They also have a good assortment of wood-burning stoves, the De Dietrich and Jøtul models, and a Franklin fireplace. MO

X-5
C&D DISTRIBUTORS, INCORPORATED
P.O. Box 766
Old Saybrook, CT 06475

Hearth Mate, the Fireplace Stove, free brochure, illustrated, color.

The Hearth Mate is adaptable to almost any fireplace and comes with a cover panel, held in place by lintel clamps, for the fireplace opening. It takes logs up to 22″ and a load of hardwood on the correct damper setting burns for twelve hours or more. The stove has a flat top that can be used for cooking. Among available accessories are a see-through steel mesh door screen, baking oven, log holder, and a specially designed poker (called a fire tender). There is also a free-standing model of the stove for those who have no fireplace. Write for the name of your nearest dealer. RS

X-6
THE CEILING FAN GALLERY
108 East 82nd Street
New York, NY 10028

The Ceiling Fan Gallery, 50 cents, published annually, 12 pages, illustrated, color.

At the beginning of the catalogue are two pages of questions and answers on the installation of ceiling fans. These fans are energy savers both for cooling in summer and heating in winter. (They cut fuel consumption by distributing warmth evenly through the room when turned on at low speed. Rising warm air, trapped in the ceiling area, is pushed down by the fan to colder areas, recycling heat.) The savings can be astonishing as a ceiling fan operates on as little power as a light bulb, and the company claims that you can achieve up to a 25 percent saving on fuel consumption costs. Fourteen different models

Hearth Mate fireplace stove from C & D Distributors, X-5.

Ceiling fans, wood-bladed, with or without light globe; two of many to select from Periculum, X-20.

are illustrated, in wood tones, white, and chocolate brown, at prices ranging from $179 to around $340. An Adaptair mechanism that changes the angle of the blades, available on most models, adds around $60 to the cost. If you want to add a globe light, there is a light adapter kit ($12 for brown, black, and white, $20 for brass). There's also an amusing Victorian light fantastic, a brass fixture with four glass tulip shades, complete with 15-watt bulbs, pull chain, and decorative tassel, that attaches to any 52- or 36-inch ceiling fan. All fans have two speeds and a five-year guarantee. MO

X-7
EDMUND SCIENTIFIC COMPANY
7082 Edscorp Building
Barrington, NJ 08007

Edmund Scientific Catalog, *$1, published semiannually, 100 pages, illustrated, black and white and color.*

Described as having "everything for the hobbyist, schools and industry," this catalogue contains quite a few intriguing solar-energy items. There's a solar music box, a cluster of solar cells inside a 5″ acrylic cube that converts light from the sun or a 60-watt light bulb into energy (around $32); a portable solar water heater that holds 10 quarts of water and on a 70° day will heat to over 100° in three hours; a folding solar cooker and a small solar furnace that can be built from scrap parts and a special lens, and develops temperatures up to 2,000° for cooking, soldering, and other jobs. There are also powerful silicon solar panels at prices ranging from around $60

for a small 4½″ x 5″ panel to almost $2000 for a 21″ x 21″ panel. Then there's a flue pipe exchange heater, aluminum fins that slip around a flue pipe and divert normally lost heat into the room (around $11), and a gadget that detects heat loss by tracking air currents to their source. The company also has books on solar energy that explain how it all works. MO

X-8
ENCON INDUSTRIES, INC.
2629 Whitmore Street
Fort Worth, TX 76107

Presenting the Encon Collection, *color brochure, 25 cents.*

Eight Encon ceiling fans are shown—three in the Classic Series of plain fans and five in the Decorator Series, which incorporates a variety of lighting fixtures from Tiffany and Victorian to simple globes. The fans come in 42″, 48″ and 56″ sizes and the blades are curved for more efficient air spread. Among the notable features are self-lubricated ball bearings, 100 percent copper-wound direct-drive electric motor, and solid steel drive shaft. When writing for information, request the name of your nearest Encon distributor. RS

X-9
ENERGY HARVESTERS CORPORATION
Route 12, P.O. Box 19
Fitzwilliam, NH 03447

Energy Harvesters Wood Stove, *folder with brochures, $1, 17 pages, illustrated, color.*

Cast iron woodburning stoves: a new design from Energy Harvesters, X-9; and the Norwegian-made import from Kristia Associates, X-15.

Traditional wood-burning cast iron stoves in two basic models, both 26¾" high x 18½" wide x 34½" deep. They will take logs up to 22" long. Special features are the large interior smoke baffle and primary and secondary air regulators to increase heat. The stoves cost $448, shipping costs are extra. An optional accessory is a spark screen that enables you to enjoy the pleasures of an open fire ($15.50, plus shipping and handling cost of $3). MO

X-10
FAIRE HARBOUR LTD.
44 Captain Pierce Road
Scituate, MA 02066

Faire Harbour Ltd., $1 *(refundable with purchase), 12 pages, illustrated, color.*

This company sells Aladdin kerosene heaters of different types with safety guards and automatic shutoff devices in case the heater is overturned. A gallon of fuel will heat 3,000 cubic feet for about 15 to 20 hours. The heaters are easily portable and fill short-term, small-space or supplementary heating requirements. One of the more attractive models is a compact red-enameled radiant heater with parabolic dish reflector. Prices range from under $100 to around $170. MO

X-11
FIRE-VIEW PRODUCTS INC.
P.O. Box 370
Rogue River, OR 97537

Free brochure, 6 pages, illustrated, black and white.

Fire-View's wood heaters have tubular fire boxes of hot-rolled steel and their patented design provides the largest possible heat-radiant surface. Among their unusual features are an end door at right or left for loading the firewood, a tempered glass window that is removable for cleaning, and two flat cooking surfaces on top of the heater. A firebrick lining acts as an insulation barrier that protects both the bottom of the firebox and the floor and helps to retain heat, so no special grate is needed. The heaters are available in three sizes for wood lengths of 20" to 30". This is one of the neatest looking models we've seen. RS

X-12
GEORGETOWN FAN COMPANY, INC.
P.O. Box 2128
Denver, CO 80201

The Ceiling Fan, brochure, 25 cents.

Georgetown has two versions of the standard

ceiling fan, available in walnut, oak, yellow, and white—$69.95 for the plain model and $84.90 for one with a frosted globe attachment to hold a light bulb. Each one measures 44″ from blade tip to blade tip and both are made of heavy-duty resin plastic with rods of polished chrome. MO

X-13
GLEN RAVEN MILLS, INC.
Glen Raven, NC 27215

Sunbrella Fabrics Can Save Energy, *50 cents, 12-page brochure, illustrated, color.*

If you had never thought of awnings as energy-savers, the brochure points out that they can save up to 25 percent on air conditioning costs by blocking out 75 percent of the sun's heat and reducing room temperatures by up to 15 degrees. Different types of awnings to suit various exposures are shown, as well as other ways to use Sunbrella 100 percent acrylic fabric for upholstery, tents, screens, and cabanas. Sunbrella fabrics are sold by canvas products dealers listed in the Yellow Pages under "Awnings and Canopies." RS

X-14
HEATHDELLE ASSOCIATES, INC.
Box 1039
Meredith, NH 03253

Nashua Doubleheat Woodstoves *and* ***Elite Fireplace Insert,*** *brochures, $1, illustrated, black and white and color.*

The Nashua stoves are free-standing models fitted with blowers that recycle room-temperature air through super-heated manifolds within the stove itself. They are constructed of boilerplate steel with firebrick lining and some have a large, heat-resistant window so you can see the fire. The Elite fireplace insert, a porcelain-finished steel stove (color choices are charcoal or cranberry) with antique brass trim, is designed to fit into most standard fireplaces from 24½″ high x 27″ wide to 33″ high x 51″ wide. A screen-protected glass fire-viewing area gives you the visual charm of a fireplace plus the warmth and comfort of circulatory and radiant heat. Write for the name of your nearest dealer. RS

X-15
KRISTIA ASSOCIATES
P.O. Box 1118
Portland, ME 04104

The Homeowners Resource Book on the Art of Heating with Wood, *$1, published annually, 64 pages, illustrated, black and white.*

The company has been importing the famous Jøtul cast iron wood-and-coal burning stoves, combi-fires (fireplace stoves combining contemporary design and high heat output), and cook stoves since 1970. The book introduces the stoves, shows the various models with dimensions, log length, heating capacity, and so on, provides installation and operating advice, and is a mine of information on heating with wood and coal. At the back is a list of sources of wood-burning information. Well and clearly written and attractively illustrated with photographs and sketches, this book is well worth owning if you are interested in heating with stoves. When writing to the company, request a list of retail sources in your area. RS

X-16
MAJESTIC COMPANY
P.O. Box 800
Huntington, IN 46450

Built-In Fireplace Catalog, *free, published seasonally, 10 pages, illustrated, color.*

These prefabricated steel built-in fireplaces cost about one-half as much as a masonry fireplace, which, together with the extra energy efficiency, makes them a valuable addition to both new and existing homes. The key element is the triple-wall air-cooling system. This is carefully explained in a technical section at the back of the book, which also describes the easy installation

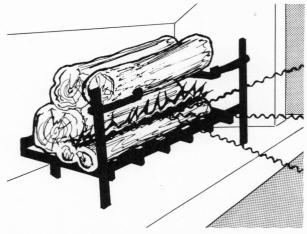

To give more fireplace heat, the Fireframe grate from Texas Fireframe, X-25.

procedures. There are four basic models of fire-box, which can be combined with the mantel of your choice and finished in any style. Additional information on customized fixtures is available from Majestic dealers. RS

X-17
MARTIN INDUSTRIES
P.O. Box 128
Florence, AL 35630

Fireplaces by Martin, Built-in, and Octa-Therm, brochures, 25 cents, illustrated, color.

Martin's "Build-in-Anywhere" fireplaces are designed to be installed by do-it-yourselfers and come with illustrated instructions for building the fireplace into or out from any wall. The Octa-Therm is an energy-saving fireplace that heats more efficiently by drawing in outside air for combustion (unlike a masonry fireplace, which uses room air for combustion). Almost no heated room air is drawn into the fireplace to go up the chimney; instead, the heating air-flow system takes already warm room air through intakes near floor level, reheats it, and returns it to the room through outlets above the fireplace. Outlets are provided for ducting heated air to as many as three rooms with optional blowers for improved heat distribution. Write to the company for dealer information. RS

X-18
MOHAWK INDUSTRIES, INC.
173 Howland Avenue
Adams, MA 01220

Coal and Wood Energy, free booklet, 24 pages, illustrated; also free leaflets on Mohawk products.

If you are thinking of switching to a stove as an alternate form of heating, you will find a lot of pertinent information in this well-written and well-researched booklet put out by a stove manufacturer. For instance, there is a chart that rates the cost of hardwood against other forms of heating, another that shows the BTU output of the different common firewoods and rates them on this, on splitting ease, coals, and sparks. Another section discusses the selection of a wood stove and coping with creosote in the stovepipe and chimney. If you are planning on cutting your own firewood, the booklet tells you what tools are needed, how to cut and trim a tree, and how to split and season the logs. There is a final section on Mohawk's Tempwood stoves, which are

also shown with accessories in a product information leaflet. All of the stoves burn wood; the Tempcoal model also burns coal. Another leaflet covers a damper panel kit that combines with the stove to fill in and seal off a fireplace opening and includes step-by-step installation instructions and a list of the required tools. A third leaflet shows the "Wood Lion" chain-saw adaptor unit, an updated version of the old saw horse. A throttle actuator assembly clamps on to the chain-saw handle and special notches on a tilt-table indicate log lengths. As each log is sawed it drops clear by way of a curved rail. The unit takes logs and trees up to 12' long and 1' in diameter. RS

X-19
NUTONE DIVISION, SCOVILL
Madison & Red Bank Roads
Cincinnati, OH 45227

NuTone—Making Homes Better, $2, published annually, 164 pages, illustrated, color.

NuTone's whole-house ventilators save energy by cooling your house without air conditioning in temperate climates. Hot stale air is pulled from the living areas and exhausted through attic vents, while cooler fresh outdoor air is drawn in through open windows, creating a steady breeze that helps to lower the temperature. An automatic timer shuts the fan off when you don't need it. Louvers in the ceiling open and close automatically with fan operation. The ventilators can be useful even in warm climates, as they mean you use your air conditioner, which uses higher wattage, much less. RS

X-20
PERICULUM
P.O. Box 15
Yellow Springs, OH 45387

Periculum, The Ceiling Fan Specialists, free brochure, published periodically, 8 pages, illustrated, color.

Periculum sells ceiling fans made by Hunter, Emerson, and CasaBlanca plus light fixtures and accessories that you can add to them as you wish. The fans, which range in price from around $90 to over $500, not only cool during the summer but also help to circulate warm air through the room in winter. There are many models from which to choose, in 36" or 52" sizes, with various finishes such as white with white

A vacation house living room planned and decorated to save energy. The wood- and coal-burning stove acts as focal point and a giant decorative cloth window canopy/blind keeps warmth in or keeps sun out. Photographer: Otto Maya.

painted wood blades, brown with natural wood blades, pecan wood finish with natural cane inserts, deep walnut finish, wood and cane, or brass. The light fixtures include a simple white globe (around $30), clusters of frilly Victorian lamp shades, and Tiffany-type shades in various colors and shapes. Any one can be fitted to the fan with the aid of a light adaptor kit. A swag kit enables you to mount a ceiling fan when there is no electrical connection in the ceiling by means of a light cord looped through a chain, a good idea if you want to install a fan in an apartment. A solid-state speed control that allows for variable speeds on all models is also available. MO

X-21
PREWAY, INC.
1430 Second Street North
Wisconsin Rapids, WI 54494

Sensible Fireplaces by Preway, free
brochure, 8 pages, illustrated, color.

The brochure shows Preway's two types of energy-conserving fireplaces, the built-in Energy-Mizer and the free-standing Provider, both with glass doors to keep heated room air from escaping and radiate additional heat. The Energy-Mizer has an air intake that uses outside air for combustion and a built-in warm air return. The Provider has a built-in air circulating fan for rapid home heating as well as an optional air intake kit. To complete the fireplace installations, Preway offers a complete U.L.-listed chimney system. RS

X-22
ROYAL WINDYNE LTD.
1316 West Main Street
Richmond, VA 23220

America's Finest Ceiling Fan, $1, 8 pages,
illustrated, black and white.

Royal Windyne's ceiling fans are hand-built, with blades of tulip poplar, the wood that was used in fans in the late 1800s and early 1900s, and solid brass appointments. The gracefully curved blades, based on turn-of-the-century designs, are cut one at a time, not mass produced, then sanded individually, given five protective coats of finish from stain to sealer to lacquer over

Mini fan, which uses only 15 watts, quietly and
efficiently evens out heat or cold from woodstove or air
conditioner. Ship's Wheel, V-21.

a period of several days, waxed, and hand-buffed. These and other details of hand craftsmanship make these fans more expensive than those of other companies. The fans come in two models, Regular and Supreme, both in 39" and 52" diameters. The Supreme is rather more elaborate and costly—$377 for the 39" size as against $297 for the regular model. There are also five different solid brass light attachments with shades or globes, at an additional charge. Royal Windyne will also make fans to your specifications. MO

X-23
SIERRA WOOD STOVES
P.O. Box 346
Harrisonburg, VA 22801

Hearthstove by Sierra, free color brochure.

Engineered to fit on your fireplace hearth or to be used as a free-standing unit, these wood-burning stoves are made of heavy steel plate with high-density firebrick lining and have cast iron doors and draft regulators. There are three models—the Classic, the Cricket, and the Contemporary—each with slightly different details. They come in two sizes, to take 22" or 27" logs, and cost less than $550. The name of your nearest dealer will be sent on request. RS

X-24
SOUTHPORT STOVES
959 Main Street
Stratford, CT 06497

Free brochures, illustrated, color.

The company imports stoves from Belgium and Denmark. The versatile Efel Kamina from Belgium, an airtight, controlled-draft, long-burning stove and fireplace combination, has both air-circulating heat and radiant heat (from the cast iron construction and glass door). The stove is so constructed as to transfer 85 to 90 percent of its heat into the room and is extremely compact and attractive, 32¼" high x 15" deep x 28" wide with the exterior steel cabinet porcelainized in red, blue, white, beige, dark green, gold, brown, or charcoal gray. When the exterior hood is raised, the cast iron firebox hood can be used as a cooking surface and there is also a barbecue grill attachment. The stove burns either coal or wood; one load of dry hardwood will burn for 12 to 15 hours.

The Danish Morsø cast iron stoves come in seven different models. Some are stove and fire-

Wind-N-Sun shield, a reversible drapery lining for insulating windows against cold and heat. X-26.

place combinations with a bricklined fire chamber. Others are box stoves made with traditional Scandinavian design, some with a heat exchanger—an arch-shaped device that increases the heat output 50 percent by holding the hot smoke in the stove longer and radiating more heat without additional fuel consumption—on top. All the stoves have a porcelain finish. For further information about prices and dealers, write to the importer. Also available at a cost of $1 is the *Morsø Wood Heat Handbook* by Lee Gilchrist. RS

X-25
TEXAS FIREFRAME COMPANY
P.O. Box 3435
Austin, TX 78764

Texas Fireframe Grate, free literature.

For addicts of the open hearth, this grate invented and patented by a Texas physicist offers something new, simple, and eminently practical. The specially-designed grate with adjustable arms for positioning the logs provides a fire that starts more easily and quickly, burns steadily, and throws more heat into the room. Instead of piling the logs one on top of the other, you put

two small logs in the front, a large one at the back, and an upper log on the arms, a more efficient way of arranging wood. There are five different sizes, for small, shallow, standard, large, and extra-large fireplaces, at prices ranging from around $35 to around $80 (shipping extra). MO

X-26
WIND-N-SUN SHIELD, INC.
Box 1434
Melbourne, FL 35935

Silver Lining, free brochure.

The silver lining is the material used in these drapery-liner panels, a silvery reflective polyester on white vinyl backing. When the reflecting side is turned toward the window it throws summer heat outward; reversed, it radiates room heat inward. The panels are 36″ wide x 95″ long and can be joined by adhesive strips for greater width or be cut to desired length. They hook on under draperies and can be pinch-pleated into the same folds. The price per panel is around $18. The company also produces roller blinds of the same material with two sets of brackets for a cost of around $15. MO

Window Quilt, an insulated window shade to winterize rooms and save heat and air conditioning loss. Appropriate Technology, X-1.

WindowBlanket draperies, another decorative way to insulate windows against heat and cold. X-27.

X-27
WINDOWBLANKET COMPANY, INC.
Route 1, Box 83-Y
Lenoir City, TN 37771

Free folder (or 50 cents with fabric swatches), illustrated, color.

By keeping warmth in during cold months and heat and noise out in warm weather, these vertically quilted curtains with polyester fill and polished cotton finish offer an attractive solution to one aspect of the energy problem. They come in white, rust, or tan in a standard 45″ x 84″ size that fits most windows, have tabs that slip over a café-curtain rod, and are protected by Scotchgard into the bargain. One windowBlanket is $51.50 (this includes shipping and handling). Longer curtains can be ordered at a cost of $5 for each 6″ of additional length. MO

Build in Anywhere, a fireplace designed for do-it-yourself installation. Martin Industries, X-17.

XI
Kits, Crafts, and Craft Supplies

XI-1
AEROGEN INDUSTRIES, INC.
P.O. Box 36462
Houston, TX 77036

Build an Heirloom, *free brochures, illustrated, black and white and color.*

The heirloom is a solid wood traditional four-poster bed in kit form, ready to assemble and finish, in twin, double, queen, and king sizes at prices ranging from around $150 for twin to around $250 for king size. Aerogen will also custom-make a kit to any other size you request. Each kit, which the manufacturers say takes only an hour's assembly time, contains four posts, headboard, frame, slats, and hardware. Footboards are optional extras at a slight charge. Two accessory pieces, a two-shelf nightstand and four-shelf étagère, also come in kit form, with spindle posts to match the beds and clear acrylic shelves, at very reasonable prices. MO

XI-2
AMERICAN ART CLAY COMPANY, INC.
4717 West 16th Street
Indianapolis, IN 46222

Art, Craft and Toy Products, *no charge, published annually, 8 pages, illustrated, color.*

This company started over sixty years ago manufacturing Permoplast, a modeling clay for schools. Now in addition to various clays they have other modeling materials, such as Crea-Stone, a lightweight stonelike material in powder form that is mixed with water and cast into shapes, and Claycrete, which has all the qualities of the original papier-mâché but is much easier to prepare. In the do-it-yourself field, they are probably best known for their decorative fin-ishes—Rub 'n Buff metallic finishes, Stain 'n Buff wood finishes, Brush 'n Leaf, a leafing metallic for interiors or exteriors, and Antique 'n Glaze, specially formulated to "age" a surface. These are all simple to use, needing just to be rubbed or brushed on, and can be applied to a wide variety of surfaces. There is also a Batikit Craft Kit—cold water fabric dyes and dye waxes and an introduction to batik techniques with patterns, instructions, and ideas. A Decorative Inspiration Book, $2, shows in 24 color pages how to use all the Rub 'n Buff finishes, which are sold in craft supply shops. MO

XI-3
BENJANE ARTS
320 Hempstead Avenue
West Hempstead, NY 11552

Seashells and Natural Sea Life Specimens, *$3, published annually, 32 pages, illustrated.*

In addition to many beautiful shells and sea life specimens, Benjane sells craft shell packs, collections of shells, and directions for projects such as making a coral wreath, shell mosaic, box or mirror, or decorating a basket. Send $1 and a large self-addressed stamped envelope for each project, specifying the number shown in the four-page brochure. A seashell sampler of 200 assorted shells with shellcraft ideas booklet is $13.50. MO

XI-4
ADELE BISHOP, INC.
P.O. Box HDC
Dorset, VT 05251

Stenciling by Adele Bishop, *$1, published annually, 20 pages, illustrated, color.*

Adele Bishop has long been known for her contributions to the revival of stenciling as an art

Adele Bishop's easy-to-use stencil kit includes precut stencils, brushes, instant-drying paints, and complete how-to instructions. XI-4.

form—particularly her discovery of the see-through stencil and the addition of inked-on register marks that make it possible to place the stencil perfectly, eliminating guesswork and lost time. In this catalogue, probably the best and most professional around, you will find designs that would have been impossible to execute just a few years ago and now can be stenciled on walls, floors, fabrics, and furniture. The stencil kits are mostly traditional American designs; however, one of five Japanese designs taken from ancient family crests would look delightful on a bedspread, screen, canopy, chest, fabric, or wall. There are Early American designs for boxes, tinware, furniture, and walls; Pennsylvania Dutch designs; a rose wreath with tulip design taken from an old quilt that could be used on a floor, fabric, or wall hanging; and some very handsome eighteenth-century designs for stenciling floors or floorcloths (suggested materials for these are canvas, heavy cotton duck, heavy linen, and woven grass or straw matting, protected, like floors, with coats of varnish after stenciling). A Folk Art kit enables you to create your own designs from thirteen stencils—singly, repeated, or in combinations. An incredibly large number of objects and surfaces can be stenciled (note the suggestions on the reverse side of the order sheet). A complete kit contains stencil designs, instructions, brushes, and the instant-drying japan paints produced by Adele Bishop for decorative stenciling, or you can order just the designs and instructions. Prices range from $5.95 to $49.95 according to the number of designs and whether or not you order a complete kit. The paints can be ordered separately in 1-ounce jars or 8-ounce cans (the latter will stencil

four or more average size rooms). Many colors are available, as well as professional brushes in ½", 1" and 1½" diameters, transparent unprinted stencil sheets, a special knife for tracing and cutting your own stencils, and an instructional booklet, *Adele Bishop's Creative and Comprehensive Stenciling Course.* MO

XI-5
BOYCAN'S CRAFT SUPPLIES
P.O. Box 897
Sharon, PA 16146

Boycan's Craft Supplies, *$1 (refundable with purchase), published annually, 116 pages in ring binder, illustrated, black and white.*

A catalogue featuring all manner of supplies for découpage, beadwork, macramé, tole painting, weaving, string art, basketry, needlework, and more offbeat things, such as floral arrangements of artificial materials, dried flowers and foliage, and silk and cloth flowers. There are also wood items and papier-mâché forms for decorating and kits for latch-hook rugs and pillows. Prices are inexpensive. MO

XI-6
BRAID-AID, Dept. HD2
466 Washington Street
Pembroke, MA 02359

Catalogue of Braiding and Hooking Materials, also Quilting, Shirret and Weaving, *$1.50, published quarterly, 88 pages, illustrated, black and white.*

Braided wool rug and hooking kits from Braid-Aid, XI-6.

Braid-Aid offers a complete line of kits for braiding and hooking rugs, pillows, chair seats, footstool covers, runners, and bell pulls, plus all the necessary materials and accessories, as well as books and booklets. They have a collection of over 200 hooking designs—florals, fruits, orientals, and geometrics included—and also sell designer's catalogues of hooking patterns. There's a starter set for shirret, a rug-making technique that combines shirring and crochet; quilting supplies, instructions, and patterns; and yarns, looms, accessories, instructions, and patterns for weaving. There's a great deal of information and equipment packed into this catalogue. Prices are reasonable. MO

XI-7
COUNTRYSIDE BOOKS, Dept. CDC
200 James Street
Barrington, IL 60041

Free catalogue and brochures.

The catalogue lists mainly special-interest books on houseplants, gardening, and landscaping. There are both large format (8¼" x 10½") paperbacks and a series of "Little Books," paperbacks measuring 5½" x 8" at $1.49 each. One of these, *Houseplant Housecrafts,* with text and color photographs by Derek Fell, is full of ideas for offbeat ways to display your plants other than in a plain old pot. There's a hanging planter with diagram and directions that would be very easy to construct. Other containers are shells, lava rock, driftwood, coffee cans covered with wood slats, coconuts, sawn-off wine jugs, even eggshells for miniature plants. The book also covers dish gardens, terrariums, and bottle gardens. Lists of plants suitable for certain containers and planting instructions are provided where necessary. If you can't find it at your bookstore, order it directly from the publishers. MO/RS

XI-8
CREATIVE NEEDLE
Box 8104
Dallas, TX 75205

Creative Needle, $3 (refundable with purchase), published annually, 50 pages, illustrated, color.

Unusual needlepoint kits, designs hand-painted on French canvas and packaged with Persian yarns, that include oriental designs taken from antique porcelains, oriental symbols, exquisite floral designs, shells, butterflies, quilt and zo-diac designs, and samplers. There are also gingham needlepoint pillow designs combined with ribbon stitched to the canvas. Prices range from $4 for a 2" x 4" Christmas ornament tag that could be put on a package to $330 for rug kits with oriental motifs. Designs can be painted to specified colors or on larger canvases than those in the kits. MO

XI-9
DOVER PUBLICATIONS, INC.
180 Varick Street
New York, NY 10014

The Complete Dover Needlecraft Catalogue, free, published annually, 80 pages, illustrated, black and white.

This catalogue contains illustrated descriptions of over 100 craft books in the Dover Needlecraft Series on quilting, patchwork, appliqué, sewing, knitting, crocheting, tatting, and embroidery. Other subjects not related to needlecraft, such as collage and découpage, woodcraft and home improvement, stencils, and stained glass, are also listed. All are paperbound and modestly priced, from $1.50 to $5. MO

XI-10
FURNITURECRAFT, INC.
Box 285c
Stoneham, MA 02180

FurnitureCraft, Inc. Distinctive Early American Furnishings, 50 cents, published semiannually, 32 pages, illustrated, color.

FurnitureCraft has for $38 a charming stylized Americana wall stencil kit composed of five patterns developed in New England during the early nineteenth century. The kit contains precut vinyl stencils, reusable velour applicators, oil paints in six period shades of red, green, blue, yellow, brown, and black, spar varnish, instructions, and a 15-page decorating guide to give you ideas for using the stencils. MO

XI-11
GUILD OF SHAKER CRAFTS, INC.
401 W. Savidge Street
Spring Lake, MI 49456

Shaker Furniture Reproductions, $2.50 (refundable with purchase), published seasonally, 28 pages, illustrated, black and white and color.

Listed under Stitchery are needlepoint and

crewel kits for the famous "Tree of Life" wall piece, for which you can also get a simple pine frame (6" x 6" size is $18 for the kit, $8.50 for the frame). In needlepoint there are the "Dove of Peace" and "Basket of Apples." The "Tree of Life" is also available in a 21" x 27" x 24" (half-moon shape) latch-hooked rug kit, $36. MO

XI-12
HAGERTY COMPANY
38 Parker Avenue
Cohasset, MA 02025

Cohasset Colonials by Hagerty, $1, published semiannually, 38 pages, illustrated, color.

Hagerty offers a wonderful selection of American Colonial furniture copied from originals in museums and private collections that comes in kit form with assembly instructions. A pine blanket chest kit (from an original in Old Sturbridge Village) complete with handmade nails and stencil pattern is $110, plus color pack of the special paint colors, $8.50. A harvest table with pine top and maple legs is $195. There are also such popular pieces as Windsor chairs and settees, a butterfly table, and a hutch cabinet. The catalogue has a two-page section on finishing and books on Early American furniture and lighting, and stenciling. MO

XI-13
HISTORIC CHARLESTON REPRODUCTIONS
51 Meeting Street
Charleston, SC 29401

Historic Charleston Reproductions, $3.50 (refundable with $25 purchase), 56 pages, illustrated, black and white and color.

The needlepoint kits in this catalogue have designs inspired by Charleston architecture, paintings, textiles, prints, birds, and flowers. There's a delightful "Camellia Basket" doorstop or bookend design, taken from an oil painting in the historic Nathaniel Russell house; kits with motifs of Low Country birds such as the white egret, oystercatcher, and blue heron; a kit for a bench cover with a design taken from an exquisite plasterwork ceiling in Drayton Hall; and "Canton Harbor," from an early nineteenth-century Chinese glass painting designed to fit a trumeau mirror or small stool or make a needle-point picture. Prices for the kits range from $12.95 to $95. MO/RS

Interior decorating do-it-yourself kit from Interiors by Arden, XI-14.

XI-14
INTERIORS BY ARDEN
P.O. Box 1503
La Mesa, CA 92041

Arden Graff's Interior Design Kit, $10.95 (includes postage and handling).

Interior designer Arden Graff's do-it-yourself kit contains the basic materials and simple instructions for drawing your own floor plans and working out room settings. It includes a 16" x 21" sheet of graph paper, a large selection of ¼"-scale furniture cutouts, a professional scale ruler with fixture and door-opening templates, and 72 gradated color samples that let you compare different color harmonies and visualize a color scheme. The kit, in softcover book format, also contains pages of decorating tips, guidelines on the use of color and different lighting techniques, a questionnaire to help you determine the most efficient use of available space, and advice on keeping records of home improvement expenses and paid receipts for income tax purposes. MO

XI-15
IROQCRAFTS, LTD.
RR2
Ohsweken, Ontario,
Canada NOA IMO

Indian Crafts, $1 (refundable with purchase), 32 pages, illustrated, black and white, with 2-page color insert.

A large selection of traditional and ceremonial arts and crafts from the Six Nations Reserve, among them Iroquois paintings, watercolors and limited-edition prints, limited-edition Eskimo prints, burlap murals and wall hangings, stohe carvings, baskets, ceramics, wood carvings, masks, and musical instruments. Many are collector's items, some are strictly souvenirs. Craft supplies and books are also included in the catalogue, which could be better organized—it is difficult to correlate the uncaptioned illustrations with their categories and prices. MO

XI-16
LEMAN PUBLICATIONS, INC.
Box 394, Dept. FR
Wheatridge, CO 80033

Quilts & Other Comforts, 50 cents *(refundable with purchase), published annually, 20 pages, illustrated, black and white with some color.*

Everything a dedicated quilter could need. Besides a wide range of metal template sets, plastic and paper patterns and stencils, there are quilt-making supplies including frames, hoops, needles, thread, and batting as well as books on quilting. For beginners there's a patchwork pillow starter kit for around $11, or a patchwork quilt kit with precut 6″ calico print squares and directions that runs from around $16 for a twin-bed coverlet to around $28 for king-size. MO

XI-17
MASON & SULLIVAN COMPANY
39 Blossom Avenue
Caterville, MA 02655

Catalogue of Clock Kits, Movements and Dials, $1, *published seasonally with supplements, 46 pages, illustrated, color.*

The great thing about the clock kits offered by

Family hobby room has weaving looms and yarns from Nasco Handcrafters, XI-18.

Wall clock kits of wood slices are available in choice of woods with battery movement from Weird Wood, XI-36.

Shaker-style precut pine tall clock case kit from Erastus Rude original at Old Chatham Shaker Museum. Mason & Sullivan, XI-17.

Mason & Sullivan, a company that has been in business almost seventy-five years, is the scope they give for all levels of craft skills, from beginning woodworkers to master craftsmen. Simplest is the precut kit, which includes precut frame and base, dial, hardware, and assembly instructions and requires only a screwdriver. The do-it-yourself kit includes blueprint, lumber, and hardware. Other kits have no lumber, just the components, or blueprints only, with specifications, materials list, and assembly instructions. Cases come assembled and either finished or unfinished. Movements and dials are fully assembled. Just about every type of clock kit is available, from wall and mantel types to grandfather clocks. A Willard banjo clock precut kit is $132.50 in mahogany, $143 in walnut; the do-it-yourself versions are $89.60 and $109.50. A simple rectangular desk clock precut kit is a mere $14. There are various dial and movement options for each clock. Mason & Sullivan also sell assembly tools, clock maintenance kits, and books on clock assembly and woodworking. MO

XI-18
NASCO HANDCRAFTERS
1 West Brown Street
Waupun, WI 53963

Arts & Crafts Catalog, 50 cents, published annually, 392 pages, illustrated, black and white.

You should be able to locate just about anything you need for craft projects in this huge catalogue of art and craft supplies. It would be impossible to list all the categories and items, which include supplies for metal enameling, etching, bead- and leathercraft, weaving, and making ceramics, carvings, candles, and tiled accessories. Nasco must have one of the most complete collections of looms, from large professional models (around $500) to small tapestry looms (under $10).

Of special interest to do-it-yourselfers is the section on "decorator crafts" where you'll find lots of useful products such as cork in various sizes and shapes, including cork sheets from 1/16" to 1/4" thick; peel-and-pat velours to apply to walls or accessories; pressure-sensitive foil sheets with a textured metallic plastic-film surface that reflects colors; stained glass; iron-on transfers. The catalogue also features decorator's burlap in every color for 95 cents a yard (77 cents for 50 or more yards), monk's cloth, unbleached muslin, and felt. Nasco sells a few craft books and the Butterick crafts program—audiovisual kits that come with color filmstrips, cassettes, charts, and teaching guide—covering stitchery and appliqué, needlepoint and bargello, patchwork and quilting, off-loom weaving and basketry, and decorative machine stitching, $65 each or a complete set of five for $275. MO

XI-19
OLDSTONE ENTERPRISES
77 Summer Street
Boston, MA 02110

Oldstone Enterprises Rubbing Materials,
free brochure, illustrated, black and white.

Oldstone sells two complete rubbing kits, "The Original Oldstone Rubbing Kit," $9.50 postpaid, and a child's rubbing kit for $3.50 postpaid. The Oldstone kit contains five sheets of rubbing paper, two cakes of rubbing wax in black and brown, tape to hold the paper, a bristle brush for cleaning the surface, and *Oldstone's Guide to Creative Rubbing,* all packaged in a leatherette case. Also available are sheets of rubbing paper, cakes of rubbing wax in red, orange, blue, green, brown, black, silver, and gold, and pie-shaped wedges of the same colors. MO

XI-20
PEACOCK ALLEY
650 Croswell Street, SE
Grand Rapids, MI 49506

Needlepoint brochure, $2, 20 pages,
illustrated, color.

Interesting and original designs hand-painted on single-mesh white French canvas, Persian yarns, a needle, and complete instructions come in the needlepoint kits from Peacock Alley. There are straps for luggage with a design of pineapples or strawberries ($33.50 the set of 3), a shell motif cover for a brick doorstop ($22.50), enchanting sachet covers complete with backing, ruffle, and sachet ($11), and many Christmas items—tree ornaments, stockings, wall and door hangings, and a tree skirt panel. The many pillow designs are especially enchanting—Swiss wildflowers, a Persian bird, a black and white Moses Eaton stencil design, oriental motifs, a Rousseau-like cheetah, owls and a pussycat up a tree, a bargello fish, a Hawaiian quilt design, and a cluster of morning glories. Rugs include a 3' x 4' size with panels and border of wildflowers, and a 36"-diameter round rug patterned with tulips ($153). Custom designing is also available. Write for estimates. MO

Stone-rubbing kit from Oldstone Enterprises, XI-19.

XI-21
PEERLESS RATTAN
P.O. Box 8
Towaco, NJ 07082

Peerless Rattan Catalogue, no charge, 16
pages, illustrated, black and white.

If you are wondering about the difference between cane and rattan, cane is the outside bark of rattan, a jungle vine of Borneo, Sumatra, and Malaysia. Peeled and shaved to a proper width and thickness, cane has been used for centuries for chair seats (prewoven cane webbing was not used until the end of the nineteenth century) and if the chair seat has drilled holes around it, it must be caned by hand with strand cane. Peerless sells strand cane in various diameters to fit the holes, binding cane for finishing, plus various types of cane webbing—open, close-woven, radio net, and medium Swedish loose weave for chairs with a routed groove around the top of the seat opening. The webbing comes in widths from 12" to 36" and is sold by the foot or in 10- or 25-foot rolls. Other items in the catalogue include fiber rush, seagrass, reed and ash splits, reeds for basketry and basketry bases, natural rattan and raffia, caning tools, a chair caning kit at $4.95, books on resplinting, recaning and rerushing chairs, restoring wicker furniture, and weaving chair seats. Peerless points out that chair caning is a skill easily learned and one that can become a profitable business. They also offer stool and chair frames and kits at very reasonable prices. A cane stool kit costs around $15, a rush stool kit around $13; a simple basic stool frame costs only $4 or $5, a child's chair frame around $10. MO

XI-22
PLAN-IT-KIT, INC.
Box 429
Westport, CT 06880

Free folder, illustrated, black and white.

The 3-D Plan-It-Kit for room arrangements enables you to work out on graph paper possible furniture combinations with lightweight styrofoam miniatures, made to scale. The kit, which costs $9.98 plus $1.25 postage, comes with 57 furniture modules, cardboard walls, windows, and doors in standard sizes with gummed backs, and an 8-page illustrated booklet with instructions and design pointers. For $13 plus $1.25 postage you get the kit plus a punch-out template furniture arranging kit. MO

XI-23
THE PRINCETON COMPANY
P.O. Box 276
Princeton, MA 01541

The Princeton Company—Tools For Proud Craftsmanship, $1, published annually, 30 pages, illustrated, color.

A superior collection of woodworking devices, large and small. Their two all-wood cabinetmaker's work-center benches look great. One, for $395, in red beech and white birch, incorporates its own full-sized cabinet and drawer system. The other, for $399, in darker kiln-dried Danish beech, is designed around a "four-point bench dog surface hold" that can grip every conceivable workpiece, no matter how oddly shaped, up to 51". The smaller items include beautiful selections of German chisels and other carving implements such as a five-piece Firmer gouge set for $53, screwdriver sets, vices and saws, a jumbo bag of 1600 springs for $3.95, and a professional latex paint spraying kit for $89.95. Sections on garden hardware, woodworking books, and tool-care equipment are also included. MO

Three-dimensional room arrangement Plan-It-Kit. XI-22.

XI-24
RAINBOW ART GLASS, Dept. CHC2
49 Shark River Road
Neptune, NJ 07753

Adventures with Color and Light, $1 (refundable with purchase), published semiannually, 14 pages, illustrated, color.

Most of the styles and models of Tiffany-type lamps, stained-glass ceiling panels, clocks, mirrors, and terrariums offered assembled by Rainbow Art Glass are also available in kit form at a lower cost. The glass has already been cut to shape—all that remains is to copper-foil the pieces, solder, and assemble according to the instructions. All necessary materials are included. Prices range from around $21 to just over $300 for a lamp with shade containing 850 glass pieces. MO

XI-25
ROBERTS INDIAN CRAFTS
& BEADING SUPPLIES
404 West Virginia Street
Anadarko, OK 73005

Free price lists.

Craft supplies including beads, bells, thongs, shells, horsehair, fringe, feathers, needles for beading, and thread are Roberts' stock in trade. MO

XI-26
SCANDINAVIAN RYA RUGS
P.O. Box 447
Bloomfield Hills, MI 48013

Cum Rya, $2, published every 3 or 4 years, 32 pages, illustrated, color.

The color catalogue shows 27 rya rugs and nine pillows, available in kits complete with woven rya backing of the required size, 100 percent wool yarn, a gauge for the knotting, needles, pattern, and directions. Two pages of the catalogue illustrate the rya technique and give instructions. The rugs come in various sizes from 2' x 4' to 6' 9" x 10', round and square. The kits are fairly expensive, ranging from $89 for a 2' x 4' rug with ¾" pile to $698 for the largest rug with 1½" pile, but backings and yarn are available separately, and it is possible to make your own designs if you have some skill. MO

XI-27
JANE SNEAD SAMPLERS
Box 4909
Philadelphia, PA 19144

Jane Snead Samplers, 35 cents, published annually, 48 pages, illustrated, black and white.

A comprehensive and charming collection of samplers and sampler kits in all sizes and shapes to enliven bedroom, bathroom, kitchen, and nursery. Some are amusing, some patriotic, some inspirational, some personalized, some traditional. There are also pincushion sampler kits, 4" x 4¾" at $1.60, plus sawdust stuffing ($1). Prices are very reasonable. MO

XI-28
STEARNS & FOSTER
P.O. Box 15380
Cincinnati, OH 45215

Stearns & Foster Catalogue of Quilt Patterns, Designs and Needle Craft Supplies, $2, published periodically, 72 pages, illustrated, black and white.

The catalogue is beautifully illustrated with clear sketches of the 130 quilt patterns offered by Stearns & Foster and sold through the Creative Quilting Center of the company. The patterns extend from antique to modern, floral to geometric, and include the old-fashioned Double Wedding Ring, Tree of Paradise, and Lone Star, some interesting Hawaiian designs like the Hala Tree, an appliqué quilt, and a quick-to-make bandanna quilt for beginners. There's an interesting description of each pattern and, where applicable, its history and background. At the back of the catalogue are basic instructions for making quilts or comforters and advice on how to care for them. MO

XI-29
STENCIL MAGIC
8 West 19th Street
New York, NY 10011

Stencil Magic, 50 cents, published quarterly, 10 pages plus flyers, illustrated, black and white.

Stencil Magic offers a variety: precut, re-usable plastic stencils in natural motifs, 9½" x 12½", packaged with instructions ($2.50); modular precut stencils containing different motifs that can be combined in designs of your own creation ($3.98); patterns from which you can cut out your own stencils; and stencil kits for aprons, labels, Christmas and note cards, and place mats (the stencils, of course, are re-usable for other projects after you have made the apron or mats that come with the kit). Kits include paints, stencil brush, and instructions. The company sells supplies such as stencil paper, brushes, and knives, as well as a *Beginner's Guide to Stencil Decorating* with fifteen projects for fabric, wood, walls, and floors based on six decorator stencils ($2.98). MO

Rollerwall design kit for easy wall decorations. II-26.

XI-30
THE STITCHERY, Dept. E-900
204 Worcester Turnpike
Wellesley, MA 02181

The Stitchery, 50 cents, published seasonally, 64 pages, illustrated, color.

A large selection of needlecraft designs and kits for pictures, tablecloths, pillows, place mats, quilts, guest towels, boxes, rugs, bookmarks—even a needlepoint backgammon board (around $40; cups, dice, and playing pieces extra). Cross-stitch, embroidery, needlepoint, and crewel are included, as are some attractive latch-hook rugs and an afghan knitted in a pattern stitch that creates a reversible design, 42" x 62", $32.50. There's a lovely white-on-white pineapple pattern quilt top, stitched in squares so it makes an easily portable project. You'll also find handsome quickpoint pillows, easy enough for beginners, delightful red, white, and green calico holiday decorations in kit form, and crewel tree ornaments. MO

XI-31
SUDBERRY HOUSE
Box 421
Old Lyme, CT 06371

Sudberry House, $2 (refundable with purchase), published annually, 24 pages, illustrated, color.

Sudberry House specializes in wood products to complement and contain needlework—trays with glass or plexiglass to cover the work, game boards, coasters, tray tables, a luggage rack, mirrors that display the needlework in the upper part of the frame, a screen, picture frames, footstools, a magazine rack, and various boxes. They now have a section of gift items in which art prints are used to decorate a magazine rack and trays, plus trays and mirrors for other crafts, such as a shell collection, tinsel painting, and theorem painting. Then there's the Sudberry yarn palette, which organizes 23 yarn colors for easy access when you are working on needlepoint. A useful list of sources for the needlework designs illustrated in the catalogue is included. The sizes listed with each item give the exact measurements of the visible design area, but designs should be outlined and stitched at least ½" larger than this. Prices range from around $8 for a trivet to $120 for a child's chair. MO/RS

XI-32
T.I.E. LTD.
P.O. Box 1121
San Mateo, CA 94403

Creative Caning, brochure, 25 cents (refundable with purchase).

Kits of prewoven cane for repairing chair seats, screens, stereo speakers, door panels, and so on, complete with materials, instructions, and one sheet of cane. There are three basic sizes: a 12" x 12" cane sheet kit is $9 postpaid, an 18" x 18" kit is $13, and a 24" x 24" kit is $18.50; other sizes can be made to fit your needs. You can also order prewoven cane in different widths (priced by the linear foot) and other caning supplies such as round reeds, split reed, and paper rush. MO

XI-33
THE UNICORN
P.O. Box 645
Rockville, MD 20851

Textile and Craft Books, list and order form, $1, published annually, 24 pages.

A very wide selection of books and booklets on crafts are carried by The Unicorn, a company that will also obtain for you books not in the catalogue, provided they are still in print. Among the subjects covered are weaving, macramé, North American Indian crafts, folk art, Navajo rugs, spinning and dyeing, embroidery and needlepoint, appliqué and patchwork, quilting, batik, basketry, glassworking, metalworking, woodworking (which includes cabinetmaking, carpentry, and building), and enameling. MO

XI-34
VIKING CLOCK COMPANY, Dept. HD
P.O. Box 490
Foley, AL 36535

Viking Clock Catalogue, $1, published semiannually, 16 pages, illustrated, color.

Many and varied clocks, in kit form or assembled and finished. There are grandfather clocks, an 8-day key-wind schoolhouse clock, a carriage clock, a banjo clock, an amusing Victorian teardrop mantel clock, eccentric in shape ($125 for kit with movement, $168 finished), and a Bavarian regulator wall clock. The company also sells some furniture, in kit form or finished. MO

XI-35
WAKE'DA TRADING POST
P.O. Box 19146
Sacramento, CA 95819

Beads, Feathers, Indian Craft Supplies, 50 cents, 12 pages, illustrated, black and white.

The Trading Post specializes in American Indian crafts and craft supplies of all kinds—beads, bells, feathers, hides and furs, and shells. The

Chilkat blankets, silk-screened on a burlap-like material, make unusual wall hangings. The catalogue lists hundreds of items with prices. There are also books on Indian crafts. Should you want to make your own Sioux tipi, you can get the poles, covers, liners, a grommet kit, canvas, and stovepipe ring. MO

XI-36
WEIRD WOOD
Green Mountain Cabins, Inc.
P.O. Box 190 CD
Chester, VT 05143

Weird Wood, brochure, 25 cents, illustrated, black and white.

This company has some interesting clock kits made from pieces of round-edge plank, with plain or rough-sanded face, cut 8″ to 12″ wide x 14″ long and routed at the back for the clock movement supplied. Black or brass hour and minute hands and matching markers, finishing instructions, and clock face template are included. These are priced from $17.95 for white cedar to $22.95 for maple or cherry. Finishing materials and kits are also available. MO

XI-37
JANE WHITMIRE
2353 South Meade Street
Arlington, VA 22202

Museum Masterpiece Needlepoint, $1, published annually, 16 pages, illustrated, black and white.

Jane Whitmire's needlepoint kits are unusual because they are based on designs derived from folk art, art, and needlework she discovered on her world travels, or on original designs that echo modern art trends. The fascinating collection of designs includes a Byzantine eagle from the eleventh century; a Coptic cupid; a Greek peacock from peasant embroidery; a Scythian horse; Imari and Persian patterns; a rhinoceros from a Dürer etching; an adaptation of an Ashanti chief's richly patterned robe; an American primitive cat; and William the Conqueror's boat from the Bayeux tapestry of the Norman invasion of England. There is also a vibrant modern collage, an unusual mixture of 26 pure bright colors and subtle neutrals on a white background. The kits include imported canvases and Persian wools, Irish linen and English crewel wool for crewel kits. Prices range from $10 for pincushion kits to $150 for a 5′-long wall hanging

Stenciled window shades, trim, wall, and floor from precut design kits. Stencil Magic, XI-29.

Decorative needlework pillow kits by Jane Whitmire, XI-37.

adapted from a West African textile pattern. The catalogue also offers Sheraton footstools and a firescreen to display your needlework. MO

XI-38
WORLD ARTS
Box 2008
Covina, CA 91722

Catalogue, 20 cents, 12 pages, illustrated, black and white.

Despite the grandiose name, the World Arts catalogue has a limited selection of items with no apparent theme, among them stained glass lamp kits in two styles at $37.95. They will also transfer your photos to fabric or canvas for crewel or needlepoint pictures. MO

XI-39
YIELD HOUSE, INC.
Route 6
North Conway, NH 03860

Yield House, free, published quarterly, 74 pages, illustrated, color.

This catalogue contains a very extensive collection of traditional pine furniture, sold either finished or in Easy Kit form, ready to assemble and finish at a considerable saving. The kits require only a screwdriver and hammer to assemble the presanded, unfinished wood pieces. Screws, hardware, and instructions are included. Yield House also sells finishing kits with stain, sealer, wax, buffing supplies, and instructions, as well as stencil kits. The pieces of furniture available in kits are too numerous to mention, but include just about everything from a rolltop desk to a magazine rack. MO

Authentic Shaker reproductions in prefinished, ready-to-assemble kits from Cohasset Colonials, Hagerty, XI-12.

XII
Kitchens and Bathrooms

XII-1
ABITARE
212 East 57th Street
New York, NY 10022

Abitare, $10, published annually, 234 pages in ring binder, illustrated, black and white.

Abitare's collection of stunning international designs in home furnishings includes beautifully spare and extremely functional bathroom accessories, which mount to the wall with expansion plugs. The toilet tissue holder is the only one we have seen that really makes sense—a twist of chromed brass over which the roll slips easily. The towel holders are equally practical and simple. MO/RS

XII-2
ALLMILMÖ CORPORATION
P.O. Box 629
70 Clinton Road
Fairfield, NJ 07006

Allmilmö Main Square Catalogue, and Aktuell brochure, $3, 55 pages and 24 pages, illustrated, color.

Allmilmö is a European company with branches in many countries and the kitchen cabinets they produce, mainly of wood but also of high-quality plastic, are fantastic examples of contemporary and traditional design. Their catalogue is magnificently produced and filled with pictures of marvelous kitchens, each one a temptation. Craftsmanship and styling are impeccable and the contemporary designs far exceed anything we have seen recently. Write for the name of your nearest dealer. RS

XII-3
ARISTOKRAFT
P.O. Box 420
Jasper, IN 47546

Center of Family Living, 50 cents, folder of 23 loose pages, illustrated, black and white and color.

AristOKraft cabinets are available in various wood finishes and include all the usual kitchen wall and base cabinets, plus a linen closet with or without hamper, cabinets to take ovens, ranges, and sinks, and cabinets with partitioned drawers. There's also a sheet of assembly instructions for making a hutch from wall and base cabinets. Cabinets are shown in color and in sketch form on specification sheets. RS

XII-4
ARTISTIC BRASS
3136 East 11th Street
Los Angeles, CA 90023

Decorative Bathroom Faucets and Accessories, $2, 26 pages plus loose sheets on different collections, illustrated, color.

Luxurious and expensive bathroom accessories are the specialty of Artistic Brass. You'll find tub, sink, and shower sets, tissue holders, towel rings and bars, drawer knobs, soap, tumbler, and toothbrush holders, tank handles, and bidet fittings. Plain or etched brass fixtures are combined with crystal, porcelain, fine-grained lacquered ash, malachite, marble or onyx. A fabulous Gem collection incorporates 11 different semiprecious stones, including rose quartz and tigereye. The Tomorrow line is sleek, clean-lined, and contemporary in design; Delicious! is a far-out collection of sculptured chrome and Lucite bath faucets and accessories with sphere handles in brilliant decorator colors. There's something for every taste here. Specifications are included, but as the company sells only through wholesalers you should write for the name of your nearest dealer. RS

XII-5
BRADLEY CORPORATION
FAUCET DIVISION
P.O. Box 348
Menomonee Falls, WI 53051

Vanity Top Catalogue, no charge, 10 pages, illustrated, color.

The catalogue shows the company's marbleized vanity tops and two-handle or single-control faucets and shower controls. They also have a free brochure of nine decorator faucets of various types and finishes for kitchen and bath. Parisian, a delicate pattern of violets on white china, is especially charming. RS

XII-6
CONRAN'S MAIL ORDER
145 Huguenot Street
New Rochelle, NY 10805

Conran's, $2.50, published annually, 112 pages, illustrated, color.

Kitchens, kitchen equipment, and cookware figure largely in Conran's comprehensive catalogue. The Country Kitchen line features attractive, simple cabinets and shelf units in natural pine with protective clear lacquer finish. Drawers have the Conran touch—fingerholes instead of knobs—and are lined with easy-to-clean white plastic. A base cabinet costs around $250, a shelf unit, $85. Worktops for the base cabinet are available in two finishes—cream laminate or iroko, a tough African hardwood, oiled for easy care. Units come QA (quickly assembled), packed in cartons, and you complete the assembly at home. Other good kitchen items are metal grids to hang on a wall or overhead for pan and tool storage and handsome plain wood pieces such as a slatted rack for draining dishes, towel holders, spice racks, and simple shelves with hooks for cups or slots for knives.

For bathrooms, there are numerous accessories in light sunny pine finished in polyurethane lacquer, or white or dark-brown plastic, running the gamut from cabinets to towel rails, with holders for everything imaginable. There's also a practical solid beech slatted bath mat that could be used indoors or out, 16" x 24", around $14. Towels and shower curtains are included in this section. MO/RS

XII-7
COUNTRY FLOORS
300 East 61st Street
New York, NY 10021

Ceramic Tiles for Floors and Walls, $5 (refundable with purchase), published annually, 34 pages in folder, illustrated, color.

Country Tiles has oval and round sinks designed to coordinate with their Mexican wall or countertop tiles, plus a line of matching accessories including soap, paper, and toothbrush holders, hooks, and switch plates. There are also porcelain bath accessories from Italy, sleek, contemporary, and functional in style, available in white and colors. MO/RS/ID

XII-8
ELJER PLUMBINGWARE
Wallace Murray Corporation
Three Gateway Center
Pittsburgh, PA 15222

The Gallery Collection by Eljer, 25 cents, updated as necessary, 8 pages, illustrated, color.

These modern lavatories, tubs, sinks, and toilets are available in four attractive decorator shades of fiberglass, enameled cast iron, and vitreous china. One of the tubs is a total-immersion circular model, another is fitted with whirlpool hydrojets. There are also two lines of contemporary crystal and brass fittings. Schematic diagrams and measurements are included for all fixtures. RS

XII-9
ELON, INCORPORATED
198 Saw Mill River Road
Elmsford, NY 10523

Elon Tiles, $1, 16 pages, illustrated, color.

In addition to their charming rustic Mexican floor and wall tiles, many of which would add a decorative touch to a kitchen or bathroom, Elon has a line of Carillo handmade round or oval sinks designed to coordinate in color and design with a tiled countertop. A faucet and spout set

and various accessories such as a towel rail, soap dish, toilet-roll holder, and toothbrush-and-tumbler holder can also be found here. Prices on request. MO/RS/ID

XII-10
HAAS CABINET COMPANY, INC.
625 West Utica Street
Sellersburg, IN 47172

Do It Yourself Kitchen Guide, 50 cents, 10 pages, and *Haas Design Guide: Kitchen Cabinets, Vanities, Modular Wall Units,* free, 8 pages; both illustrated, color.

The kitchen guide provides ideas for planning different arrangements of equipment and cabinets, as well as sketches of the different types of wall, base, and corner cabinets available, with dimensions, and a graph for working out your plan. There's also a step-by-step guide to the installation of Haas cabinets.

The design guide shows the various styles of wood cabinets offered by Haas with sketches of all the types available, complete with measurements and technical specifications. RS

Geneva custom-fitted kitchen cabinets in oak with rollout or stationary shelves by Rutt, XII-20.

Limoges porcelain lavatory set from Artistic Brass, XII-4.

White porcelain basin set from Guerin, IX-18.

Mirrored chrome free-form sculptural turn-taps, door knobs, and drawer pulls from Sherle Wagner, XII-21.

XII-11
JACUZZI WHIRLPOOL BATH, INC.
P.O. Drawer J
Walnut Creek, CA 94596

The 1980 Jacuzzi Whirlpool Baths, free, 26 pages, and The 1980 Jacuzzi Whirlpool Spas, free, 10 pages; both illustrated, color.

The ten whirlpool baths in the first catalogue are shown in photographs and full-color schematic diagrams, with accompanying text. The tubs are standard or outsize and hold from one to four people. The three spas featured in the second catalogue are roomier—the largest seats up to eight; it comes in kit form, but should be installed by a professional. Also shown are two redwood hot tubs with Jacuzzi hydromassage and portable water-circulating units. As these catalogues are revised every year, the current offerings may be somewhat different. RS

XII-12
KITCHENAID DIVISION, HOBART CORPORATION
World Headquarters Avenue
Troy, OH 45374

KitchenAid Does Beautiful Things for a Kitchen, free brochure, 8 pages, illustrated, color.

Four models of dishwashers—the Custom, Im-perial, Patrician, and top-of-the-line Superba, which has more cycles and features than the others, such as a 16-position upper rack, small-items basket, and fast-wash cycle—are shown. Specifications, installation data, water consumption, and other useful information are given. Also shown are the newest 190°F hot-water dispenser, waste disposer, and trash compactor, again with specifications, dimensions, and other information. RS

XII-13
KOHLER COMPANY
Kohler, WI 53044

Kohler Elegance. Great Ideas for Bathrooms, Powder Rooms and Kitchens, 50 cents, published annually, 40 pages, illustrated, color.

Kohler is a highly respected name in plumbing products and the latest idea-book-cum-catalogue we received is a fantasy of the most luxurious and beautiful bathroom equipment. Excellent color photographs show off Kohler fixtures in settings from Victorian nostalgic to rustic avant-garde. There's an amazing variety of baths, including whirlpool baths; a chin-deep steeping bath; a biggest-ever bathtub, nearly 5½' x 7'; a corner bath; and a marvelous old-fashioned cast iron tub, glossily enameled in red, black, parchment, or white with feet and faucets that can be given a 24-karat gold finish for sheer elegance. Most spectacular and alluring of all, though, are the specialized environment modules—wall booths that can be programmed for heat, sun, rain, steam, and warm breeze effects to provide a synthesis of man's natural environment (with optional stereo radio and tape player). This has to be the ultimate in climate engineering and health equipment. In addition, there is an extensive collection of Kohler's other fixtures, such as lavatories in various shapes and colors, toilets, a bidet, fiberglass bathing modules, kitchen and bar sinks and faucets, bathroom faucets, and shower heads. A well-conceived booklet that provides product information, color choices, and decorating ideas in a most inspiring way. RS

XII-14
MERILLAT INDUSTRIES, INCORPORATED
2075 West Beecher Road
Adrian, MI 49221

Merillat Kitchen Cabinets, 75 cents, 12 *pages, illustrated, color.*

The brochure shows and describes Merillat's five lines of cabinets in oak or oak-grain plastic laminate. The cabinets offer such features as self-closing hinges, adjustable shelves, wipe-clean interiors, slide-out trays, and Lazy Susan wall and base cabinets. Each line is shown in a kitchen setting. RS

XII-15
THE NATIONAL KITCHEN CABINET ASSOCIATION, Dept. CM
P.O. Box 2978
Grand Central Station
New York, NY 10017

Kitchen and Bath Planning, 35 cents, 16 *pages, illustrated, color.*

A booklet that tells you how to provide for your storage needs with different types of cabinets and gives general advice on planning a new or remodeled kitchen and bath. There is a useful sketch showing work heights and cabinet dimensions. MO

XII-16
NUTONE DIVISION, SCOVILL
Madison & Red Bank Roads
Cincinnati, OH 45227

NuTone—Making Homes Better, $2, *published annually, 164 pages, illustrated, color.*

Keystone oak cabinets in a country kitchen from AristOKraft, XII-3.

NuTone has been developing new products for the home and updating existing ones for over forty years. This extensive catalogue contains a sizable selection of bathroom cabinets (over 78 models) and accessories, such as shower rods, towel rings and bars, soap dishes, scales, switch plates, and valance lighting for mirrors, vanities, and storage cabinets.

Some of the other items in this jam-packed catalogue are kitchen range hoods; the NuTone food center, a built-in machine that takes a food processor, blender, mixer, and other electrical appliances; a central cleaning system that keeps the vacuum motor permanently out of sight and operates by means of a hose for the tools that plugs into outlets in the various rooms; and electronic garage-door openers. Each of the products is shown in a color photograph, with detailed specifications. RS

XII-17
PERIOD FURNITURE HARDWARE COMPANY, INC.
123 Charles Street
Boston, MA 02114

Heritage Collection of Fine Hardware and Bath Accessories, $2, *published biennially, 124 pages, illustrated, color.*

The Heritage Collection covers designs to complement any style of bathroom from colonial to

Store tall and bulky bottles neatly in wasted space under refrigerator shelves in vinyl-coated cradle. Organize your flatware in a five-compartment white vinyl-coated wire tray. Both from The Silo, VIII-18.

contemporary. Materials and finishes are equally varied—polished brass and chrome, French bronze, pewter, porcelain, clear or colored acrylic, wrought iron, and wood. There are faucets, fittings for tubs and showers, lavatories, hooks, mirrors, switch plates, towel rails, soap holders, and a good selection of door and cabinet hardware. No prices. RS

XII-18
POGGENPOHL USA CORPORATION
P.O. Box 10
Teaneck, NJ 07666

The Ultimate Kitchen, *144 pages, and* ***Poggenpohl Bath Catalogue,*** *20 pages, $5.50 for the two catalogues, published annually, illustrated, color.*

Poggenpohl, a German company that has been manufacturing trendsetting kitchen furniture for over eighty years and built one of the first mass-produced modern fitted kitchens as early as 1950, has produced one of the most stunning and beautiful kitchen catalogues we have ever seen. Their lines encompass a tremendous variety of cabinets that incorporate the latest improve-

ments in international conceptual design, in traditional as well as contemporary styles. The catalogue shows many examples of beautifully designed and handsome kitchens, suitable for different spaces and families, that provide infinite inspiration for the kitchen planner. It includes close-ups of different worktop surfaces, suggested color combinations for worktops and front finishes, kitchen information for home builders with checklists of the requirements, and pages on pages of the finishes, units, accessories, and other equipment available (with metric measurements, so be prepared to convert).

While not as extensive as the kitchen catalogue, the bathroom catalogue offers some great designs and ground plans for contemporary bathrooms using Poggenpohl cabinets and storage units in a choice of six laminate fronts in color and four solid wood fronts; countertops; and self-rimming sinks in white or colors. RS

XII-19
THE RENOVATOR'S SUPPLY
71 Northfield Road
Miller's Falls, MA 01349

The Renovator's Supply, *$2 (refundable with purchase), 48 pages, illustrated, black and white.*

If you are looking for Victorian faucets with porcelain caps for your restored house, Renovator's Supply has them, as well as solid brass Victorian towel holders, tissue and toothbrush-tumbler holders, an old-fashioned brass faucet set, and a hard-to-find brass tub drain and overflow. Prices are reasonable. MO

XII-20
RUTT CUSTOM KITCHENS
Route 23
Goodville, PA 17528

Contemporary Kitchens by Rutt, *$1, 18 pages, illustrated, color.*

Rutt's classic and contemporary cabinets, in oak or cherry wood, are made to the highest quality specifications, of 6 percent moisture content wood, and hand finished. The contemporary lines are beautiful, especially the Geneva, which uses ultramodern styling to emphasize to an extraordinary degree the lush natural characteristics of the wood. Authorized dealers will custom-design and install cabinets, appliances, and accessories, with all plumbing and electrical connections. RS

XII-21
SHERLE WAGNER INTERNATIONAL, INC.
60 East 57th Street
New York, NY 10022

Sherle Wagner Catalogue, $5, 82 pages, illustrated, color, with supplement on **The Sherle Wagner Tile Collection.**

The Sherle Wagner name in bath fittings and accessories is the equivalent of Rolls Royce—the finest, most luxurious, and expensive. This superbly produced and illustrated catalogue presents the full line of traditional designs and contemporary designs in basin and tub hardware—in such materials as brushed chrome, antique pewter, 24-karat gold plate (often combined with onyx, malachite, rose quartz, and other precious minerals)—and a fabulous assortment of basins and lavatories. The China Collection has beautiful hand-painted porcelain bowls and matching accessories—soap dishes, towel bars, switch plates, even coordinated wallcoverings, tiles, wastebaskets, doorknobs, and drawer pulls. There are counters of semi-precious stone with matching basin sets, shell-shaped pedestal lavatories, marble lavatories, hand-painted lavatories with sinuous Art Nouveau curves, and console lavatories with slim bamboo or reeded metal legs. Everything for the well-dressed bathroom has been gathered together in this catalogue down to elaborate sconces, crystal ceiling lights, door levers and knobs, hinges, medicine cabinets, and chaises percées. Even Hollywood couldn't top this. Prices, naturally, are high. MO/RS/ID

XII-22
THERMADOR/WASTE KING
5119 District Boulevard
Los Angeles, CA 90040

Waste King, Quality Kitchen Appliances, free brochure, *and* **Thermador,** *free, 20 pages, illustrated, black and white.*

The Waste King brochure features three dishwasher models, two of which have an innovative steam-clean cycle that softens food soil on dishes. One also has an electronic-delay start button that enables you to operate the dishwasher during off-peak hours or when you are away from home. Also shown are five waste disposers, two gas-fired barbecues with optional rotisserie, and trash compactors with optional cutting board tops.

The Thermador catalogue features a wide variety of microwave and conventional oven combinations, microwave ovens with a self-cleaning conventional oven below, and separate microwave and self-cleaning ovens, as well as regular and Thermaglas cooktops, warming ovens, gas-fired barbecues, hoods, dishwashers, trash compactors, ventilators, turbo-fan heaters for walls, and a built-in can opener. Specifications come with each model and complete installation instructions are available. RS

XII-23
TOUCH OF CLASS
North Hampshire Common
North Conway, NH 03860

Touch of Class, $1 (refundable with purchase), published semiannually, 20 pages, illustrated, color.

Touch of Class has some unusual and attractive bathroom accessories in solid oak, among them a standard-size toilet seat, wall cabinet, towel bar, switch plates, wastebasket, holders for tissues, toilet paper, and toothbrushes, and even an oak bathroom scale ($33). We also noticed a pretty hand-painted porcelain tumbler and soap dish set ($10), shower curtain, and boxes with a rainbow motif, as well as two very amusing shower curtains, one with Kliban's Supercat as a motif, the other with a telephone booth screen-printed on vinyl ($18). A good source for something different for the bathroom. MO

Victorian-style white china wash basin and faucet set in a pretty bath designed by Keith Irvine and Thomas Fleming. Sherle Wagner, XII-21.

Solarium/bath custom designed of slip-proof ceramic tile by American Olean, II-5.

Rose-colored onyx center-of-the-room tub with hand-painted porcelain fittings in a luxurious bath designed by Keith Irvine and Thomas Fleming. Sherle Wagner, XII-21.

Compact, contemporary kitchen with cabinet fronts of laminated plastic, pulls and trim of light oak. Allmílmö, XII-2.

XII-24
TUB-MASTER CORPORATION
413 Virginia Drive
Orlando, FL 32803

Tub-Master Folding Shower Doors, free 8-page color brochure.

Tub-Master makes pleated doors that operate on the bypassing principle of standard glass doors for showering, but can also fold completely back for bathing so the tub area is open (this also makes tub cleaning easier). The styles: "B" deluxe; "F" standard; and "FD," standard with built-in swing-out drying rack for light laundry. Frames come in gold or silver anodized aluminum, panels in translucent white, gold flake, or silver flake with a choice of decorator color hinges. Tub-Master also has folding doors for small shower stalls and will make custom enclosures for corner tubs and showers. No matter what size or shape your tub or shower is, the company probably has a door available to fit. Custom units are available on special order through Tub-Master dealers. Write to the company for the name of your nearest retail source. RS

XII-25
THE VIKING SAUNA COMPANY
P.O. Box 6298
San Jose, CA 95150

The Whirlpool Bath by Viking, free, published annually, 8 pages, illustrated, color.

Whirlpool baths are designed primarily for indoor use, and provide luxurious hydromassage in a wide selection of tub shapes, sizes, styles, and prices. For minor additional charges, these baths can be customized to match your bathroom scheme. RS

XII-26
WHITE–WESTINGHOUSE
APPLIANCE COMPANY
930 Fort Duquesne Boulevard
Pittsburgh, PA 15222

Space Mates Laundry Designer Ideas, free color brochure.

The brochure shows the White–Westinghouse Space Mates combination of washer and dryer which can be installed under the counter or stacked in a space 27" x 27" x 71" high. The front-loading, tumble-action washer uses less water per load and therefore consumes less electricity for heating water. Both the washer and dryer have energy-saving cycles. Another handy model, the Space Mates II laundry twins, is designed for limited space. Each unit is only 24" wide and 25" deep, and the top-loading washer has a roll-out track that enables you to pull it out easily for use and store it under the dryer when not in use. RS

Space Mate washer and dryer built into a linen closet. White–Westinghouse, XII-26.

XIII

Do-It-Yourself, Remodeling, and Building

XIII-1
ANDERSEN CORPORATION
Bayport, MN 55003

Beautiful Rooms Begin with Andersen Windows and Gliding Doors, 26 pages, illustrated, color, and three brochures, The Window and Gliding Door Answer Book, Andersen Energy Facts, and Easy Window and Gliding Door Installation, all free.

This leading manufacturer of windows and gliding doors has put out a series of consumer booklets and brochures designed to answer any questions you have about their products. The 26-page book shows Andersen windows in exterior and interior settings of all kinds and gives rough-opening sizes for the different types: double-hung, casement, awning, gliding, angle bay and bow, and gliding doors. Inquiries for the booklet should be addressed to Dept. L-2 at the company's address.

The first two brochures provide general information about the construction of the windows and the energy-saving qualities of double-pane insulating glass and triple-glazing systems, useful if you are planning to build or remodel your home. The brochure on installation, however, is undoubtedly the most practical. If you plan to do the work yourself, you will learn about the tools and materials you need and how to prepare the rough opening—and be able to see the whole procedure in step-by-step sketches with installation instructions. The windows are readily available through dealers and building centers. RS

XIII-2
BENDIX MOULDINGS, INC.
235 Pegasus Avenue
Northvale, NJ 07647

Kitchen Cabinets, Door Decorating, Furniture Projects, and Picture Framing, each 25 cents, 8 pages, illustrated, two-color.

Four do-it-yourself booklets that show how to use Bendix moldings in a variety of ways—as trim for kitchen cabinets and drawers, on interior and exterior doors, to add trim to pieces of furniture, and to make mirror and picture frames or coffee table borders. The tools needed, step-by-step mitering, and the way to add a liner to a picture frame are illustrated. There's also a page on professional solutions to mistakes in mitering. If you don't want to go to the trouble of cutting your picture frames yourself, Bendix also has an instant picture-frame kit, described on page 123. RS

XIII-3
BROOKSTONE COMPANY
Vose Farm Road
Peterborough, NH 03458

Hard-to-Find Tools and Other Fine Things, free catalogue, 68 pages, illustrated, black and white.

All kinds of tools are clearly illustrated and described in meticulous detail, with suggested uses. If you can't find a tool for a particular job in here, chances are it doesn't exist. Prices are reasonable. The "other fine things" include all

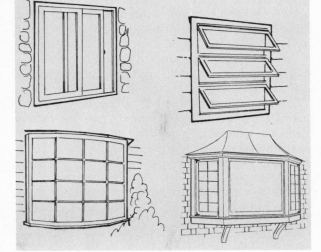

Vinyl-sheathed window frames and sashes come in a variety of styles from Anderson, XIII-1.

sorts of items from a door-closing device to a fire escape ladder. MO

XIII-4
SAMUEL CABOT, INC.
1 Union Street
Boston, MA 02108

Cabot's Stains, 25 cents, published periodically, 16 pages, illustrated, color.

This useful little booklet on wood and wood stains contains information about exterior stains, stain wax for interior woodwork and paneling (it stains, waxes, and seals in one operation), bleaching oil and stain for a weathered driftwood look, solid color stains, finishes for redwood, decking and fence stains, cement floor stains, and latex stains. Cabot also makes gutter paint, house and trim paints, and tree-healing paint. A one-page guide to successful staining covers color selection, preparation of new wood, application, and maintenance. RS

XIII-5
CALIFORNIA REDWOOD ASSOCIATION
1 Lombard Street
San Francisco, CA 94111

Redwood Homes/Redwood Interiors, $1, and Renew It with Redwood, 50 cents; each 12 pages, illustrated, color.

The manifold uses of versatile redwood for exteriors and interiors are shown to good advantage in these brochures. *Redwood Interiors* concentrates on paneling with a guide that shows how to create patterns with the wood and contains information about grades and grain, finishes, and special color effects; *Redwood Homes* is more concerned with striking contemporary architecture. *Renew It with Redwood* illustrates ways redwood can be used on porches, on decks, and indoors, with a description of two projects—an add-on garden room and a room where paneling is used on walls and for storage areas. RS

XIII-6
CAROLINA LOG BUILDINGS, INC.
P.O. Box 368
Fletcher, NC 28732

Real Log Homes, $5, 36 pages, illustrated, black and white and color.

This company, founded in 1963, has become the nation's top producer of log homes, and their

XIII • *Do-It-Yourself, Remodeling, and Building*

Above, out-of-date family room before remodeling.
Below, transformed with easy-to-cut redwood paneling.
A do-it-yourself project from California Redwood, XIII-5.

fine catalogue contains an extensive introductory section explaining the insulating capacity of wood, building systems, log peeling and treatment, and the many advantages of an all-log home. The main section lists the various home models, all with technical specifications and floor plans; many are shown in photographs, some in color. The sizes range from 887 to 2,834 square feet. Blueprints may be ordered in advance at $25 per set, which can be credited to the purchase price of a home. Specifications are also provided for windows and doors, as well as outbuildings of various sizes: lean-tos and 2- or 3-car garages. A price list is included, and the company will ship direct.

Further information and advice may be obtained by calling one of their six manufacturing facilities, where you will be told the name of your nearest dealer. MO/RS

XIII-7
ALBERT CONSTANTINE AND SON, INC.
2050 Eastchester Road
New York, NY 10461

Constantine's Woodworker's Catalogue, 50
*cents (or $1 with 20 wood samples), published
annually, 100 pages, illustrated, black and
white and color.*

A catalogue with many products for the woodworker, craftsperson, and home handyman. One
of the specialties is the selection of fine wood
veneers in standard thicknesses, and versatile
flexible veneer, $\frac{1}{64}$" thick, mounted on a paper
backing, which makes it a simple matter to cover
beat-up furniture or an inexpensive painted
piece. There are 15 different veneers to choose
from, including teak, figured walnut, and zebra-
wood, in 8' rolls and three widths, 18", 24" and
36", at prices ranging from $17.50 to $74.95, depending on the wood and the size. An introductory veneering kit costs $5.75. The catalogue
contains a variety of woodworking and carving
tools, imported cabinet woods and American
hardwoods, plywood panels, refinishing materials, wood moldings and carvings, wood inlay
borders, various types of hardware, woodworking plans and patterns (including full-size plans

*Bedroom wall storage and under-the-stairs cedar closets,
do-it-yourself ideas from Giles & Kendall, XII-11.*

for Early American furniture), and craft books.
There are also upholstery tools and materials,
lamp parts, caning kits and materials, picture
frame moldings, marquetry kits, and clock
kits. A veritable treasure trove for the do-it-
yourselfer. MO

XIII-8
CURVOFLITE
RFD 2, Box 145A
Kingston, NH 03848

Color brochure, $1.

The brochure gives construction specifications
for Curvoflite's wood spiral staircases, which
come in oak for interiors or mahogany for exteriors, sanded and ready to stain or lacquer. You
can choose balusters and handrails to suit contemporary or traditional houses. Examples of installation are also shown. Write for the name of
your nearest dealer. RS

Oak spiral staircase from Curvoflite, XII-8.

XIII-9
GALAXY KITCHENS, INC.
6727 N.W. 16th Terrace
Fort Lauderdale, FL 33309

U-Do-A-Door, $1.95 for brochure and samples (refundable with purchase), illustrated, black and white.

With this kit you can resurface metal, wood, or painted kitchen cabinets with preglued panels of pecan, walnut, butternut, or white cherry woodgrain vinyl that come with raised moldings. The brochure shows step-by-step illustrated installation techniques and has a chart for measuring your door panel sizes and an order form with door and drawer dimensions, plus samples of the vinyls. MO

XIII-10
GEORGIA–PACIFIC COMPANY
900 S.W. Fifth Avenue
Portland, OR 97204

The Paneling Book, $1, 28 pages, illustrated, color.

Installing wall paneling is one of the simplest and most satisfying do-it-yourself projects. This new illustrated booklet, a complete guide to installing paneling, tells and shows you how to panel standard and problem walls, arches and alcoves, stair walls, ceilings, and attic areas. Detailed procedures, material lists, and diagrams are included for all paneling projects, with instructions for handling uneven surfaces, slanted studs, and out-of-square walls. There are also tips on selecting paneling and on thermal and sound control insulation. Eight pages of color photographs provide ideas for the use of paneling in different rooms and ways. MO

XIII-11
GILES & KENDALL, INC.
P.O. Box 188
Huntsville, AL 35804

The One Scent in a Thousand, no charge, and *Build your Own Aromatic Cedar Closets,* 25 cents, illustrated, color.

The free brochure describes Giles & Kendall's 4' x 8' closet panels of Eastern red cedar, considered the best material for indoor closets because of its moth-repelling qualities. The 25-cent color brochure gives step-by-step plans for building four different cedar closets with information on installing and cutting the panels. One is a bedroom storage wall, the others a free-standing closet suitable for a garage, basement, or guest room, an under-stair closet, and a linen closet. RS

XIII-12
GREEN MOUNTAIN CABINS, INC.
P.O. Box 190 DC
Chester, VT 05143

Free brochure.

The brochure shows a selection of Green Mountain Cabin's typical log home designs, which are priced two ways—for the basic log package and the more complete full shell house package. Prices for the full shell house package designs range from $14,167 to $28,284. If you prefer to design your own house, they sell a $4 kit and manual, *Designing Your Own Green Mountain Log Home,* which tells you how to draw the floor plan and select the parts you need from their catalogue of walls, porches, balconies, roofs, etc. These are all priced, so you can compare their prices with those of local suppliers. Green Mountain will also do custom designs. MO

Conventional home before remodeling, above, and after re-siding with new logs, below. Wilderness Log Homes, XIII-35.

XIII-13
HARDWOOD PLYWOOD MANUFACTURERS ASSOCIATION
P.O. Box 2789
Reston, VA 22090

Price list of brochures, free.

This list offers individual brochures relating to plywood and plywood paneling, laminated hardwood block flooring, and floor tile, as well as do-it-yourself plans for a bookcase-room divider, child's desk and chair unit, a planter, a hanging wall desk, and a hi-fi-bar unit. Brochure prices range from 15 cents to $5.79. There are also audio-visuals on various aspects of hardwood.
RS

XIII-14
HERITAGE HOMES PLAN SERVICE, INC.
550 Pharr Road, N.E., Suite 830
Atlanta, GA 30305

The Plans Book, $12.50, 296 pages, illustrated, black and white.

Almost 300 house designs with floor plans are shown in this portfolio by Henry Norris, A.I.A. The designs utilize mainly stock parts and standard lumber dimensions, so they are practical and economical, and they come in a great variety of styles—traditional, contemporary, rustic, and Spanish among them. A package offer of four sets of plans (for owner, builder, building permit, and mortgage source) costs around $150. Included are the foundation, basement, and floor plans, exterior elevations, fireplace and stair details, but not plumbing and heating plans, which vary regionally and should be obtained from a local subcontractor. An introduction to the book by Mr. Norris gives relevant information on building and financing a home and on dealing with realtors and contractors. MO

XIII-15
HOME PLANNERS, INC.
23761 Research Drive
Farmington Hills, MI 48024

English Tudor Homes, $2 (refundable with purchase), published quarterly, 98 pages, illustrated, color.

Half-timbers, stucco, sculptured chimneys, high peaked roofs, muntined casement windows, brick and stone exteriors; these are some of the distinguishing characteristics of what has come to be known as the "Tudor" house. This cata-

New, rambling, two-story Geodesic Dome that two people can build. Monterey, XIII-20.

logue contains a large selection of modern-day adaptations of this popular style, 135 in all, presented in line-and-wash drawings and with floor and ground plans; if you see a design you like, you may order a complete set of blueprints, a materials list, and a complete specifications outline, for $60. The company also provides similar catalogues for 1-story homes, 1½- and 2-story homes, split levels, and vacation homes. MO

XIII-16
HYDE MANUFACTURING COMPANY
54 Eastford Road
Southbridge, MA 01550

Hyde Tools Catalog, no charge, 34 pages, How to Use Hyde Tools, no charge, and How to Prepare Surfaces for Painting, Decorating, Wallcovering, $1, published annually, 28 pages; all illustrated, black and white.

The manufacturers of Hyde tools for surface preparation of walls have come up with three nifty booklets for those who are remodeling or redecorating a home.

The tools catalogue shows their different tools, including putty knives, trowels, scrapers, brushes, hand knives, wallpaper tools, and equipment, including folding table, magnesium straight-edge, chalk line, zinc strip, and plate—to be used for, among other things, cutting materials, hanging wall coverings, and refinishing furniture.

How to Use Hyde Tools sketches them in action and gives directions for removing paint, preparing and finishing walls, repairing windows, and removing and hanging wallpaper.

The large how-to booklet on preparing surfaces for home maintenance, remodeling, and

Acrylic skylights from O'Keefe, XIII-25.

Acrylic Sunbubble window. T-M Corporation, XIII-30.

restoration provides clear sketches and straight-forward copy showing and telling how to remove paint and prepare surfaces, replace broken windows, cut clear plastic, tape and finish wallboard joints, and lay brick and block walls.

Hyde tools are stocked in paint and hardware departments, hardware stores, building centers, and paint stores, and these booklets will help you to identify and use them. RS

XIII-17
LINDAL CEDAR HOMES
P.O. Box 24426
Seattle, WA 98124

Lindal Homes—Quality Living With Cedar, $3, published annually, 50 pages, illustrated, color.

Lindal, the world's largest manufacturer of cedar homes, control their building packages from the Lindal sawmills all the way through to your building site; the elegant packages that result give rise to some remarkable houses, well represented in the excellent color photography of this catalogue. The standard models fall into three basic categories—chalets, 2-story gambrels, and contemporary homes—but some custom designs are also shown. Each house is provided with a stylized floor plan, and described in the text. The company has headquarters in both the U.S. and Canada, where you may write for the name of your nearest Lindal dealer. You can also order a Lindal Plans Package with three sets of blueprints for $50, which will be deducted from the purchase price of the house. MO/RS

XIII-18
MANNINGTON MILLS
P.O. Box 30
Salem, NJ 08079

Remodeling with the Floor in Mind, free 12-page booklet, illustrated.

This booklet from a manufacturer of resilient vinyl flooring gives suggestions on how to go about a remodeling job, depending on your budget and skills. It covers such things as making a floor plan, finding a reputable contractor, outlining the job and determining the price, getting time estimates, a guarantee, and a service clause, or, if you are doing the job yourself, how and where to shop. While it doesn't tell you how to do the project, there may be some pointers here that you have overlooked. MO

XIII-19
MARTIN INDUSTRIES
P.O. Box 128
Florence, AL 35630

Fireplaces by Martin, Built-In, and Octa-Therm, brochures, 25 cents, illustrated, color.

This company makes fireplaces that can be installed without any masonry work and supported and surrounded by standard materials. The fireplaces come with illustrated instructions for building them into or out from any wall. RS

XIII-20
MONTEREY DOMES, INC.
P.O. Box 5621-J
Riverside, CA 92517

Monterey Domes Catalog and Plans Book, $4 for two booklets, published annually, 78 pages, illustrated, color.

A thorough and persuasive introduction to an entirely new concept in housing—the self-built geodesic dome. The shape makes it by far the most efficient form of living space to heat or cool and the price makes it possible to own a house as spacious as required for a small fraction of what was previously possible, but the particular strength of this catalogue lies in the myriad design and decorator schemes Monterey has developed to suit its product to a variety of tastes. The old image of a glass-and-girder bowl is now replaced by rambling, two-story modules with simulated shake roofs, tiny one-room domes that resemble fairytale cottages, or larger multielement structures which can be extended ad infinitum.

Two people can build a complete Monterey Dome shell from start to finish, with the help of an instruction package that includes three sets of blueprints and a certified structural engineering package that enables prospective owners to apply for a building permit anywhere in the U.S. The ground-plans booklet is comprehensive, and demonstrates the various ways in which a circular floor plan can be divided into rooms. Dome packages start as low as $3,995, and the numerous options include solar panels (prices range from $2,145 to $2,745 for 6), foam insulation, special deep frames for higher insulation, shingling, base walls, and extension packages. MO

XIII-21
NATIONAL PLAN SERVICE, INC.
435 West Fullerton Avenue
Elmhurst, IL 60126

Free list of publications.

The National Plan Service offers low-cost blueprints for house plans, plus books on all kinds of subjects relating to the home. They have guides to bathroom and kitchen planning, plumbing repairs, home carpentry, remodeling and building projects, as well as furniture upholstery and re-

pair and storage. There are also books on designing and building a solar house and solar water heater. Prices start at $1.25. MO

XIII-22
NATIONAL WOODWORK MANUFACTURERS ASSOCIATION
℅ Sumner Rider and Associates, Inc.
355 Lexington Avenue
New York, NY 10017

Free brochures.

Among the consumer brochures issued by the National Woodwork Manufacturers Association, two we found had most to offer—a leaflet reprint of an article on installing wood shutters, "The Open and Shut Case for Interior Wood Shutters," because of its practical information; and *Remodeling with Wood Windows and Panel Doors,* a brochure that illustrates and describes the various types of windows and styles of panel doors and compares wood windows with metal in terms of insulation and condensation, durability, maintenance, and appearance. MO

Folding louvre and panel doors from National Woodwork Manufacturers' booklets. XIII-22.

Inexpensive, easy-to-build complete home sewing center that neatly disappears behind roller shades. Designed by James DeMartin for Woman's Day Magazine.

XIII-23
NORTHEASTERN LOG HOMES, INC.
P.O. Box 46
Groton, VT 05046

Northeastern Log Homes Brochure, *$4, 62 pages, illustrated, color.*

Northeastern Log Buildings are made from white pine logs that are precut, numbered, notched, submerged in wood preservative, and then shipped in a Log Home Materials Package directly to the building site. Each of the 38 models is shown in full-color line drawing, and in schematic floor plan. It is also possible to make changes to suit your individual requirements— Northeastern is in fact willing to provide a scaled floor plan drawing designed to meet any applicable building codes, together with a price quotation, free of charge and with no purchase obligation. Prices for the standard models range from the 5-room Retreat Camp ($10,195) to the 17-room, two-car garage Bristol ($47,825). There are also solid log and log siding garages, from $3,585 to $7,025. MO

XIII-24
OAK FLOORING INSTITUTE
804 Sterick Building
Memphis, TN 38103

Hardwood Flooring Installation Manual, *and* ***Hardwood Flooring Finishing/ Refinishing Manual,*** *each 50 cents, 8 pages, illustrated, black and white.*

In addition to a wood-care guide for 25 cents that tells you about the types of hardwood used for floors and discusses finishes, cleaning, and care, the Oak Flooring Institute (part of the National Oak Flooring Manufacturers' Association) will also supply on request two manuals listed above on hardwood flooring installation and hardwood flooring finishing and refinishing that would be of great assistance to the do-it-yourselfers. The manuals are clearly and simply written, without technical jargon, and have good illustrations of techniques of installation, finishing, and refinishing, including stenciling. MO

XIII-25
O'KEEFFE'S, INC.
75 Williams Avenue
San Francisco, CA 94124

O'Keeffe's Skylights, *$3, published annually, 40 pages, illustrated, black and white.*

This manual was prepared to provide complete and reliable information relating to the design, detailing, and specifications of skylight construction; it is divided into two parts covering glass and acrylic skylights. Some of the more commonly used skylight configurations are shown in both plan and elevation drawings keyed to the sectional details. There are many photographs of O'Keeffe skylights in use in commercial centers throughout the country. RS

Custom-designed contemporary cedar and glass home by Lindal, XIII-17.

XIII-26
THE OLD HOUSE JOURNAL

69A Seventh Avenue
Brooklyn, NY 11217

The Old House Journal, *annual subscription $12, published monthly, illustrated, black and white, and* ***The Old-House Journal Catalogue,*** *$9.95 (includes postage).*

The Journal, a monthly newsletter devoted exclusively to pre-1914 antique houses, covers interior and exterior decoration in authentic period styles and the preservation and restoration of old houses. You will find practical, do-it-yourself information and sources for products. A free sample copy of the newsletter and the Journal's *Field Guide to Old Houses,* which provides illustrations of the most common old-house styles with characteristic architectural details, will be sent on request. As more and more restorers of old houses want to locate appropriate materials and items such as plaster moldings, wide plank flooring, and tin ceilings, the Journal has published *The Old-House Journal Catalogue,* a directory of 830 sources, many of them small and hard to find, whose products or services have been verified by the editors.

XIII-27
PRE-BUILT HOME SYSTEMS, INC.

P.O. Box 116
Healdsburg, CA 95448

Pre-Built Home Systems, *$2, published annually, 55 pages, illustrated, black and white.*

A catalogue of prefabricated house "shells," 29 in all, from the Laguna, 960 square feet ($7,263) to the Elmwood, 1,936 square feet with carport ($21,422). There is precise construction and installation information plus a full-page line drawing and floor plan for each house model. MO

XIII-28
THE RENOVATOR'S SUPPLY

71 Northfield Road
Miller's Falls, MA 01349

The Renovator's Supply, *$2 (refundable with purchase), 48 pages, illustrated, black and white.*

This company was established in response to a need for availability of products and information by those engaged in restoration and renovation work. They offer a complete line of renovation

Coffee table made of plywood with bamboo-covered base and vinyl-treated fabric top. Photographer: Otto Maya.

items including hardware, plumbing, building, and electrical supplies, decorative moldings, mantels, corner cabinets, even reproductions of old-fashioned embossed leather seats for chairs. In most cases the products are reproductions of items found in old houses and museums; some are made from molds and with tools and machines that have been in use for over 100 years. Renovator's Supply is staffed by people with firsthand renovation experience who can answer questions concerning installation of their products. The catalogue, a sampling of what they stock, includes locks, keys, handles, a letter box-knocker, iron and brass knockers, door bells, even foot scrapers for outside the door. There are old-style sash fasteners, an art glass window, antique reproduction sheet glass with wavy texture and bubbles, bathroom accessories, lighting fixtures and lanterns, etched glass shades, brass wallplates, and a good selection of brass cabinet hardware, brass hooks, shutter hinges, wrought iron hardware, and hard-to-find brass and bronze screws. There are also tools and supplies for care and repair. If you want something not in the catalogue, the company will help you find it. A discount is given on orders over $1500. MO

XIII-29
SYLVAN PRODUCTS, INC.
4729 State Highway 3 SW
Port Orchard, WA 98366

Hainesway II Log Homes, no charge, 12 pages, illustrated, black and white and color.

Every Hainesway home, chalet, or commercial building is custom precut, so any modern or traditional decor or finish may be used. The smallest home, the Pueblo, is 672 square feet; the largest, the Shenandoah, offers 2,114 square feet on two floors, but the customer is allowed tremendous latitude as to the final form the house will take, and is advised to consult with his local dealer to take maximum advantage of this opportunity. The color section gives a number of examples of finished exteriors and interiors, both simple and elaborate. MO/RS

XIII-30
T-M CORPORATION
413 Virginia Drive
Orlando, FL 32803

What You Should Know About Skylights, free, 6 pages, and *Skymaster Skylights,* free, 4 pages; both illustrated, color.

The first leaflet is an admirably simple yet thorough guide to skylights—what they are, what they are for, what kinds are available, and what is involved in the installation. The photographs provide useful examples for anyone contemplating such a step. The second leaflet is a list of Skymaster skylights available in three models—curb-mounted, self-flashing (no curb), and Sunbubbles (which also make interesting windows)—in a variety of sizes. Both pamphlets contain a fair amount of technical information as well. RS

XIII-31
TRUE-CRAFT LOG STRUCTURES, LTD.
60 Riverside Drive
North Vancouver, B.C.,
Canada V7H IT4

True-Craft Catalogue, $2 (refundable with purchase), 12 pages, illustrated, black and white.

True-Craft buildings can be erected on any kind of approved foundation and adapted to virtually any type of terrain; the kit includes everything needed to build the basic structure, including floors, windows, and insulation. The basic building material is Western red cedar. The catalogue offers 35 models, from 256 to 1654 square feet. Price information and customized plans are available from the company. MO

XIII-32
WATCO–DENNIS CORPORATION
1756 22nd Street
Santa Monica, CA 90404

How to Beautifully Finish Wood, and *Beautiful Wood Staining and Finishing,* free brochures.

The first brochure shows Watco's Danish oil finish, which comes in natural; also in medium, dark, or black walnut, applied to oak and ash. Then it gives the four basic steps in application. There's a listing of other Watco products, including finishes for exterior wood, wood floors, red-

wood, and porous masonry, as well as satin wax and a teak oil finish. The other brochure shows the wood and decorator colors available in Watco 5-minute wood stains, gives simple directions for their use, and describes the Danish oil finish and some of the other products. RS

XIII-33
WEIRD WOOD
Green Mountain Cabins, Inc.
P.O. Box 190 CD
Chester, VT 05143

Weird Wood, brochure, 25 cents, illustrated, black and white.

This company offers woods in many and various styles, shapes, widths, lengths, and thicknesses for shelves, table tops, countertops, and

Beach house has living room sleep-sofas and wall cabinets built of old boardwalk planks. Coffee table is driftwood log with top of discarded cable spool. Designed and built by owner/designer Willard Ching.

benches. Also available are clock blanks, ovals cut diagonally, for which you can purchase battery movements, brass or black hands, and self-adhesive numerals. They also have complete clock kits and wood finishing materials and kits. The wood isn't ordinary lumber but pieces specially cut from the log to give a particular form and grain, each one different. On the order form you specify your needs and the wood you want. The woods available are white pine, butternut, black cherry, sugar or rock maple, basswood; small quantities of native ash, oak, white cedar, and yellow birch; some from the West Coast (redwood, red gum eucalyptus, walnut, olive, and buckeye); and several Central American hardwoods. You can also buy handmade black iron legs for the table-top wood slabs that complement the rustic look, $7.50 for the 13″ length, $8 for the 17″. Each piece of wood is individually priced according to the grade, size, and type and includes planing on at least one side unless you request otherwise. MO

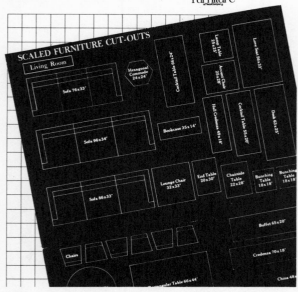

Scaled furniture cutouts and ½″ graph paper, included in many furniture catalogues, help you solve room arrangement problems. The above is from Stanley, I-75.

XIII-34
WESTERN WOOD PRODUCTS ASSOCIATION
1500 Yeon Building
Portland, OR 97204

Ideas for the Home Craftsman, free list.

The list offers 35 plans and booklets for remodeling and improving your home and garden, mostly using Western Wood products, at prices ranging from 25 cents to 50 cents. Included are such subjects as making storage units, paneling walls, adding on rooms, and building wood decks. There are also booklets on extending and adding to mobile homes. MO

XIII-35
WILDERNESS LOG HOMES, INC.
Route 2, SCHD-80
Plymouth, WS 53073

Wilderness Log Homes Brochure/Plan Book, $5, published semiannually, 20 pages, illustrated, black and white.

Wilderness Log Homes offer both traditional log homes and a unique "Full Log Look" half-log design (which allows for a very high energy efficiency) with full log corners. Designs featured run from one to twelve rooms; prices range from $5,900 to $34,090 for the basic units, and options such as knotty pine paneling, cedar shake shingles, or porches are always available when not already part of the design. The written section on construction details and specifications includes a good explanation of the various foundation systems that can be used. MO

XIII-36
WOOD MOULDING & MILLWORK PRODUCERS
P.O. Box 25278
Portland, OR 97225

How to Work with Wood Mouldings, 25 cents, 16 pages, illustrated, black and white.

A useful and easy-to-follow booklet with illustrated, step-by-step instructions for selecting, estimating, and installing moldings. It explains mitering, coping, splicing, and the materials required in a very clear way. Highly recommended for anyone about to undertake this ticklish task. MO

XIV

Problem Solvers, Decorating Ideas, and Services

XIV-1
THE AMERICAN CANVAS INSTITUTE
10 Beech Street
Berea, OH 44017

Ten Terrific Things Canvas Can Do, color brochure, 35 cents.

Four pages of ways in which to use canvas, including some you might not have thought of. It is shown stretched in billowing panels on wires that adjust to the sun's angle as shelter for a deck, draped around a room like a tent, as curtains for a four-poster, as an overhead screen for a pool or at poolside, as a terrace awning, to shield an entrance or porch and as a marquee, open on four sides, for outdoor dining. Canvas awnings can also help you save up to 25 percent on energy costs, if your home is air-conditioned. MO

XIV-2
AMERICAN OLEAN TILE COMPANY
1000 Cannon Avenue
Lansdale, PA 19446

Decorating Ideas with Ceramic Tile, 50 cents, published annually, 16 pages, illustrated, color.

Ceramic tile is one of the oldest decorative materials and this idea booklet illustrates the many uses of quarry tile in natural clay color, bright and matte glazed tiles, ceramic mosaics, and textured glazed tile for walls, floors, and countertops, bathtub and shower areas, as well as for a patio and outdoor bench. There is a discussion of each type of tile, including sheets of pregrouted tile which save considerable time when you are doing a wall, advice on care, and a section of color schemes showing how American Olean ceramic tiles can be coordinated with bathroom fixtures and appliance colors. (For more information on the wide range of American Olean tiles, see page 52.) RS

XIV-3
ANTIQUE TRUNK CO.
3706 West 169 Street
Cleveland, OH 44111

Antique Trunk Restoration Parts Catalog, 25 cents, 12 pages, illustrated, black and white.

If you have an antique trunk in bad condition and want to repair it yourself, here's the place to find everything you need, from tacks, nails, and split rivets used on locks and corners to leather handles, hardware, keys, and solid brass embossed trunk coverings. There's also a plastic mender reinforced with steel for repairing metal trunk coverings, plans and instructions for making a stagecoach trunk, circa 1840, a price and identification guide for antique trunks, and a comprehensive repair manual for $2.50 postpaid, which includes a free catalog. Prices are very reasonable, from 25 cents to about $6 for a nineteenth-century style trunk lock with drop, escutcheon, and key. Shipping, handling, and insurance are extra. MO

XIV-4
W. GRAHAM ARADER III
1000 Boxwood Court
King of Prussia, PA 19406

W. Graham Arader III, Rare Maps, Books and Prints, $24 for six catalogues a year, single issues $5 each (refundable with purchase), illustrated, black and white.

In addition to selling maps, books, and prints, Mr. Arader offers his customers conservation and restoration services for all works of art on paper, including globes. For a free estimate, write or call and describe the work desired. When the print, map, or globe is received, its condition will be analyzed and the recommended procedure and cost submitted in writing. Sample prices start at around $50. The firm will also do hand binding in vellum, leather, or cloth, and book repairs. MO

XIV-5
ARMSTRONG CORK COMPANY
P.O. Box 2477
Boulder, CO 80321

Good Ideas for Decorating, $6 for a 1-year subscription, published quarterly, illustrated, color.

This colorful quarterly magazine is primarily devoted to family living and homemaking, with tips and ideas from interior designers who create rooms for Armstrong. In addition to the many attractive and livable room settings, there are various how-to projects, from designing and making your own lamps to simple cabinetwork to stretched fabric art for the super-graphic look. MO

XIV-6
BALL AND BALL
463 West Lincoln Highway
Exton, PA 19341

Fine Quality Hardware by Ball and Ball, $4, 108 pages, illustrated, black and white.

Certain special services are offered on the back page of the price list in Ball and Ball's catalogue. They will repair hinges of all types, door locks, lights, lanterns, andirons, firetools, and furniture hardware at a considerable saving on the replacement cost. For a firm quotation, send the item to be repaired. Copies can also be made to match your original. MO

XIV-7
BIGELOW–SANFORD, INC.
P.O. Box 3089
Greenville, SC 29602

Everything You've Always Wanted to Know About Carpet . . . but Were Afraid to Ask, 25 cents, published annually, 22 pages, black and white.

Bigelow's booklet should be a great help to carpet seekers who are confronted with a bewildering array of styles, fibers, and backings and need basic information before buying. You'll learn the difference between a plush, a twist, a tweed, a saxony, a sculpture, and a tip or random-sheared carpet, as well as the trade names of manmade

fibers, the types of backing available, how to estimate the amount of carpet you'll need, and how to care for the carpet once you've bought it. MO

XIV-8
BLACK MAGIC CHIMNEY SWEEPS
Drawer 250
Stowe, VT 05672

Is Your Chimney a Fire Hazard? and Do-It-Yourself Chimney Sweeping Kit, $1, 14-page booklet and flyer, illustrated, black and white.

Is Your Chimney a Fire Hazard? is a homeowner's guide to chimney safety and maintenance that tells you about the problems associated with wood burning, the dangers of creosote buildup, and ways to check your wood-burning stove or chimney for safety and keep it clean—using the Black Magic do-it-yourself kit offered in the flyer. Included in the kit are a stiff spring steel wire brush of the right size for your flue (flue sizes are indicated on the price list), seven flexible fiberglass rods plus connectors and a 27-page manual, everything you need to do a professional job yourself. With all the wood burning going on these days, this would be a useful kit to have around. MO

XIV-9
BUTCHER POLISH COMPANY
120 Bartlett Street
Marlborough, MA 01752

More Handy Tips on Wood Care, 50 cents, published annually, 24 pages, illustrated; also free leaflet on fireplace cleaners and polishes.

The wood-care booklet provides practical answers to basic questions on how to care for wood floors, furniture, and paneling. It tells how to get rid of white rings and scratches on furniture,

Fireplace, hearth, stove, and glass cleaners, and paste wax—a few care and cleaning products from Butcher Polish Company, XIV-9.

how to remove spots and stains from marble tops, and how to care for antiques. The free leaflet shows and describes Butcher's wood stove and fireplace polishes, and cleaners for fireplace, stove glass, and hearth that are specially formulated to remove soot, smoke, creosote, and dirt and water stains from brick, stone, marble, and other hard surfaces. MO

XIV-10
CHEM-CLEAN FURNITURE RESTORATION CENTER
U.S. Route 7
Arlington, VT 05250

Color brochure, 25 cents.

The brochure describes the wood-finishing products used in the Furniture Restoration Center that are also sold by mail—a floor stripping kit, paint and varnish removers, bleaching cream for wood, brush cleaner and reconditioner, and satin-finish polyurethane varnish—and gives refinishing tips. Included on the order form are other necessities for furniture restoration—cane, pegs, a how-to booklet for caning chairs, a special glue for furniture joints, steel wool pads, and tack cloth among them. MO

XIV-11
CYRUS CLARK CO., INC.
267 Fifth Avenue
New York, NY 10016

Everglaze Chintz Makes a Beautiful Wallcovering, *free booklet.*

Glazed chintz makes an attractive and practical wallcovering that is resistant to creasing, stretching, and soil. Dust can be whisked away with a soft brush. The booklet gives step-by-step directions and sketches for applying chintz to the wall. You can hang it like wallpaper, except that the paste is applied to the wall, not the fabric. Cyrus Clark Everglaze chintz comes in a variety of patterns, 36" wide, and may be found in fabric shops and department stores; you can write for the name of your nearest retail source. RS/ID

XIV-12
THE CLASSIC BINDERY
P.O. Box 399-D
Mendham, NJ 07945

The Classic Bindery, *25 cents, brochure, published annually, 4 pages with order form, illustrated, black and white.*

Seamless vinyl flooring, easy to install and maintain, from Mannington, XIV-26.

This company specializes in custom bookbinding in leather or cloth in three styles, with gold stamping and gold edges, if desired. Price is determined by the size and bulk of the book. For a standard size book, you can pay as little as $15 for a book bulking under 2" bound in cloth to $85 for full leather binding of a book bulking 3". They will also resew and repair deteriorated volumes and make slip cases. MO

XIV-13
CONSUMER INFORMATION CENTER
Pueblo, CO 81009

Consumer Information Catalog, *free, published quarterly, 16 pages.*

The catalogue lists and describes a number of booklets prepared by the U.S. Consumer Information Center on a variety of subjects from automobiles to food to gardening to housing, heating, and home maintenance, many of which can help you save money. In the gardening realm, there are booklets on building hobby greenhouses, growing bonsai, indoor gardens, and house plants. In the housing category you can get designs for low-cost wood homes and a comprehensive illustrated handbook of detailed instructions and basic principles for building and insulating wood-frame houses. There are also booklets on indoor and outdoor painting, simple home repairs, the burning characteristics of different firewoods, and the installation, operation, maintenance, and costs of the most commonly used heating systems. *The Energy-Wise Home Buyer* tells you about twelve energy features to look for in a home, with detailed energy checklists, charts, and maps for figuring your energy costs and needs. Especially valuable to have on hand are the *Consumer's Resource Handbook,* which tells you how to complain and get results, and *Shopping by Mail,* an explanation of Federal regulations on merchandise ordered through the mail. There's even a booklet on removing 180 common stains from fabrics. Some of the booklets are free, others range in price from 35 cents to $3.50. Order blanks are included for the individual booklets, which are also available in Spanish. MO

XIV-14
CROWN PUBLISHERS, INC.
1 Park Avenue
New York, NY 10016

Staple It! Easy Do-It Decorating Guide, by *Iris Ihde Frey, paperback, $8.95, 180 pages, illustrated, black and white photographs and sketches, 8 color pages.*

Staple-gun decorating projects are something anyone can do, and this very practical and attractive book tells and shows exactly how, with diagrams, directions, and photographs. Here are techniques for covering walls and floors with fabric; making wall hangings, draperies, shades, and super-graphic panels; covering furniture, boxes, picture frames, and screens; even making seating modules with a wood frame, plywood seat panel, foam cushion, batting, and fabric. Photographs of finished rooms show how the techniques may be applied. The book also contains information about supplies and materials; charts; tables for figuring yardage; and facts about working with pattern repeats, and back-tacking so the staples don't show. Designer Iris Ihde Frey has done a nifty job of covering the possibilities of decorating with a staple gun in this informative book, a must for do-it-yourselfers. If you can't find it in your local store, write to the publishers. MO/RS

XIV-15
E. I. DU PONT DE NEMOURS
& COMPANY, INC.
1007 Market Street
Wilmington, DE 19898

Creating with Corian, $2, 28 pages, illustrated, color.

An idea booklet showing many different ways to use Du Pont's Corian—a solid, strong, hard, nonporous polymer building material that is eas-

ily cut and shaped for counter tops, vanity tops, desk and table tops; or wall surfaces in bathrooms and shower stalls. The material has a pleasant opalescent quality reminiscent of alabaster, and comes either in Cameo White, delicately veined Dawn Beige and Olive Mist, or dappled-yellow Autumn Gold (the colors and pattern run right through the material). There are color photographs of Corian in bathrooms and kitchens; on ceilings and walls; around a fireplace; on tables and bars; and used in many original ways for lamps, planters, and bathroom accessories. Included in the booklet are a kitchen and bath planning guide and a list of standard Corian products such as kitchen counter tops and sinks, bar top and sink, vanity tops and bowls, and bathtub wall kits. RS

XIV-16
EASTMAN KODAK COMPANY,
Dept. 412L-539
343 State Street
Rochester, NY 14650

Decorating with Photographic Art. An Idea Book, no charge, 20 pages, illustrated, color.

The booklet shows a series of attractive room settings in which photographs are used as art, or in unusual ways. Examples are a grouping of framed family photographs lining a stairway, a large photomural of the Southwest on one wall of a guest room, framed photographs of plants hung on a screen, a cube end table decorated with butterfly photographs, close-ups of pasta shapes in a kitchen, and enlargements of flower transparencies backlighted in a room divider unit. Professional photographs can be given smooth or textured protective lacquer finishes that eliminate the need for glass, or mounted directly on canvas. There are many ideas here to inspire you, and Eastman Kodak will work with you to create a work of photographic art of just the right size, shape, mood, color, and finish, and mount and frame it if you wish. MO

XIV-17
EMERSON BOOKS, INC.
Reynolds Lane
Buchanan, NY 10511

List of books, 25 cents, 16 pages, illustrated, black and white.

Among the subjects on the Emerson list are books on crafts, carpentry, antiques, clock repairing, and a guide to what you need to know when buying a house. MO

Family portrait photographs turn an uninteresting stair wall into an exciting gallery. Eastman Kodak, XIV-16.

XIV-18
F.O.S.G. PUBLICATIONS
P.O. Box 239
Oradell, NJ 07649

Factory Outlet Shopping Guides, $2.95 each plus 60 cents postage and handling, published annually, and Factory Outlet Newsletter, $5 subscription for 8 issues a year.

Factory-outlet shopping is the smart, money-saving way to buy that has really caught on, and the six available guides each cover a different East Coast area—New England; New Jersey and Rockland County; New York City, Westchester, and Long Island; Pennsylvania; Washington, DC, including Maryland, Virginia, and Delaware; North and South Carolina. They are revised every year to keep the information up to date and supplemented by current listings in the newsletter. The Guides are well organized. First comes a definition of outlet shopping terms which tells you such things as the difference between types of outlets—factory, distributor's or wholesaler's, importer's, manufacturer's outlets and clearance centers—and words such as jobber, job lot, overcuts, overstock, and overruns. Then there are suggestions about shopping, sav-

ing time, and keeping records of purchases, even making complaints. The stores are listed alphabetically, with a description of the merchandise, discounts, what payment or credit cards are taken, hours and days they are open, and how to get to the location. In the back of the book outlets are listed by types of merchandise and by area. The Guide we received for New York, Long Island, and Westchester, contained a great many listings in the home furnishings, fabrics, china and silver, and yarn and crafts categories, among them a butcher block factory outlet, furniture clearance centers, discount wallcoverings, and a piano factory that gives a 20 to 38 percent discount. MO

XIV-19
FUNWOOD, INC.
P.O. Box 670
Wilmington, DE 19899

Calico Corners Guide to Do-it-Yourself Decorating, $2, 40 pages, illustrated, black and white.

Packed with detailed instructions and professional tricks, this clear and informative little book on decorating with fabric is put out by a

Easy, quick staple gun projects, from Crown's Staple It! Easy-Do-It Decorating Guide, *XIV-14. Five mini-print fabrics create pedestal tables, fabric "paintings," and shirred door panels by designers Jerry Janauer and Joseph Minicucci.*

franchise store with branches all over the country. (Calico Corners sells drapery, slipcover, and upholstery fabric seconds at savings of up to 50 percent off the original price.) The book tells you how to cover walls with fabric, using starch, glue, wallpaper paste, or a staple gun (including how to backtack to hide the staples); how to build a frame of furring strips to which the fabric can be attached; how to shirr fabric on rods between ceiling and baseboard. Also covered are the use of fabric on floors and ceilings; various window treatments; mounting decorative fabrics as "instant art" for walls; making pillows, tablecloths, runners, and shower curtains; a shortcut method of patchwork; and assorted projects like covering a screen, shelves, door panels, Parsons tables, or an old trunk with fabric. Did you know you can even give your old refrigerator a new custom look by starching fabric to it and then varnishing the fabric with polyurethane? You'll find all these ideas and more, plus detailed sketches of step-by-step procedures, in this book. MO/RS

XIV-20
GUILD OF SHAKER CRAFTS, INC.
401 W. Savidge Street
Spring Lake, MI 49456

Shaker Furniture Reproductions, $2.50 (refundable with purchase), published seasonally, 28 pages, illustrated, black and white and color.

The Guild has a service for repairing and restoring original Shaker pieces. Estimates are given on request. For additional information, call them at 616-846-2870.

XIV-21
INTEXT/ICS
(International Correspondence Schools)
Scranton, PA 18515

Free brochure.

The brochure is a brief outline of the school's Interior Decoration and Design Career Program, which is divided into five modules, starting with the principles of interior design and going through design elements and room decor to the work of the interior decorator. MO

XIV-22
JOHNSON WAX, Dept. CHC2
Consumer Services Center
P.O. Box 567
Racine, WI 53403

Furniture Care, 24 pages, and Album of American Furniture Classics, 40 pages, illustrated, black and white. No charge for either booklet.

If you have any furniture cleaning problem, the care booklet should provide the answer. You are told how to clean and care for antiques; plastic, acrylic, and painted furniture; real and imitation

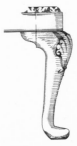

Queen Anne leg detail drawing from Album of American Furniture Classics booklet. Johnson Wax, XIV-22.

marble; wood with an oil finish or super finish (sealed and heat-cured to be more resistant to spills and stains); lacquered furniture; vinyl and leather upholstery and self-adhesive vinyl coverings; and combinations of materials such as metal and glass, slate and mosaic, or wood and leather or plastic. The booklet discusses the different cleaning products including spray polishes, liquid and paste waxes, and household solvents and tells how they treat scratches, blemishes, burns, alcohol spots and rings, water marks, paint stains, and heat marks on wood furniture.

The *Album of American Furniture Classics*, compiled in consultation with Marvin D. Schwartz, shows examples and gives descriptions of styles and pieces from 1650 to 1930, interspersed with cleaning tips for antique furniture. MO

XIV-23
KENNEY MANUFACTURING COMPANY
1000 Jefferson Boulevard
Warwick, RI 02887

Creative Windows, Volume II, *$1.95 plus 25 cents postage, 112 pages, illustrated, color.*

The 30-page how-to section in this decorating booklet contains detailed directions and sketches to help you create your own window treatments. There are instructions for the measuring and mounting of many types of curtain rods—decorative and conventional traverse, café, sash, and other types—and measuring techniques for standard windows, bay and bow windows, angled bays, corner windows, and French doors. Further sections cover the selection of hooks, rings, clips, and holdbacks as well as the making of lined and unlined draperies, shirred curtains, café curtains, pleats, and valances. There is also a cutting chart for fabric. MO

XIV-24
KIRSCH COMPANY
Dept. GU
Sturgis, MI 49091

Windows Beautiful, Volume VII, *$2.50, published every two years, 140 pages, illustrated, color.*

This book devoted to window treatments using Kirsch drapery hardware contains an informative how-to section on measuring for rods and draperies and making your own curtains, with a useful chart of yardage required. RS

Rejuvenate an old trunk with new hardware, paint, and stencil designs. Antique Trunk Company, XIV-3.

XIV-25
LEVOLOR LORENTZEN, INC.
720 Monroe Street
Hoboken, NJ 07030

Window Magic, *$1, published annually, 42 pages, illustrated, color.*

In the center of this decorating idea book about the uses of Levolor blinds is a 16-page Designer's Handbook full of helpful advice. There are suggestions for using blinds to solve design problems and information on measuring windows and installing horizontal or vertical blinds and shades. You are given instructions, with sketches, for painting a blind, covering the slats with fabric, plastic, or wallpaper, and removing a blind and taking it apart. RS

XIV-26
MANNINGTON MILLS
P.O. Box 30
Salem, NJ 08079

Decorating with the Floor in Mind, *free 12-page booklet, illustrated.*

Mannington Mills is a manufacturer of resilient vinyl flooring and this idea booklet shows the ways in which it can be used throughout the house. For a bedroom with a colonial look, a planklike design is teamed with a needlepoint rug; for an entrance, a brick or flagstone pattern takes over. Suggestions for using leftover flooring include lining kitchen shelves and drawers, making a backsplash, coasters, and place mats, or covering cubes or end tables, using Mannington's latex adhesive. RS

XIV-27
MINWAX COMPANY, INC.
Box 995
Clifton, NJ 07014

Tips on Wood Finishing and color cards, free booklet and leaflets.

Information about stripping, sanding, and finishing wooden surfaces, from furniture to paneling to floors, is packed into this handy booklet. You are told how to raise shallow dents and gouges by steaming with a damp cloth and an electric iron, or fill deep ones with animal glue and sanding dust. Minwax makes a wide variety of finishes in wood tones and colors which are shown in color in the leaflets (one covers exterior finishes), plus a special Blend-Fil pencil for covering nail holes and imperfections, paste and liquid waxes, an antique oil finish, and polyurethane finishes. RS

XIV-28
OAK FLOORING INSTITUTE
804 Sterick Building
Memphis, TN 38103

Wood Floor Care Guide, 25 cents, 16 pages, illustrated, black and white.

A useful pamphlet from the Oak Flooring Institute that tells you about the open- and close-grain hardwoods used for flooring and how to care for them. It discusses the finishes used on flooring, including penetrating seals and surface finishes (polyurethane, varnish, shellac, lacquer); gives advice on cleaning special surfaces, such as distressed wood (wire-brushed to give it an antique, textured look); deals with removing stains and wax buildup, repairing a finish, and refinishing a floor; and tells you what to do if your floor develops cracks or squeaks. MO

XIV-29
OLIN CORPORATION/OMALON
120 Long Ridge Road
Stamford, CT 06904

The Carpet Report, $1, 12 pages, illustrated, black and white.

Carpet is a costly investment and this brochure by a company that makes carpet underlay tells you how to judge well and buy wisely. It contains advice on finding the right carpet retailer and what he should provide in the way of information and services; how to select carpet in terms of color, fiber, style, use, price, and underlay; identification of natural and manmade fibers; pointers on how carpet is made; density, pile height, backing, styles, and textures; cost; and a short history of the various kinds of underlays, up to and including Omalon. MO

XIV-30
PLAYER PIANO COMPANY, INC.
704 East Douglas Street
Wichita, KS 67202

Player Piano Company, Inc., $3.50, published every three years, 182 pages, illustrated, black and white.

A complete and comprehensive catalogue for anyone interested in player pianos from a company that offers the largest selection of parts and accessories for this instrument in the world. The list of contents starts with tubing and hoses and goes on to cover tools, parts, reed organ supplies, piano supplies, music rolls, and books on reed organs, pianos, player pianos, and automatic musical instruments. There's a slew of technical information and an extensive list of player piano brands and actions of different manufacturers. Each listing is informative, with the item numbered and priced; there is also a very good index. The company has an enormous number of player piano rolls, including Duo-Art, Ampico, and Recordo, ranging in price from around $2.40 to $5.30. MO

XIV-31
RIVERSIDE FURNITURE CORPORATION
P.O. Box 1427
Fort Smith, AR 72901

Getting it all Together, free booklet, published annually, 10 pages, illustrated, black and white and color.

Riverside is a furniture manufacturer with over 8,000 dealers in 50 states and in Canada. Their helpful and informative booklet is designed to tell you how to go about planning rooms and room schemes, use color effectively, solve space problems, and, above all, what to look for when you buy furniture. It contains definitions of

Fabric flows on walls, floors, window shades, and cushions to widen a narrow room designed by Adrienne Wasserman and James R. Patterson. Instructions for all the ideas are in Calico Corners' Guide To Do-It-Yourself Decorating *from Funwood, XIV-19.*

manufacturer's terms you'll find on the label or hang tag, explanations of furniture construction and how to judge quality, even a detailed sketch showing the inner construction of a sofa. A section telling you how to care for wood furniture is also included. RS

XIV-32
THOMASVILLE FURNITURE INDUSTRIES
P.O. Box 339
Thomasville, NC 27360

Founders Guide to Modern Decorating, $2, 96 pages, illustrated, black and white and color.

This breezily written paperback book by three home-furnishings experts, Frances Heard, Harriet Burket, and Joann Francis Gray, covers a lot of ground. It gives a brief description of twentieth-century furniture and design and tells you, with sketched floor plans and photographs of Thomasville's "Founders" contemporary furniture, how to decorate in the modern way. The basic and useful information in the book includes a description of different woods and finishes, metals, plastics, upholstery fabrics, and synthetic fibers plus advice on how to shop for quality modern furniture. MO

XIV-33
WOOD-MODE CABINETRY
Kreamer
Snyder County, PA 17833

Picturebook V of the Loveliest Rooms in America, $2, published every three years, illustrated, color.

The rather grandiose title doesn't explain the true purpose of this booklet, which shows the custom-designed and custom-built cabinets made by Wood-Mode in many different settings —kitchens and bathrooms, family rooms, dens, sewing rooms, bedrooms, and dining rooms. The designs vary from traditional to sleekly contemporary and there are many specialized cabinets for storage of clothes, shoes, sewing machine and supplies, canned foods, and appliances. You can find practical suggestions here if you are building or remodeling and want ideas for storage planning. The cabinets are sold through a network of dealers, most of whom provide a full range of services, including design and installation. RS

XV

Outdoor Living, Gardening, and House Plants

XV-1
ARTHUR EAMES ALLGROVE
281 Woburn Street
Wilmington, MA 01887

The Twentieth Register, *50 cents, published annually, 16 pages, illustrated, black and white.*

The Twentieth Register is a folksy little publication on the kits for terraria and saikei (miniature Oriental dish gardens), plants, and terrarium supplies that Arthur Allgrove sells. A bottle garden kit with pint bottle and cork stopper, soil mix, moss, partridge berries, rattlesnake plantain, and ¼″ dowel with directions is only $3.50 plus postage; a larger half-gallon bottle garden is $6.50. Kits for terrarium bowls include plants and materials. If you are not going to plant your terrarium immediately, Mr. Allgrove advises that you keep it intact in the vegetable bin of the refrigerator. He also has terrarium plants, mosses, and supplies listed by item; insectivorous plants such as the Venus Fly Trap, Northern Pitcher Plant, and Cobra Lily; air plants; bonsai and saikei plants and accessories; and a wide variety of native wildflowers, ferns, orchids, and ground covers. His own *Wildflower Planting Guide* ($2) gives explicit directions for the care and planting of 119 different wildflowers, shrubs, ferns, and ground covers for naturalizing. An interesting and offbeat variation on the usual indoor and outdoor garden. MO

XV-2
ALMOST HEAVEN HOT TUBS
P.O. Box C-1
Renick, WV 24966

Redwood Hot Tubs and Jacuzzi Baths, *free brochure.*

This is basically an informational brochure about hot tubs, their construction and accessories. The different tub sets offered by the company include the tub, heater, pump, Jacuzzi filter, massage and suction jets, two benches, chine joists, water-test kit, and 24-hour timer, and range in price from $1,220 to $2,550, according to diameter and depth. There is also a wading tub for $395 and various hot tub accessories. MO/RS

XV-3
ALUMINUM GREENHOUSES, INC.
14605 Lorain Avenue
Cleveland, OH 44111

Everlite Aluminum Greenhouses, *free, published annually, 28 pages, illustrated, color.*

Everlite's were the first standard prefabricated aluminum greenhouses manufactured here. The catalogue shows the variety of free-standing and lean-to models, with diagrams of installation and specifications. The glazing is double-strength clear glass, with fiberglass as an optional alternate. The company also sells all the usual accessories and equipment, including humidifiers, vents, misting systems, benches for plants, aluminum shelves, soil-heating cables, and roll-up shades. A bay-shaped window greenhouse is priced from $255 to $480, according to size. MO

XV-4
BARREL BUILDERS
1085 Lodi Lane
St. Helena, CA 94574

Hot Tubs by Barrel Builders, *free, published annually, 16 pages, illustrated, black and white.*

The Barrel Builders coopers build their tubs to Wood Tank Institute specifications, and supply pumps, tub tops, hydrotherapy jets, filters, heaters, and blowers. Solar power panels are also

Dutch-design greenhouse with sloping sides of fiberglass/acrylic redwood framed panels. Peter Reimiller, XV-27.

Freestanding Orlyt curved eave design with seven glazed sections. Lord & Burnham, XV-17.

available. The tubs, from 4' to 12' in diameter, cost from $460 to $1787 and are shipped in kit form or preassembled. They offer 2"-thick new tubs and 2" and 3" recycled tubs (the latter are less costly). MO

XV-5
T. E. BROWN INC.
14361 Washington Avenue
San Leandro, CA 94578

Free color brochure.

For over seventy-five years, T. E. Brown's craftsmen have been building redwood tanks and mastering the secrets of the cooperage art. For example, they seal the ends of each stave with a patented formula that virtually eliminates small splits that might lead to leakage. This expertise, originally employed for water storage tanks and wine vats, goes into making their hot tubs, which are distributed to selected dealers throughout the country. They have a wide range of standard sizes in stock at all times for quick delivery, although no specifications are included in this brochure, which merely shows hot tubs in construction and in action. RS

XV-6
CALIFORNIA COOPERAGE
P.O. Box E
San Luis Obispo, CA 93406

Architectural Guidebook to Hot Tub Environments, $4.95, 60 pages, and Hot Tubs, free, 20 pages, and Spas, free, 12 pages; published quarterly, illustrated, color.

Easy-to-erect lean-to model from J.A. Nearing, XV-21.

The architectural guidebook, a companion volume to California Cooperage's line of hot tubs, is a tour-de-force in its own right—a handsome and well-executed collection of design concepts for owners and builders. It shows in both a full-page drawing and a stylized blueprint 26 deck-enclosure settings with hot tubs in three price categories—low cost (under $500), medium range ($1000 to $2000), and sky's-the-limit luxurious professional installations, some of which might be added to an existing or additional part of the house. No specific prices are offered; this is strictly an inspirational idea book, and a good one. The company's hot-tub catalogue offers redwood, cedar, or mahogany tubs together with the supporting equipment—gas or electric heaters, air switch, time clock, and massage jets. The tubs are from 4' to 7' in diameter and package prices run from $1,795 to $3,245.

A spa differs from a hot tub only in being made of a different material, in this case a fiberglass and tile tub that can be used indoors or out. California Cooperage has spas in 3 sizes—5' square, 5½' round, and 6' octagon (with tile rim and deck)—and varying depths, priced from $2,465 to $2,995. They incorporate gas or electric heaters, automatic skimmers, and time clocks and can be equipped with optional hydrojet or air-bubble attachments. MO/RS

XV-7
CHILD LIFE PLAY SPECIALTIES, INC.
15 Whitney Street
Holliston, MA 01742

Quality Play Equipment, free, published annually, 24 pages, illustrated, color.

Just about every kind of backyard play equipment is shown in this neat catalogue, starting with a three-ladder swing set that combines swings, rings, a trapeze, and three ladders for crawling up and over. Then there's a swing set that teams with a jungle gym, one with rope ladders and a slide, a fireman's gym for the climbing set, all kinds of playhouses, slides, sandboxes, and seesaws, even a space trolley with a bosun's chair that runs on double wires between trees ($54 plus $17 for ladder for boarding the trolley). Most of the equipment can be ordered unpainted and unassembled, or assembled at a slightly higher cost. Some of the sets come in kit form. Prices are reasonable for most items, the most expensive being the playhouses and the complete Fire Chief Swing Set ($460). MO

XV-8
CORNING GLASS WORKS
Houghton Park
Corning, NY 14830

Plant Helpers, free 12-page color brochure, illustrated.

Corning, better known for cookware, has come up with a line of good-looking and practical aids to growing house plants, specifically a new type of pot and saucer, made of tinted glass and designed so the pot is elevated above the saucer to give better drainage and prevent overwatering. Optional additions are a glass dome that fits over saucer or pot to create a mini-greenhouse for starting seedlings or revitalizing ailing plants and glass rooter marbles that can be put in the saucer for starting bulbs, cuttings, or an avocado plant. There is also a macramé plant hanger, and

Plant Helpers tinted glass pots and saucers from Corning Glass Works, XV-8.

you can get a windowsill planter tray with brackets and glass shelves to hold the pots. The smoky-brown color of the glass is much more attractive than plastic and scientific tests have shown that the light penetrating the container has no detrimental effect on growth; in fact, plants actually grow better in these pots. The pots, domes, and saucers come in 5", 7" and 9" sizes, and are generally available through retail sources that sell Corning products. RS

XV-9
COUNTRY FLOORS
300 East 61st Street
New York, NY 10021

Ceramic Tiles for Floors and Walls, $5 (refundable with purchase), published annually, 34 pages in folder, illustrated, color.

While Country Floors specializes primarily in imported floor and wall tiles, they also sell handsome sculptured terra-cotta planters from Tuscany in a variety of sizes and shapes, based on antique designs and decorated with classic themes, plus garden seats, friezes, and columns. MO/RS/ID

XV-10
DESERT PLANT COMPANY
P.O. Box 880
Marfa, TX 79843

Cacti of the Southwest U.S.A., $1, 38 pages, illustrated, black and white.

The catalogue shows many varieties of cacti suitable for terraria or gardens and gives growing instructions. Each item is named, numbered, described, and priced. Prices range from under $1 to around $25, with a minimum postpaid shipment of 10 small plants. Leaflets are also included for special offers on assorted cacti, quantity price offers, and desert driftwood and cactus wood. MO

XV-11
EDMUND SCIENTIFIC COMPANY
7082 Edscorp Building
Barrington, NJ 08007

Edmund Scientific Catalogue, $1, published semiannually, 100 pages, illustrated, black and white and color.

Weather instruments are just one of the many useful items in this catalogue. Among them are various outdoor and indoor-outdoor thermometers, such as the Min-Max, which tells you the highest and lowest readings and the present temperature at a glance; one that also gives you the humidity reading; and a digital time-and-temperature indicator with an alarm to alert you to a preselected temperature setting so you can rush out and protect your plants (around $90). There are wind speed monitors and indicators; a wind chill meter; a weather computer that with the aid of a barometer enables you to predict the weather 24 hours in advance; and a digital rain gauge that never needs emptying, for which you can take a remote reading on an indoor counter (around $50). MO

XV-12
FOUR SEASONS SOLAR PRODUCTS CORP.
672 Sunrise Highway
West Babylon, NY 11704

Four Seasons Solarium & Passive Solar Greenhouse, free, published annually, 24 pages, illustrated, black and white and color.

A carefully designed alternative to the traditional energy-wasting single-glazed greenhouse, the Four Seasons solar greenhouse uses double and triple glazing, solar collectors, and specially tailored climate control and heat exchange systems to provide year-round energy savings. The

Family-size redwood hot tub from Viking Sauna, XV-36.

greenhouses come in all standard sizes, and many of them are photographed in color; the accompanying text is extensive, covering such areas as tax credits, warranties, and suiting your greenhouse to your climate. There is also a special greenhouse-spa kit to turn the interior of your greenhouse into a steamroom/spa/hot-tub center. Technical specifications and price list included. MO

XV-13
GIRARD NURSERIES
P.O. Box 428
Geneva, OH 44041

Catalogue, free, published annually, 36 pages, illustrated, black and white and color.

Girard has a good selection of evergreen trees and shrubs, bonsai trees, and flowering shrubs such as azaleas, rhododendrons, forsythia, and lilacs, as well as ground covers, climbing vines, and ornamental and shade trees. All the baby bonsai trees are two and three years old, root-pruned and potted in 2″ and 3″ pots. A bonsai starter collection of 16 trees is $17.50. MO

XV-14
GOTHIC ARCH GREENHOUSES
P.O. Box 1564
Mobile, AL 36601

Gothic Arch Greenhouses, free brochure, illustrated.

Designed in the shape of a Gothic arch as opposed to the usual gable design, these greenhouses allow plenty of space for multi-level growing and take advantage of a curved surface's ability to transmit more light without harsh shadows or hot spots. The prefabricated, ready-to-assemble greenhouses come in four sizes, with either redwood or redwood-and-cedar framing and fiberglass glazing panels, and range in price from $574 to $3,571. Heating and cooling systems are extra. MO

XV-15
GREAT LAKES ORCHIDS
P.O. Box 1114
Monroe, MI 48161

Orchid Species, free, published semiannually, 24 pages, black and white.

There are no illustrations in this catalogue, just an alphabetical listing of the orchids with their prices—but the descriptions are detailed and indicate the country of origin and the temperature recommended for culture under lights or on windowsills. The company also sells books on orchid growing, plus fertilizers, fungicides, and pesticides, nutrient solutions, and potting materials. They have an annual space-making sale when plants may be bought at a special price. MO

XV-16
LITTLE GIANT PUMP COMPANY
3810 N. Tulsa Street
Oklahoma City, OK 73112

Landscaping with Light and Water, free, 32 pages, illustrated, color.

This pamphlet shows how to plan and install Little Giant fountain jets and rings, waterfalls, pumps, and outdoor lights (both above ground and submersible). Many of the design suggestions are illustrated with color photographs. RS

XV-17
LORD & BURNHAM
Division Burnham Corporation
2 Main Street
Irvington, NY 10533

More than a Greenhouse, free, 36 pages, and Sunlyt, free, 8 pages; published annually, illustrated, color.

Lord & Burnham has a greenhouse for every setting: backyard, terrace, small apartment, condominium, and penthouse. Each greenhouse is shown in color, with a schematic drawing. Prices range from $904 to almost $7,000. A solar model for the window costs $200 to $245. The greenhouse catalogue gives extensive technical information to do with insulation, heating, and ventilation, and there is a selection of accessory equipment.

The Sunlyt is a build-it-yourself greenhouse, either lean-to, free-standing, or a window model. The brochure describes the do-it-yourself procedures in text and with pictures. MO

XV-18
MCGREGOR GREENHOUSES
1195 Thompson Avenue, P.O. Box 36
Santa Cruz, CA 95063

Free booklet, published seasonally, illustrated, black and white.

The McGregor redwood-framed and fiberglass greenhouses bolt together for strength and por-

Cedar-log frame backyard play structure from Northwestern, XV-23.

tability and come free-standing or attached. Prices start at about $180 for the small Green Room attached model. One of the features is a "double-layer design" that permits easy installation of an inexpensive polyfilm liner that can save up to 40 percent on heating costs. A selection of essential accessories is also available. MO

XV-19
MERRY GARDENS
P.O. Box 595
Camden, ME 04843

The Merry Herbs, brochure, 50 cents, published annually.

In addition to a good selection of potted herbs, which includes all the familiar ones like rosemary, tarragon, thyme, and mint and some less common, such as lemon grass, elecampane, and hyssop, Merry Gardens has a large number of scented leaved geraniums, miniature and dwarf geraniums, and ivies. Ivies are around $1, geraniums $1.25 to $2. There's a minimum order of $8 plus postage and prices are subject to change. The plants are in 2" to 3" pots and are shipped after March 15 through April and May and again in September and October, with limited shipping in June and November. MO

XV-20
MEYCO PRODUCTS, INC.
255 Park Avenue
Hicksville, NY 11801

Meyco Safety Pool Covers, and Meyco Tensional Tennis Curtain, free, illustrated, color.

Meyco offers mesh swimming pool covers (with safety anchors and springs) precut to fit most rectangular pools. You can provide additional information using materials enclosed in the folder to make it possible for this company to custom-cut a cover for any pool, regardless of size or shape. Prices range from $258 to $977 according to the size of the pool. The company also includes in the folder a handy little brochure on pool maintenance.

The Meyco Tensional Tennis Curtains are windscreens designed to survive storms of up to hurricane strength without damage. A sample of the mesh material is included in the brochure. RS

XV-21
J. A. NEARING CO., INC.
9390 Davis Avenue
Laurel, MD 20811

Janco Greenhouses, $1.50 (refundable with purchase), published semiannually, illustrated, color.

This catalogue shows a very extensive selection of easy-to-erect greenhouses of all shapes (lean-to, free-standing, or even span) and sizes (from a 16"-deep window box to an elegant two-story model). Prices range from $190 for the smallest window box to $6404 for the 52' Chesapeake 21. The catalogue also shows every kind of accessory including misters and plant-gro-propagation mats. MO

Freestanding redwood hot tub from Spring Mountains, XV-32.

XV-22
NOR'EAST MINIATURE ROSES, INC.
58 Hammond Street
Rowley, MA 01969

*Nor'East Miniature Roses, free, published
semiannually, 16 pages, illustrated, color.*

These dwarf roses grow only 12" to 15" tall at
most, sometimes only 5" to 8", and reflect, in
miniature, the classic hybrid teas. They are cared
for like any other roses but have the added advantage of being growable both indoors and out
—miniatures in the garden can be potted in the
fall and brought inside. Prices for these exquisite, colorful little roses are very reasonable, from
around $2.75 to $3.50 each. You can order a basic
indoor kit—four plants, four pots, three quarts
of potting mix, and instructions, $13.75—and
various collections selected by Nor'East Roses. A
collection of twelve of the highest-rated miniature roses is around $30. Some of the roses make
splendid plants for hanging baskets. Nor'East
also sells their own special potting mix and *The
Complete Book of Miniature Roses* by Charles Mar-
den Fitch ($12.95), which tells you all you need
to know. MO

XV-23
NORTHWESTERN DESIGN PRODUCTS INC.
(BigToys)
3113 S. Pine Street
Tacoma, WA 98409

*Backyard BigToys, free, published annually,
8 pages, illustrated, black and white.*

A complete line of playstructures specifically designed for backyard use. The cedar-log frame-
works, in sizes ranging from 7' x 8' to 18' x 20',
feature swings, slides, ropes, and ladders, and
can be assembled without professional help. The
catalogue is comprehensive and includes a photograph of each structure, suggested age groups,
ground plans, basic building instructions, and
an illustrated list of accessories. Prices on request. MO/RS

XV-24
ORCHIDS BY HAUSERMANN, INC.
P.O. Box 363
Elmhurst, IL 60126

*Orchids by Hausermann, $1, updated
annually, 72 pages, illustrated, black and
white and color.*

Orchids may not be commonly thought of as
house plants, but they can be grown in an east,
west, or south window. The Hausermann catalogue tells you about the conditions, temperature, light, and care different varieties need and
which are suitable for home growing. Hausermann's listing of species orchids and related hy-
brids, imported from tropical countries around
the world, represents the widest possible color
choice. Plants are sold potted in 3" to 5" pots,
with the exception of a few larger or smaller varieties. Most adapt easily to various growing
conditions. Some are collector's items and a chal-
lenge to grow and bloom. In addition to the variety, the listing gives color, blooming season,
and price range of the orchids, many of which
are shown in color photographs. MO

XV-25
PACIFIC COAST GREENHOUSE
MANUFACTURING COMPANY
8360 Industrial Avenue
Cotati, CA 94928

*Greenhouses and Solariums; Greenhouse
Equipment, three free brochures, illustrated,
black and white.*

The three brochures describe the company's
products and equipment supplies, their standard
greenhouse and lean-to solarium models, their
recently designed "Luther Burbank" economy
greenhouse with panels of fiberglass reinforced
acrylic, and a great deal of equipment including
gas and electric heaters, thermostats, humidi-
stats, magnetic water valves, and air-circulating
fans. Their higher priced greenhouses, from 6' to
18' wide, and their small economy greenhouse
are all framed with redwood (specially treated to
eliminate termites and fungus) and meticulously
carpentered, and all are prefabricated. The company claims that all you need to erect one of their
models is a ladder, a screwdriver, a hammer, a
friend, and one page of instructions. No prices
are included in the brochures, but further information will be sent on request. MO

XV-26
PERICULUM
P.O. Box 15
Yellow Springs, OH 45387

*Periculum, The Ceiling Fan Specialists, free
brochure, 8 pages, illustrated, color.*

Although Periculum's chief product is the ceiling
fan, they also have a ready-to-assemble garden
bench with cast iron sides and fir slat seat and

back that comes primed, sanded, and ready to finish. The supply of these is limited, according to the leaflet that came with the fan brochure, so best inquire about availability. MO

XV-27
PETER REIMULLER—THE GREENHOUSEMAN
980 17th Avenue
Santa Cruz, CA 95062

These Are my Greenhouses, $1 (refundable with purchase), published annually, 24 pages, illustrated, color.

The brochure describes the full line of greenhouses, which have redwood frames and fiberglass-acrylic panels or, in the case of the Gothic arch Crystalaire model, a fiberglass or polyethylene cover. Among other models are a Dutch design with sloping sides that let in more sunlight, a lean-to greenhouse, and a most intriguing geodesic dome, 15' in diameter, easiest of all to erect because all you need to do is bolt the rigid triangles together. All the greenhouses have preassembled doors, ridge beams, and vent supports, and precut panels, and can be put together by the novice. There are also accessories such as exhaust fans, humidifiers and heaters, heating cables, and shade screens. A chart tells you the BTUs needed per hour to keep the greenhouse at 55°F at night. For indoor gardeners, Reimuller has a mini-greenhouse, 2½' wide and 4' long with 15 cubic feet of growing space that can be used on a windowsill. Request price list when writing. MO

XV-28
THE RENOVATOR'S SUPPLY
71 Northfield Road
Miller's Falls, MA 01349

The Renovator's Supply, $2 (refundable with purchase), 48 pages, illustrated, black and white.

The Renovator's Supply has some Victorian-style garden accessories, such as a Venetian fluted urn that is still being manufactured as it was before the Civil War, a French reservoir urn, and a classic Greco-Roman urn. A cast iron reproduction of an old railroad bench in bird-of-paradise motif comes in 5' and 8' lengths, assembled or unassembled; the large size is $280 unassembled, $360 assembled. MO

Blue Blanket polyethylene Ethafoam hot tub cover from Tubmakers, XV-34.

XV-29
SANTA BARBARA GREENHOUSES
390 Dawson Drive
Camarillo, CA 93010

Santa Barbara Greenhouses, free brochure, illustrated, black and white.

Inexpensive free-standing and lean-to greenhouses of redwood with fiberglass glazing, precut and ready to assemble in a variety of sizes. You can have a lean-to model for just $168.50, or a free-standing model for $200. The largest free-standing greenhouse costs around $2,000. There are also redwood benches and various climate controls such as heaters, fans, humidifiers, and an automatic mist system. MO

XV-30
SANTA CRUZ FOUNDRY
Courthouse Square
Hanford, CA 93230

Santa Cruz Foundry, free 6-page brochure, illustrated, black and white.

The simple brochure illustrates the foundry's charming traditional wrought iron garden benches and table pedestals. The benches come in three models with wrought iron sides painted black or forest green and seating slats of Douglas fir with a Danish oil stain. Of these, the Empire is the most elaborate and decorative. Estate has less ornate sides and Century is like a simple park bench. The two pedestals are Victorian, the classic nineteenth-century table used in European sidewalk cafés ($124), and English Pub, a design originally struck in 1842 that became a standard fixture in British public houses ($73). Either one would be as attractive indoors as outdoors. Prices for the benches range, according to length and style, from $144 to $491. MO

XV-31
SHAFFER'S TROPICAL GARDENS
1220 41st Avenue
Capitola, CA 95010

Catalogue, free, 24 pages, illustrated, color, with supplementary lists published semiannually.

Shaffer's specializes in orchids and for their fortieth year in business they issued an attractive color catalogue. Plants of limited or constantly changing availability are written up periodically in the supplementary lists. All plants listed in the catalogue are measured by leaf spread. They also have books on orchid culture. MO

XV-32
SPRING MOUNTAINS ENERGY SYSTEMS
2617 San Pablo Avenue
Berkeley, CA 94702

Spring Mountains Hot Tubs, free literature.

If you think hot tubs are basically all the same, Spring Mountains has a new wrinkle—the energy angle. As they point out in their brochure, *Energy and Energy Efficiency,* one of the most significant yet often hidden costs of a hot tub is the energy used to heat it, which in most areas of the U.S. can be around $900 a year, or over a 10-year period considerably more than the cost of the tub. Spring Mountain aims to reduce these costs by paying particular attention to the insulative character of the tub. They use insulative blankets, extra-thick lumber, and a second, wooden lid to limit heat loss. Another of their ways to conserve energy is a copper-coil convection heater. Solar panels and special pumps are also available, and such equipment can save you money if you live in the right climate. The brochure discusses the different heating methods for hot tubs—natural gas, LP and butane gas, electric heaters, wood-fired heaters for rural areas, solar energy, convection heaters, and pump-powered heaters—in a very useful and informative way. Spring Mountain's hot tubs are made of kiln-dried all-heart redwood with 5 bolt-steel hoops and come in kit form, precut with assembly instructions, benches, covers, equipment, hardware, and piping. Tubs are priced according to size and heating system. Least expensive are a Japanese-style soaking tub with a copper-coil convection heater that uses natural or propane gas, and a rural system type that utilizes a woodburning water heater; a 5' tub is around $1,300. MO

XV-33
TEXAS GREENHOUSE COMPANY
P.O. Box 11219
Ft. Worth, TX 76109

Greenhouses, free, 18 pages, illustrated, color; and *Accessories (Cat. #14), free, 18 pages, illustrated, black and white.*

The ten different greenhouse models (each available in many sizes) are priced from $996 to $9874. Some have redwood frames, others aluminum. A few can be expanded with additional structural units. Schematic diagrams are included, and precise foundation plans and bolts are shipped out upon receipt of your order, with illustrated instructions for erection.

The Accessories catalogue lists everything from alarms to wood preservatives. Over 150 items for the maintenance and improvement of a greenhouse system are included, among them meters of all kinds, shutters, fans, heaters, misters, timers, soil warmers, and shading elements. MO

XV-34
THE TUBMAKERS
1830 Fourth Street
Berkeley, CA 94710

Brochure, 20 cents (refundable with purchase), published quarterly, 6 pages, illustrated, black and white.

This company, which has been in the business of making hot tubs since 1974, offers two types of redwood hot tub. One is the standard 4'-high model with chair-height bench, the other a Japanese-style tub, 2½' to 3' high, where you sit on the bottom or a very low bench. Both come in 5', 6' and 7' diameters, at prices ranging from $795 to $1255, with bench extra. These prices do not include cost of accessories such as tub cover, bench, hydro-jets, pump, filter and heater, preplumbing of equipment, and water-care kit. Complete hot tub system kits cost from just under $2,000 to over $3,000. These can be bought unassembled, with full instructions, for you to install yourself. MO

XV-35
VAN NESS WATER GARDENS
2460 North Euclid
Upland, CA 91786

Water Visions. The Complete Guide to Water Gardening, $1, published annually, 42 pages, illustrated, black and white and color.

A charming and unusual catalogue-cum-guide on the delights of water gardens, which can be anything from a pond with aquatic flowers and goldfish to a manmade bog garden to a water-filled tub with miniature water lilies. The guide tells you how to build and maintain a pond and make a waterfall and offers a selection of oxygenating grasses, ornamental grasses, aquatic flowers such as water lilies, water hyacinths, and water iris, and bog plants. For small spaces, there is a section on tub gardens and a Tub Garden Starter Kit for $10.95. Van Ness also sells fountains, pond-care products, and filters, pumps, and underwater lights; books on ponds, pools, and water plants; even aquatic snails, the little scavengers that eat up dead vegetation, fish waste, and algae. If you are looking for something different in gardening, this is it. MO

Lacy vinyl and tubular aluminum with baked polyester enamel finish frames for poolside activities. Brown Jordan, I-19.

XV-36
THE VIKING SAUNA COMPANY
P.O. Box 6298
San Jose, CA 95150

*The Sauna by Viking, 10 pages, and **Hot Tubs by Viking**, 8 pages, and **Spas**, 6 pages; free brochures, color.*

The sauna brochure features prebuilt modular sauna rooms priced from $1,500 to $5,000. Insulated walls, ceiling panels, flooring, carpet, heater, sauna stones, electrical controls, door, light, and benches are included in the package. You can also special-order saunas in odd shapes. These will be planned by Viking's free design service and you receive detailed specifications based on your floor plan and a custom precut sauna room package with all equipment.

The hot tubs, round or oval, in redwood or mahogany, are available in 19 stock sizes at prices from around $850 to $3,080. These can also be custom built. If you wish to assemble the tub yourself, you can purchase complete plumbing packages separately.

Spas, like hot tubs, are designed for one or more bathers to relax in warm swirling water, but are of one-piece fiberglass construction with a mosaic inlay rim. They may be installed outdoors or indoors and are available in five sizes, the largest 9' in diameter. MO/RS

Cedar tables and benches for outdoor or indoor use. Walpole, I-85.

XV-37
WALTHER'S EXOTIC HOUSE PLANTS
R.D. #3, Box 30-D
Catskill, NY 12414

Living Art Creations, $1 *(with plant list), 12 pages, revised quarterly, illustrated, black and white.*

The catalogue shows striking, individually designed horticultural art creations by sculptor John P. Walther—arrangements of stone, twig, moss, and plants set in California redwood. Most of the plants used are epiphytic Tillandsias, or air plants, which are unique in form and easy to grow. Given good light and occasional mistings, they will go through all the plant cycles including blooming and reproduction of new plants. There are some wood plaques that can be used hanging or standing, whereas the other arrangements are either centerpieces or sculptural in effect. Plaques range in size from 7″ to 14″ and in price from $15 to $28; a 12″-long centerpiece is $45, and a 12″ sculpture, $38. The list of exotic house plants features bromeliads, cacti, and succulents. MO

Poolside pavilion, terrace awning, and backyard screen panels. Ideas with canvas from American Canvas Institute, XIV-1.

XV-38
WESTERN ARBORETUM
P.O. Box 2827
Pasadena, CA 91105

Western Arboretum's New Bonsai Catalogue, $1, *published annually, 24 pages, illustrated, black and white.*

Everything for the bonsai enthusiast—living exotic trees and shrubs, imported containers, and supplies—from a company recommended by botanical gardens and bonsai societies throughout the world. There are also books on bonsai culture and related subjects such as the art of the Japanese garden. For an easy way to start, Western Arboretum sells starter, intermediate, and advanced bonsai kits. A starter kit costs $9.95. MO

XV-39
THE WOODEN SWING COMPANY
4 Tripp Street
Framingham, MA 01701

The Wooden Swing Company, free brochure, 8 pages, illustrated, black and white.

An assortment of backyard swings and gyms designed to create a physical fitness environment for children. Ladders and climbing frames are made from "industrial clear" lumber, sanded smooth and covered with two coats of lead-free, dark brown finish. The hardwood rungs are finished with a color coordinated stain. The swing seats are lightweight but durable enough to withstand weather, with adjustable nylon swing ropes. This wooden playground equipment will last for years with proper maintenance. Among the pieces shown are different swing and gym combinations, such as the free-standing Olympic gym, which has an 8′ climbing net, knotted rope, sliding pole, and two movable platforms, plus optional tent; log-cabin playhouses; an indoor climbing gym for young children with movable platforms that can be positioned to use as tables or benches; and an old-fashioned two-bench lawn swing that is large enough for four adults. No price list was included with the brochure we received, although the company apparently sells by mail. MO

XVI

A Home Decorator's Potpourri of Practical Hints

This chapter took shape after the text was completed, when what remained was a good-sized stack of tips, hints, practical how-to's, and factual information too handy to be left behind, and yet too general for inclusion in related chapters.

As most home decorators know all too well, once we become accustomed to the look of our home it is very difficult to get a new slant on how to redecorate. We all want to avoid costly mistakes, and a complete, top-to-bottom makeover is intimidating—and expensive.

If you are stuck, consider window treatments. First of all, redecorating windows pays off in more ways than just a fresh, new appearance—shades, blinds, and draperies are real energy savers. Secondly, a new look for windows will invariably change the look of the whole room, giving you something to "build on" for inspiration in other areas.

The topics that follow offer practical help and suggestions in tackling common problems when redecorating.

WINDOW SHADES CAN SAVE ENERGY AND MONEY

Did you know that plain window shades can save up to 15 percent of the costs of heating and cooling your home? They don't have to be the special insulating type, although these do an even more efficient job.

A slim trough at the base of the windows hides motorized shades in this ultra-modern bed-sitting room. The shades can be raised to any height without disturbing the dramatic line of the windows and wall. When drawn completely, the shades assure privacy and save energy.

According to scientific tests made at the Illinois Institute of Technology in winter, a drawn roller shade can prevent from 24 to 31 percent of the heat loss through glass. In summer, a translucent shade admits 44 percent less heat, a light-color opaque shade 47 to 54 percent less heat than an unshaded window. For a house with a 15 percent window area, this would mean that using ordinary window shades can reduce heat loss about eight percent in the winter, while in summer the energy required for cooling is reduced by almost 20 percent. This translates into a difference of about eight cents on every dollar spent on fuel consumption for heating, up to 21 cents for cooling. Even if your home is not air-conditioned, drawing the shades appreciably lowers the inside temperature of the rooms.

As the accompanying photographs of a modern bed-sitting room show, the use of shades need not be limited to standard windows. Architect J. R. Strignano designed a slim trough to be built into the base of the slant-topped cathedral window frame, where motorized shades disappear when not in use. They can be raised to any desired height without interfering with the basic line, or they can be closed completely for privacy and to reduce substantially the amount of heat or cold that comes through such a large glass area.

MEASURING YOUR WINDOWS FOR SHADES AND BLINDS

Measuring correctly for window shades, venetian blinds, and woven shades is both important and exacting. First of all, you should use a wooden or metal ruler; cloth tape is too flexible.

To measure the width for a new window shade to hang inside the window casement, measure the exact distance between the points where the brackets are to be placed (A). On your order, specify IB (inside bracket) mounting—the factory will allow for bracket clearance.

If you want the shade to hang outside the window casement, measure between the points where the brackets are to be placed—they should be positioned to allow 1½″ to 2″ overlap on each side of the casement (B). Again, be sure to specify OB (outside bracket) mounting on your order.

To measure the length of your window, measure from the top of the frame (soffit) to top of the sill and add 12″ (D). The extra 12″ is the safety margin that allows the shade to be pulled to full length without being torn from the roller.

If shade is to be hung from ceiling, measure from ceiling down to top of sill (E) for length. For width, measure to outer edges of casing (C).

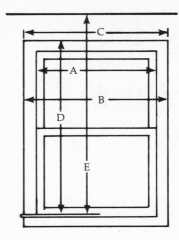

When replacing old shades, measure from tip to tip, including the little metal pins on each end. Specify "tip to tip" on your order.

Decorative trims such as scallops or fringe at the bottom should be added to the length dimension given so that they will rest against the sill and ensure privacy.

To measure the width of venetian blinds to hang *inside* the window casing, measure exact distance between inside edges of window casing (A). Do not make allowances as slats and bottom rail will be made slightly narrower at the factory to prevent rubbing against casing. Headbox will also be made narrower to fit installation brackets. Be sure to specify IB (inside blinds) on your order.

To measure the length of your window, measure distance from the top of the frame (soffit) to top of the lower sill (B). As the manufacturer makes no deduction in length, you may wish to make blind-length dimension ½″ shorter to avoid touching sill. If there is no sill, or blind is to overlap the sill, measure (E) to point to which blind is to reach.

If you want the blinds to hang on the outside of the window casing or the wall, measure the exact distance (C) between points where brackets are to be placed. Brackets need 1″-wide flat surface for mounting. Measurement (C) should be at least 3″ more than measurement (A) for privacy. Be sure to specify OB on order for this type of blind.

To find the length, measure exact distance (D) between point where top of brackets will be and top of sill. If there is no sill, or the blind is to overlap the sill, measure (F) down to point blind is to reach.

To measure a door for blinds, follow directions as for OB (outside bracket) but specify "for door"

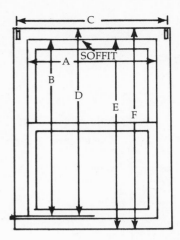

on order, since these require hold-down brackets to keep the blind from swaying when the door is opened or closed. These brackets may also be ordered as an "extra" for window blinds to prevent swaying in the breeze. Be sure to specify on your order whether brackets at each end of the bottom rail are to be fastened to top of sill, inside the jambs, or to the face of the casing, door, or wall.

To measure width of woven aluminum shades to hang inside the window casing, measure exact distance between inside edges (A). Do not make any allowance, as shades will be made slightly narrower to prevent rubbing against casing.

To measure the length, take exact distance between top of frame (soffit) and top of sill (B). If there is no sill, or shade is to overlap the sill, measure to point to which shade is to reach (E). Specify IB installation on your order.

To find width of blind to be installed on the outside face of window casing or wall, measure exact distance between points where brackets are to be placed (C). Again, this should be at least 3" more than measurement (A) for privacy.

To measure length, take exact distance between point where top of shade, including roller, will be placed and top of sill (D). If there is no sill, or shade is to overlap the sill, take measurement (F) down to point shade is to reach. The factory will include extra "wrap-around" for roller.

(Instructions and sketch on blinds: Levelor-Lorentzen)

TIPS ON BUYING FABRIC
FOR CURTAINS AND DRAPERIES

When you choose a fabric for your curtains or draperies, don't go on appearance alone. Natu-rally you want something attractive in color, pattern, and texture that will go with your room scheme, but there are other important factors to take into consideration. Ideally, the fabric should be resistant to heat, humidity, and fading caused by strong sunlight, flame-retardant, and not liable to soil easily or to sag or wrinkle. Fabrics with a special finish, such as permanent press, keep their crispness through launderings, one of the reasons so many people are using drip-dry sheets in designer patterns for curtains and slipcovers. Handle the fabric to judge the "hand" or feel (the softness, firmness, fineness) and then pull it in different directions to see if the weave stays together or separates. A fabric that is tightly woven will have a longer life than a loosely woven one. To get the color effect, hold the fabric up to daylight or strong light. Dyes should go right through the fabric, not just be printed on the surface. Scratch the print with your fingernail to see if it stays fast. Always check any special cleaning or laundering instructions and keep a note of them for future reference.

Today there are many good-looking ready-made draperies on the market, many of which can be bought by mail in a wide choice of fabrics, patterns, and styles. Ready-made draperies should be well tailored, with securely-stitched header pleats and, if the draperies are patterned, the pattern should be in the same position on each panel.

Give your rooms a custom look by making easy fabric shades to match draperies, slipcovers, upholstery, or bedspread.

HANGING CURTAINS AND DRAPERIES

Whatever shape and size your windows, there are rods to suit them. For a double-hung window, *below left,* for example, you can select from hardware suitable for many different drapery and curtain types, sill-, apron-, or floor-length. Above the window are drawings of the basic curtain rod. In addition, there are any number of more elaborate drapery and curtain rods available today for a myriad of treatments. What hardware you get simply depends on the treatment you choose. *Below right* are some of the specialized rods:

Curved hardware (1) can be fitted for any type of bow window.

For a bay window, there are single or double extension rods (2) that can adjust to fit each angle.

Brass-finished traverse rods (3), for use with cafe curtains, are made to be seen as part of the window decoration.

A double valance and traverse rod (4) holds draw draperies, as well as a stationary cornice over them. *(All sketches courtesy Ethan Allen.)*

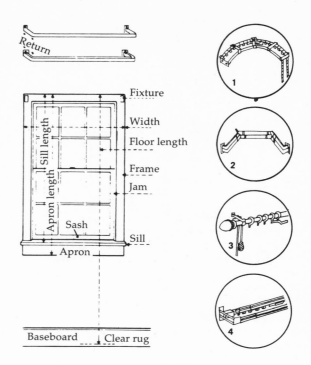

A stunning example of how drapery fabric, carefully chosen, enhances the design of a room by Angelo Donghia for Celanese House. Photographer: Otto Maya.

CUTTING CHART FOR DRAPERY MATERIAL

This unique chart has been scientifically designed to simplify cutting your drapery material. The number of spaces and pleats have been determined for double fullness. The chart is based on 1" double side hems.

If your draperies will draw one way only, consult the cutting chart for one-way draw draperies at bottom of this page. (Remember, one-way draw draperies have only *one* panel.)

Be sure to check with your fabric salesperson for proper amount of material. For example: the measurement of your rod is 36". Following the chart, the fabric for each panel should be cut to measure 48". If your drapery fabric is 54" wide, you will need one width for each panel or two widths for a pair of single-panel draperies. Drapery fabric is woven in various widths so be sure to check this measurement with your fabric salesperson.

If your windows are wide, you will need multiple widths for each panel of your draperies. For example, according to the chart a rod measurement of 92" requires the material for each panel to be cut 104" wide. You would need to cut two widths for each panel or four widths for a pair of double-panel draperies if your fabric is 54" wide. Be sure to add 1" to the cutting width measurement of the chart for seaming each width together.

This chart is based on a 4" return and a 2" overlap (or 6") for *each* panel. If the sum of return and overlap on your rod differs, adjust the cut width and finished width accordingly. Make the necessary adjustment in the first and last space of each panel. For under draperies you will need no return and should make this necessary adjustment. For example, the return on your rod measures 5" and the overlap for *one* panel is 3" for a total of 8". This time, add 2" to the cutting width and finished width for each panel (8" less 6" equals 2").

If the chart does not have your rod measurement, choose the chart measurement that's closest to it, but lower. Then subtract this measurement from your rod measurement. This is the total you must increase your drapery width. Since a pair of draperies has two panels, divide by two and add this figure to the cutting width and finished width of each panel. (*Instructions and charts courtesy of the Kinney Manufacturing Company.*)

Easy to follow cutting chart for one-way draw draperies
(One panel required per drapery)

Rod measurement between brackets	Finished width of panel	No. of 4" spaces	No. of 4" pleats	Width to cut material
36	40	10	9	80
44	48	12	11	96
52	56	14	13	112
60	64	16	15	128
68	72	18	17	144
76	80	20	19	160
84	88	22	21	176
92	96	24	23	192
100	104	26	25	208
108	112	28	27	224
116	120	30	29	240
124	128	32	31	256
132	136	34	33	272
140	144	36	35	288
148	152	38	37	304

Note: Be sure to add 1" to width measurement for every seam you will have in each panel.

Easy to follow cutting chart for two-way draw draperies
(Two panels required per drapery)

Rod measurement between brackets	Finished width of each panel	No. of 4" spaces per panel	No. of 4" pleats per panel	Width to cut material for each panel
36	24	6	5	48
44	28	7	6	56
52	32	8	7	64
60	36	9	8	72
68	40	10	9	80
76	44	11	10	88
84	48	12	11	96
92	52	13	12	104
100	56	14	13	112
108	60	15	14	120
116	64	16	15	128
124	68	17	16	136
132	72	18	17	144
140	76	19	18	152
148	80	20	19	160

Note: Be sure to add 1" to width measurement for every seam you will have in each panel.

HOW TO PREPARE THE ROUGH OPENING FOR A NEW WINDOW

If you are remodeling a room, such as an attic, and want to install the windows yourself, here are some tips from a major manufacturer of windows on how to go about it. First, consult your dealer for the precise dimensions of the window before you make the rough opening and check with him on local installation techniques, materials, and building codes, which vary according to the area you live in. Should it be necessary to enlarge the opening to take a larger window, ask your dealer about the proper header size. For a smaller window, frame the opening as in a new installation. *(Directions and sketches, courtesy Andersen Windows.)*

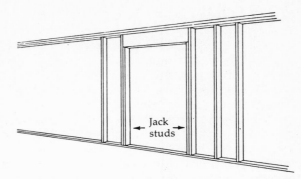

Cut jack studs to fit under header for support. Nail jack studs to regular studs.

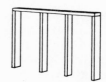

Measure rough opening height from bottom of header to top of rough sill. Cut 2" × 4" cripples and rough sill to proper length. Rough sill length is equal to rough opening width of window. Assemble by nailing rough sill into ends of cripples.

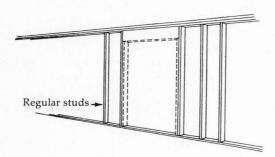

Lay out window opening width between regular studs to equal the window rough opening width plus the thickness of two regular studs.

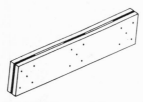

Cut two pieces of window header material to equal the rough opening of window plus the thickness of two jack studs. Nail two header members together using adequate spacer so header thickness equals width of jack stud.

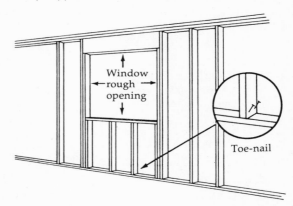

Fit rough sill and cripples between jack studs. Toe-nail cripples to bottom plate and rough sill to jack studs at sides.

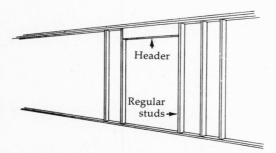

Position header at desired height between regular studs. Nail through the regular studs into header with nails to hold in place until completing next step.

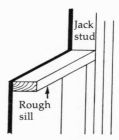

Apply exterior sheathing (fiberboard, plywood, etc.) flush with the rough sill, header and jack stud framing members.

WHAT YOU SHOULD KNOW ABOUT WALL COVERINGS

Since walls are the largest area of a room and can make a tremendous impact on its overall look, when you want to do your own decorating it's a good idea to consider some of the new wall coverings.

Prepasted papers have existed for at least twenty-five years, but the new ones are something special. The designs are well drawn and sophisticated in all price ranges. Costs compare favorably with moderately priced unpasted papers, and the expense of adhesives or paperhangers is eliminated. Do-it-yourself techniques are clearly explained in brochures available when you purchase your paper—and many prepasted coverings are also strippable.

Strippable coverings, stronger than the adhesives that hold them to the wall, are a blend of cellulose, latex, resins, synthetic and natural fibers with, often, a resilient vinyl face coating and/or a fiber backing. They're easy to install and peel off quickly for changes—making them a good investment.

Vinyl coverings are made from a liquid that is either pressed into a film or coated onto a backing of paper or fabric. The advantages are durability, cleanability, and the ease with which it can be removed to make way for new decoration.

Peel-and-stick plastics have the advantage of needing no water, paste, buckets, brushes, or seam rollers—and they can be applied on many surfaces where paper can't. As they are sold by the yard, there is little waste.

To produce a result you are proud of when covering your walls, it is important to remember that the surface must be grease-free and that any and all old wall coverings must be removed—along with all traces of old paste. To prepare a previously painted wall, chip off the old paint and spackle any holes, then seal with glue sizing. Unpainted plaster and paper-surfaced wallboard should also be sized before papering. An oil-base-painted surface should be sanded first, while new plywood must be shellacked or oil-base-painted before applying a wall covering. Be sure to paint all the trim in your room before hanging the wallpaper. Then follow to the letter the manufacturer's directions for hanging.

(All instructions and sketches: Hyde Tools.)

HOW TO HANG WALL COVERINGS

Where to start the first strip

Study the room and decide where to hang the first strip. Generally the first strip is hung on the center of a wall which is most noticed in the room. Start between 2 windows, fireplace, picture window or, if there are no outstanding openings, the first strip may be hung at a corner where an overlap is required into the corner.

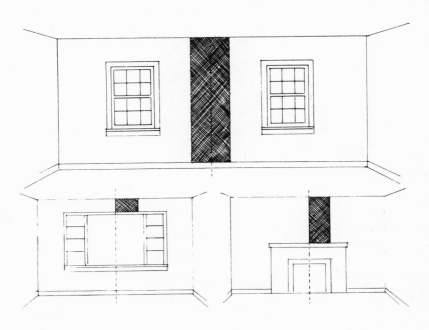

Cutting the first strips

Two sections of the paper must be cut to match pattern from ceiling to floor allowing 2″ of trim at ceiling and baseboard keeping in mind the matching of the designs in the paper.

Using the plumb bob

When the decision is made where to start, drive a tack into wall about 2″ from ceiling. Bob should hang around 2″ from floor. When bob stops swaying make a mark on wall above baseboard. Chalk line, hold line on mark and pull line out at center and release to make a vertical mark on wall. First strip of paper should align with mark. Plumb line each wall to keep vertical.

Paste application

Place the two sections of the matched paper on the table, patterns down, apply paste thoroughly to cover all areas to prevent unpasted spots, except for 2″ at the top for trimming at ceiling. Fold first section of paper, carry to the wall for hanging. Do not paste more than two sections of paper at a time.

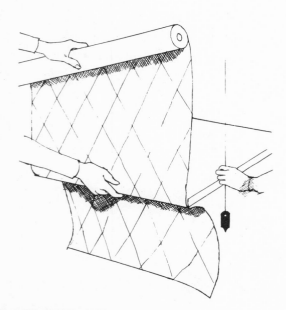

Unrolling the wallcovering

To uncurl the roll, hold it up in one hand and pull down on a section of the wallcovering over the edge of a table with the other hand.

Hanging the first strip

Unfold paper and place in position on wall using chalk line as guide allowing 2″ trim area at the top. Paper may be slid around to fit the area as planned. Starting at the top, brush paper down to smooth out wrinkles unfolding the paper as you go down the wall reaching the baseboard at the bottom, where 2″ of paper has been allowed for baseboard trim.

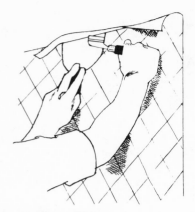

Trimming at the ceiling

Paper is trimmed where wall meets ceiling using a guide and razor knife. Follow the same procedure for the second strip of paper matching the pattern where 2" has been allowed at the top and bottom on the basis of the matched patterns.

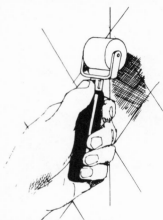

Rolling the paper and seams

Roll seam with hardwood roller. Blisters or raised paper should be gently rolled out. Pin prick covering to allow air to escape.

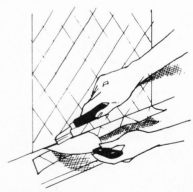

Baseboard trimming

The paper at the base may be trimmed with a serrated casing and corner knife.

Trimming around doors and windows

Concerning doors and windows, paper should be cut and trimmed as indicated using shears, casing, and corner knives.

HOW TO MEASURE FOR WALLPAPER AND BORDER PAPERS

SIZE OF ROOM* IN FEET	WALL HEIGHT TO CEILING			CEILING	BORDER 4 SIDES
	7 FT.	8 OR 9 FT.	10, 11 OR 12 ft.		
	Number of Single Rolls Needed				Yards
6 x 10	7	8	11	3	12
6 x 12, *or* 8 x 10	8	9	12	3	13
8 x 12	8	10	14	3	13
8 x 14, *or* 10 x 12	9	11	15	4	15
9 x 12	9	11	15	5	16
9 x 14	10	12	16	5	17
9 x 16	11	13	18	5	18
10 x 14, *or* 12 x 12	10	12	16	5	17
10 x 16, *or* 12 x 14	11	13	18	6	19
12 x 16, *or* 12 x 14	12	14	19	7	20
12 x 18, *or* 14 x 16	12	15	20	7	21
14 x 18, *or* 16 x 16	13	16	22	8	23
16 x 18	14	17	23	8	24
16 x 20	15	18	24	10	25
	FOR WALLS			FOR CEILING	

* *Deduct one single roll for every two doors or windows of average size in the room—or deduct two single rolls for every three openings counted.*

A GLOSSARY OF WALL COVERING TERMS

These are some of the terms you'll encounter when buying paper and vinyl wallcoverings.

Repeat. Distance from center of one motif of a pattern to the center of the next.

Matching. Hanging wallcovering strips in such a way as to correlate the design from one strip to the next. A *random match*, where the pattern looks well no matter how one panel or strip is placed in relation to another, is the simplest to hang yourself. For this you'd need a stripe or a textured or grasscloth type of covering. In a *straight match*, the pattern of one strip must be joined with a portion of the pattern on the adjoining strip to complete the pattern. In a *drop match*, a portion of the pattern appears on each strip, as in the straight match; however, the pattern will not repeat at the same distance from the ceiling line across the various strips on the wall, but matches at the same horizontal point on alternate strips.

Color run. The amount of rollage produced of a single-color combination at any one time. When the same combination is run again, it has a different run number, and there can be a slight variation in color from the previous run.

Roll of wallcovering. A bolt consisting of thirty-six square feet of wall covering, of which thirty square feet is estimated as usable. Bolts come in single, double, and triple rolls.

Foil wallcovering. A very thin sheet of flexible metal on a backing of paper or fabric.

Strippable wallcovering. One made of chemically treated, non-tearable stock with a special formulation which makes it possible to remove a strip from the wall without wetting.

Prepasted wallcovering. One with an adhesive applied to the back that is activated by dipping in water before hanging.

Pretrimmed wallcovering. One where the selvage has been trimmed from the roll at the factory.

Vinyl wallcoverings. The vinyl used in wallcoverings may be either a liquid or a flexible film. Types of vinyl wallcoverings are: (1) vinyl laminated to paper; (2) paper laminated to lightweight woven cloth and vinyl coated; (3) vinyl laminated to lightweight woven cloth, natural or synthetic; (4) vinyl laminated to lightweight non-woven cloth, natural or synthetic; (5) vinyl laminated to non-woven paper/fabric web; (6) a man-made base impregnated with vinyl.

A small bedroom alcove was turned into a charming sitting area by designer Bobbi Stuart using a pretty all-over patterned wallcovering on walls and chest, with matching fabric window shade, to open up the room visually.

A drab townhouse dining room is transformed by designer Peg Walker into a bright, garden-fresh environment. Trellised wall covering coordinates beautifully with striped shades and a fern-patterned ceiling border.

want to create, but they also help to reduce electricity consumption and prolong the life of light bulbs.

When buying a lamp, make sure that the base is sufficiently weighty so the lamp won't tip easily and the cord long enough to reach from wherever you want it to the nearest outlet. If it isn't, get the store or a hardware store to attach a longer one. Look for an adjustable "harp," the metal support that can adjust to raise or lower the shade. The shade itself should sit level on the lamp. Turn the lamp on to see if the shade allows enough light through. For this, white shades are best, and parchment or fabric (silk, linen) the preferred materials. For safety's sake, check to see if there is a label attached to the lamp socket with a UL (Underwriters' Laboratory) listing of electrical connections, such as socket, switch, plug, and cord.

Measure lamps before buying. The bottom of a desk-lamp shade should stand about fifteen inches above the desk, and a full foot away from the person working, to permit an even distribution of light.

Make sure your table lamp is proportionate to the table to avoid seeing the bulb from above when standing, below when sitting. The distance from the bottom of the shade to the floor, therefore, should measure no less than thirty-eight inches, no more than forty-two inches.

TIPS ON BUYING AND PLACING LAMPS

The proper distances of floor and table lamps from the floor and the relationship of desk and bedside lamps to work surface and bed are shown in the sketches. The purpose is always to avoid light glaring in your eyes—the bulb should not be visible when you are standing, sitting, or lying down. Hanging light fixtures should be at a height of fifty-eight to sixty-three inches from the floor, not way up in the ceiling, and wall lights down about three feet from the ceiling, or a third of the area you want to light. A fixture over a dining table should be low enough to light the table, but not so low it will obstruct sight lines—three feet is usual, two gives more dramatic lighting.

If you are buying a globe fixture, buy a larger globe than the wattage of the bulb requires. This will give you a softer, more diffused light. Incidentally, don't overlook the merits of dimmer switches (inexpensive, available at any hardware store and easy to install on a regular switch outlet). They not only control the level of light in a room, according to the activities or the mood you

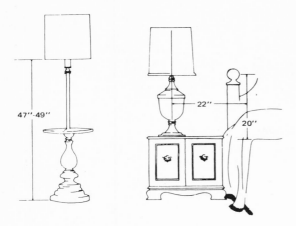

Your bedside lamp should be a maximum of twenty inches higher than the bed, measuring again from the shade bottom. Any higher, and the lamp will cast a glare. Position the bedside lamp twenty-two inches from your head and sixteen inches behind it for proper reading light.

With a floor lamp, the measurement from the floor to the shade bottom should be from forty-seven inches to forty-nine inches. Placement of it ten inches behind the chair is good for reading. *(Courtesy Ethan Allen.)*

Two well-selected simple brass lamps with matching shades add unity and provide practical light sources for chair-side and over-desk reading in an informal office-at-home.

The symmetrical arrangement of furniture and lamps in this small, elegant living room is important for balance of space and light. Designed by Sandy Blake for Celanese. Photographer: Ernest Silva.

WHAT TO CHECK FOR WHEN YOU BUY FURNITURE

When you order furniture from a reputable mail-order company or nationally known manufacturer sight unseen, you can be sure that it will be properly made and of good workmanship. However, if there is any doubt in your mind, here are some checkpoints that will help you judge the construction and comfort of the pieces.

Upholstered Furniture and Sofa Beds

Just by sitting on a piece of upholstered furniture you can discover some of the essential points—if it is comfortable and free from lumpiness and bumpiness, with a well-padded framework and good back support. Bounce up and down a few times to find out if it is sturdily made, listening for creaking joints. Then take a good look at the joint construction revealed by the underside of the frame itself. The pieces should be glued and fastened together with double-dowel joints and reinforced with corner blocks so the frame won't wobble, and the legs should be part of the framework. (See sketches opposite.)

Consider how well the upholstery fabric will stand up under daily use. Tightly woven fabrics wear better than those that are loosely woven; the lightweights, such as cotton and linen, wear better if quilted. A medium color will show least dirt. You might also find out if the fabric has been treated with a protective finish that helps to repel dirt, or ask if it can be done for you, should you be ordering a sofa or chair in your choice of fabric. Loose cushions, which can be reversed or, on a sofa, switched around, are more practical than an upholstered seat and back, while extra arm covers, or sleeves, will protect the places that get a lot of wear. Welt cording, which strengthens seams, also prolongs upholstery life.

It's easy to see what is on the surface, but what's inside counts, too. Visualize the inner workings of an upholstered piece (see the sketches opposite for the anatomy of a chair) and then look for the manufacturer's label, which identifies the wood used for the frame and other parts of the construction and gives the warranty, and the hang tag and the label on the deck (under the seat cushion) which by law must specify the contents and proportions of the stuffing or cushioning that covers the springs and frame, and the fiberfill, or padding, between stuffing and surface fabric. The most commonly used cushioning materials are polyurethane foam or foam rubber (latex); expensive upholstered pieces may have

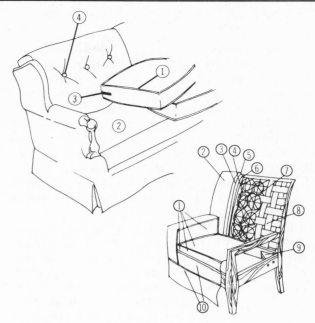

feathers or down. Fiberfill materials are usually polyester, polyester and down, or polyester and foam, and, in less expensive furniture, cotton.

Cushions may be filled with latex or polyurethane foam (the firmest seating), the softer polyester fiberfill, or polyester-wrapped down, most luxuriously yielding. To check the quality of a latex or polyurethane cushion, pick it up and feel the resiliency (it should depress and recover slowly, not quickly) and check the weight (lightness indicates poor quality). Also note the shape. If it looks flat and slabby, it was probably cut from a slab of foam rubber rather than being molded individually.

Test the comfort of an upholstered piece by sitting on it. If the piece feels good, then check its construction. The welting should be made on the bias and run straight (1). The deck under the cushions should be self-covered (2). The cushions should be reversible (3). The buttons should be sewn through the filling and strongly hold the tufting (4).

Now visualize the skeletal frame of a well-made piece of upholstered furniture. The welting is straight, crisp, and on the bias (1). Upholstery layers include surface fabric (2), cotton backing for padding (3), muslin (4), the stuffing (5), a burlap cover (6), hand-tied springs (7), and, finally, cross-lashings of tough fabric webbing (8). Screw-in wood-block braces strengthen the frame (9). The fabric pattern is well-matched, and the legs are one piece with the framework (10). *(Sketches courtesy Ethan Allen.)*

Sofa beds are of various types. The most sofa-like is the convertible, which has a concealed mattress that pulls or folds out from the seat so it can be permanently made up with sheets and blankets, and the less comfortable jackknife type, in which the back folds down to the same level as the seat for sleeping. The studio couch, an upholstered mattress on an upholstered box spring (sometimes with an extra bed tucked underneath), and the day bed are really more like beds than sofas, though they are so designed that they can serve as seating pieces, too.

Always test a sofa bed to see if it opens easily and is not too heavy or tricky for you to handle alone. It should glide out smoothly and without a lot of creaks and noise, and the metal parts should not rub against the upholstered arms of the sofa. Convertibles come with single- or double-fold mechanisms. The single-fold opens to become a wide bed the length of the sofa, so that you sleep parallel to the sofa back. The double-fold opens to a bed the width of the sofa and the sofa back becomes the headboard, an infinitely more comfortable arrangement for sitting up or reading in bed.

With the sofa bed open, test the mattress, which will be either an innerspring or foam-rubber latex or a similar synthetic. Don't just feel it with your hand. Lie on it, as if on a bed, stretch out and move around to ascertain if it is really comfortable. Like any mattress, it should not be soft and yielding, but firm enough to support your body and prevent bad posture.

Check the upholstery to see that the welting is straight, the deck self-covered, the cushions reversible, and the pattern well matched. Also check the service warranty. This is usually five years for the mechanism and wood frame, a shorter time for the upholstery and filling.

Wood Furniture and Case Pieces

Here the manufacturer's label should specify the type of wood used and any man-made components. Check chairs and tables for block-corner construction and make sure there are washers where screws are used. Look underneath a table to make sure that the joints are well secured and rock the table to see if it is well balanced and sturdy and doesn't creak. If it is an extension table, operate it a few times to find how easy it is to handle alone, and check to see that the wood and finish matches on the leaves. (See sketch opposite.) Sit in chairs and sway back and forth to ascertain if they are well balanced and won't tip over or wobble.

On chests and cabinets, the front, top, and sides should blend in color and graining. The backing of a chest should be recessed into grooves and screwed into the frames, drawers hand-fitted and easy to close, the insides smoothly sanded and sealed. Cabinet doors should fit snugly, swing evenly on precisely aligned hinges, and have magnetic catches. Check inset panels on all doors, drawers, and sides for tightness.

Look inside and out, underneath and behind furniture for signs of quality construction. Dresser should have sturdy, hand-sanded top and sides (1), floating construction that allows for expansion (2), a recessed back panel (3), dust panels between the drawers (4), hand-fitted drawers and drawer guides (5), dovetail joints (6), sturdy drawer slides (7), and drawers which resist warping (8).

Chairlegs should be firmly anchored in the corners (1). In tables, look for well-braced legs with tightly screwed on wooden blocks (1), and silent, strong slides (2) that one person can operate. *(Sketches courtesy Ethan Allen.)*

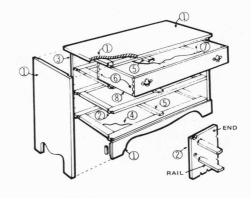

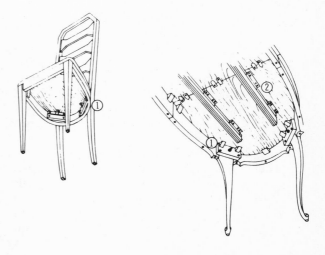

READING A BLUEPRINT

Do building blueprints bewilder you? They needn't, provided you know what the symbols mean and can "read" them in relation to the space. First visualize the two-dimensional drawing as three-dimensional space. Look at the placement of the doors, windows, closets, and appliances. Imagine yourself walking through and living in the rooms to determine whether the floor plan will suit your family's needs. Blueprints have their own visual vocabulary, with symbols which denote such things as windows, doors, plumbing fixtures, built-in cabinets, stairways, electrical wiring, heating ducts, and so on and tell the builder how the house should be constructed. The symbols shown here are those you are most likely to see on a blueprint. If there is anything you don't understand, check with your architect or builder in the initial planning stage. This is the time to make any necessary changes in the plan, not when the building is in progress. Interpreting a blueprint correctly and being able to visualize it in terms of your living requirements can save you costly mistakes.

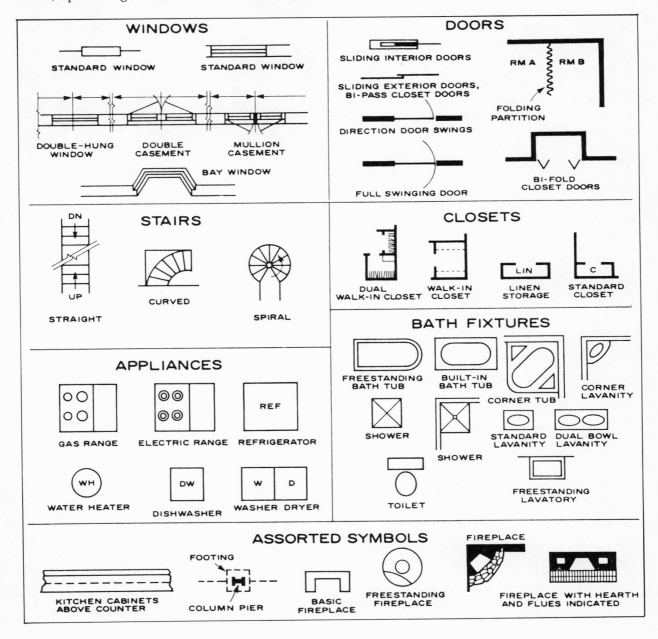

HOW TO PROTECT ART
AND OTHER VALUABLE COLLECTIONS

These days, with art thefts on the increase, insurance is no longer sufficient to protect paintings, sculpture, and other treasured objects. Now through an art registration system offered by World Art Services, Inc., 701 Beacon Building, Tulsa, Oklahoma 74103, you can register not only works of art but also such things as rare books, chess sets, and other impossible-to-replace items. Identification is established for each work being registered, and an individual identification number is issued for it. A registration certificate attached to the work warns thieves that if the object is stolen, a report will be made to local and state law enforcement agencies, the Federal Bureau of Investigation, Interpol, and a worldwide network of international art galleries. Registration for any single object, regardless of its value, is $15 for three years and registration is transferable to a new owner at a nominal transfer fee, at his cost. (Although World Art Services does not buy or sell art, the company will also put buyers and sellers in touch through a buyers' finding service called "Matchmaker.") Three-year renewal rates are half the original cost. For further information, contact the company.

Irreplaceable artwork dominates every area of this room. With today's worldwide increase in art thefts, serious collectors must take extra precautions, in the form of special registrations, to protect their valuables.

INDEX

Within the text, all sources are identified by chapter and entry number, i.e., II-1, II-2, II-3, etc. The index is keyed to these identification numbers and not to page numbers. The few references to actual page numbers are guides to general information of interest to any buyer of home decorating products or services.